THE SHAAR PRESS

THE JUDAICA IMPRINT
FOR THOUGHTFUL PEOPLE

Life

Ordinary people... facing extraordinary challenges

THE SHAAR PRESS

Lines

C. Saphir

**Their stories —
and the stories behind
their stories**

Published by **SHAAR PRESS**
Distributed by MESORAH PUBLICATIONS, LTD.
4401 Second Avenue / Brooklyn, N.Y 11232 / (718) 921-9000

Distributed in Israel by SIFRIATI / A. GITLER
POB 2351 / Bnei Brak 51122

Distributed in Europe by LEHMANNS
Unit E, Viking Business Park, Rolling Mill Road / Jarrow, Tyne and Wear, NE32 3DP/ England

Distributed in Australia and New Zealand by GOLDS WORLD OF JUDAICA
3-13 William Street / Balaclava, Melbourne 3183 / Victoria Australia

Distributed in South Africa by KOLLEL BOOKSHOP
Northfield Centre / 17 Northfield Avenue / Glenhazel 2192, Johannesburg, South Africa

ISBN 10: 1-4226-1566-9 / ISBN 13: 978-1-4226-1566-9

Printed in the United States of America by Noble Book Press Corp.
Custom bound by Sefercraft, Inc. / 4401 Second Avenue / Brooklyn N.Y. 11232

Table of Contents

Acknowledgments   9
Introduction   13

Part 1

חַיִּים אֲרוּכִים, חַיִּים שֶׁל שָׁלוֹם

Long Life, a Life of Peace

Reining in the Destroyer   19
Against the Odds   27
Alone in the Water   33
What a Lucky Boy   39
Lucky Parents, Lucky Children   47
A Listening Ear   53
Part of the Family   61
Who's on First?   71

Part 2

חַיִּים שֶׁל טוֹבָה, חַיִּים שֶׁל בְּרָכָה

A Life of Goodness, a Life of Blessing

A Forest Grows in Brooklyn   81
From Mourning to Joy   89
Barley Flour   99

From Darkness to Light   105

Dayeinu   115

Overwhelming Simchah   125

Part 3

חַיִּים שֶׁל פַּרְנָסָה. . . חַיִּים שֶׁל עשֶׁר וְכָבוֹד

A Life of Sustenance... a Life of Wealth and Honor

Fighting Fire with Fire   137

Outsourced   147

Bending the Laws of Nature   155

Wedding Spirit   165

Part 4

חַיִּים שֶׁל חִלּוּץ עֲצָמוֹת

A Life of Health

A Hole in the Heart   175

Before and After   185

From Head to Toe   193

One Good Heart   203

Silencing the Voice   213

Part 5

חַיִּים שֶׁיֵּשׁ בָּהֶם יִרְאַת שָׁמַיִם וְיִרְאַת חֵטְא

A Life in Which There Is Fear of Heaven and Fear of Sin

And the Angel Says, "Amen"   223

Life and Death   229

Computer Trouble   241

Seeing a Different Picture   249

Upstairs, Downstairs   257

Part 6

חַיִּים שֶׁאֵין בָּהֶם בּוּשָׁה וּכְלִמָּה

A Life in Which There Is No Shame or Humiliation

Quitting the Teacher   269

No Student Left Behind   279

Sheva Berachos Eulogy   289

Sticky Fingers   295
Reading the Riot Act   305

Part 7

חַיִּים שֶׁתְּהֵא בָּנוּ אַהֲבַת תּוֹרָה

A Life in Which We Will Have Love of Torah

Building My Rabbi Akiva   315
Crowning the Queen   321
Filling the Cup   331
Ice Cream for Breakfast   341

Glossary

                                         349

Acknowledgments

My first and foremost thank you goes to all of the people who have entrusted me with their *LifeLines* stories over the years. They are the true authors of this book; I am only the pen. I am continually awed by their courage, both in the way they confront their challenges and in their willingness to share those challenges for the benefit of others.

Special thanks to the *LifeLines* contributors who graciously agreed to have their stories published in this book, and especially to those who opened their hearts again to provide postscripts to their stories.

They say that parents have *ruach hakodesh* when naming a child. I wonder if the same is true when naming a magazine, because *Mishpacha* is best described as just that: a family. Like a family, the *Mishpacha* team has stood behind me loyally through thick and thin, providing unflinching support at all times. It is truly a privilege to be part of the monumental contribution this special family makes to *Klal Yisrael*.

It is rare to have an editor who is also a friend, but in Shana Friedman I have found both. Despite her impossibly busy schedule, she has consistently been there to help me generate ideas, evaluate submissions, and develop stories from outline to rough draft to polished final product. Her editorial genius is evident in the way she critiques without criticizing, edits without actually editing, and coaches so painlessly, you wouldn't even know you were being coached.

I am grateful to *Mishpacha*'s publisher, Eli Paley, for providing me with a unique weekly platform, and to Nomee Shaingarten, Hila Paley, Faigy Hutner and Lori Friedman for coordinating the various aspects of the column. Thank you, as well, to all the behind-the-scenes heroes at *Mishpacha* who brave grueling deadlines to produce a magnificent publication week after week.

Thank you to Rabbi Eytan Kobre for giving the *LifeLines* column its name.

Another family that I am privileged to belong to is the ArtScroll family. Over the years, Shmuel Blitz has provided me with a steady stream of invaluable professional opportunities, and to say that it is a pleasure to work for him is an understatement. Rabbi Nosson Scherman has been a mentor to me on many levels, and is always available to answer my questions and provide meaningful guidance. Rabbi Meir Zlotowitz is the vision behind ArtScroll, and I thank him for making me part of that vision.

Miriam Zakon is a legend and role model who calls herself a colleague. She guided this book from start to finish, going beyond the call of duty to smooth out every possible wrinkle. Her insightful editing enhanced the final product greatly.

It was a pleasure to work with Suri Brand, who did a masterful job proofreading the manuscript. Thank you to Judi Dick for reviewing the manuscript.

Thank you to Mrs. Faygie Weinbaum for her thorough proofreading, to Eli Kroen for the magnificent cover design, and to Mrs. Rivky Kapenstein for her striking page design and layout.

———————

And now to my own family.

I am forever grateful to my parents for implanting in me a love of learning and a love of the written word. Their devotion and love are the underpinnings of my every endeavor, and whatever I accomplish is to their credit. I thank my in-laws for their staunch support and for being so proud of all that I do.

My husband encouraged me, from the very beginning, to develop my writing skills, and continually propelled me to new horizons in the writing field. He first suggested that I commit to a weekly story column, and he always believed in my ability to keep the column going, even when I was sure that *this* was my last story (which happens every week, approximately). He is my sounding board, my cheerleader, and my advisory committee all in one.

I thank my children for teaching me so much and for infusing my life with joy and meaning.

I close with humble thanks to the *Ribbono shel Olam* for the opportunity to act as the pen for the remarkable people who open their hearts in *LifeLines*. I hope that He, and they, will continue to grant me this priceless gift.

C. Saphir

Shevat 5775

Introduction

If I had to isolate one theme of the *LifeLines* column, it would be that things are not always as they appear to be. Most *LifeLines* stories are about ordinary people who are facing challenges that you'd never imagine if you were to meet them.

When I began writing these stories, it was with the goal of providing a forum for those who overcame challenges, or are still struggling, and want to share their experiences with others, whether for the purpose of conveying a message, raising awareness, or providing *chizuk*.

We live in a tell-all, let-it-all-hang-out era, in which the values of privacy and personal dignity are rapidly becoming extinct. Yet the value of "*Mah tovu ohalecha Yaakov* — How goodly are your tents, O Yaakov," for their doors do not face one another — still characterizes Torah-observant society. We know how to keep personal information personal. We don't poke our noses into other people's private lives, we don't gossip about people's shortcomings, and we don't wear our problems on our sleeves.

Torah publications reflect this value. Our books, newspapers, and magazines differ sharply from secular media in that they balance the public's "right to know" with the public's commitment "not to know" if knowing will serve no purpose. This is one of the beautiful aspects of living in a Torah society.

There is a flip side to this, however. By putting a premium on privacy, we sometimes deny ourselves access to help and support, or deny others the opportunity to learn from our experiences. We might also create or reinforce unnecessary stigmas and taboos that aggravate the difficulties that others are going through.

Where can people find support and resources to cope with their personal challenges without unnecessarily disclosing private information? How can they receive assurance that the problems they are experiencing are hardly unique? Does preserving privacy have to mean that individuals in pain are hushed into silence?

LifeLines was created to give people a safe place to disclose what's truly going on in their lives, provided there is a purpose to sharing the information. Not only are the stories told anonymously (unless a particular person chose to be named), the details of the protagonists' lives are also camouflaged. And every person who submits a story to *LifeLines* is given the opportunity to review, edit, and approve the story before it goes to print.

This is what turns *LifeLines* into a "lifeline." It allows people to maintain their outward appearances and dignity, while enabling them to share their challenges and learn from the challenges of others. And, as is evident from many of the postscripts that follow the stories in this book, the stories are not over when they end. I receive innumerable requests from readers who want to contact the narrator of a particular *LifeLines* story, either because they are seeking the narrator's support or advice, or because they'd like to offer the narrator support and advice. For these people, the column is literally a lifeline.

To me, *LifeLines* is a lifeline in another way. We read about remarkable individuals who lived in previous generations, or about giants who walk among us, and we wonder how they got to where they did. Little is told about the struggles these people faced along their journey, because it is not always respectful, or within the parameters of *shemiras halashon*, to describe the challenges that great people overcame in the process of becoming great. And so we assume that they were simply born great, or that they were propelled along a lofty trajectory to which we ordinary folk cannot possibly aspire.

But that can't be the case, because in Judaism greatness is earned, not conferred. "If someone tells you, I have toiled and I have not found [i.e., succeeded in Torah] — do not believe him. I have not toiled, and I have found — do not believe him. I have toiled and I have found — believe him" (*Megillah* 6b). No credit is given to someone who didn't labor to get to where he is; sheer brilliance or talent has little significance unless it's accompanied by hard work.

In *LifeLines*, we get glimpses into this process, insights into the struggles that turn ordinary individuals into extraordinary ones. These glimpses serve not only to encourage us in our own journey, but also to shatter the popular myth that there are two kinds of people: great people like "them" and ordinary people like us.

In this sense, too, things are not always as they appear to be. Even those who look ordinary on the outside can be heroic, as many *LifeLines* stories demonstrate. And even we "ordinary" people can become great, if we choose to view our challenges as growth opportunities rather than as limitations.

Our life circumstances are not always under our control, but the choice to strive toward greatness is always ours. *Chazal* tell us as much when they say that "everything is in the hands of Heaven except for the fear of Heaven" (*Berachos* 33b).

It's telling that in the prayer of *Shabbos Mevarchim*, which encompasses all the things that enrich our existence, there is only one request that appears twice. We ask for longevity — "*chaim aruchim*"; for peace — "*chaim shel shalom*"; for goodness and blessing — "*chaim shel tovah, chaim shel berachah*"; for sustenance — "*chaim shel parnassah*"; for health — "*chaim shel chilutz atzamos*"; for a life in which there is neither shame nor humiliation — "*chaim she'ein bahem bushah u'chlimah*"; for a life of wealth and honor — "*chaim shel osher v'chavod*"; for a life in which our heartfelt requests will be fulfilled for the good — "*chaim sheyemalei Hashem mishalos libeinu l'tovah.*"

We ask for each of these things once. But for *yiras Shamayim*, fear of Heaven, we ask twice: "*chaim sheyeish bahem yiras Shamayim v'yiras cheit*" and, again, "*chaim shetehei vanu ahavas Torah v'yiras Shamayim.*"

The stories in this book discuss many of the things a Jew prays for: longevity, peace, health, prosperity, honor. But mostly, they talk about the quest for greatness, the Jew's perpetual struggle to reach upward toward his Creator.

For that is our LifeLine.

C. Saphir
lifelinesbook@gmail.com

The stories in this book were all told to me by the narrator, or by someone who knows the narrator, and originally appeared in Mishpacha magazine's weekly *LifeLines* column. The postscripts that appear after each story, which have been added for this book, contain either an update from the narrator, additional information about the story, reader feedback to the story, or insights that relate to the story.

In most of the stories in this book, names and details were changed. Real names were used in the following stories: "From Mourning to Joy"; "Ice Cream for Breakfast"; "Against the Odds" (names of some of the people in the story were changed); "Alone in the Water" (first names only); and "Fighting Fire with Fire (first names only).

To have your story told in *LifeLines*, or to share your feedback, please contact me at lifelinesbook@gmail.com

Part 1

חַיִּים אֲרוּכִים, חַיִּים שֶׁל שָׁלוֹם
Long Life, a Life of Peace

Reining in the Destroyer

It started, of course, over money. Not a lot of money; the whole fight was over $100,000, maybe $200,000, and by the time the 22-year-long court battle ended, the lawyers had eaten up practically every cent.

The court battle may have been over, but the fight was going strong, even though there was no longer any money at stake and the original fight was all but forgotten.

When I tell the story of how the fight started, it sounds almost silly. My mother's youngest sister, Shula, whose husband, Elliot, was a struggling real-estate agent, shared a two-family house with my widowed grandfather, Opa. Opa wrote in his will that his "estate," which consisted of not much more than his house, was to be divided equally among his five children. To everyone's surprise, after my grandfather's passing, a second will surfaced in which Opa had written that Shula was to receive a larger portion of the estate than the other children since she had taken care of him in his old age.

When my mother's oldest brother, Max, learned of the existence of this will, he was livid. "We all know that Papa wasn't in his right mind the last year of his life when he wrote the second will!" he fumed. Already during the *shivah*, he refused to say a word to Shula, and she responded by ordering her children not to speak to Uncle Max.

"The will is legally binding," she claimed. "If Max doesn't like it, let him try to fight it in court."

Fight it in court he did, after ostensibly receiving some sort of *heter* from his *rav*.

My mother's other two siblings, Uncle Lipa and Aunt Gertie, aligned themselves in opposite camps, with Lipa arguing that Shula deserved more money since she had been so devoted to Opa, and Gertie maintaining that Shula had lived in the house rent-free all the years and therefore owed it to Opa to take care of him without expecting a greater share of the inheritance. Looking back, it seems obvious that both arguments had merit, and a compromise was therefore in order. But the possibility of compromise was never considered.

At first, my mother avoided taking sides, telling both Max and Shula that she was satisfied with whatever portion of the inheritance she'd get. Max, however, insisted that my mother support him openly. "You know what Papa wanted," he told her. "You can't just stand by and watch his *real* will being ignored in favor of a worthless piece of paper he was forced to write when he had one foot in the grave!"

My mother couldn't withstand Max's pressure, especially since he had looked after her when the two arrived in America as refugees during the war while Opa and Oma were stranded in England along with the younger children. Reluctantly, my mother proclaimed her allegiance to Max.

So began the battle of the wills, with each side claiming to be carrying out Opa's true wishes. The tragic irony was that Opa had loathed *machlokes* of any sort, and prior to Opa's passing, my mother's family had been a loving, close-knit clan. Now the Weiss family was sharply divided, with Max's supporters pitted against Shula's supporters. There was no middle ground, no option of remaining neutral.

Since my family was officially on Max's team, Auntie Shula, Uncle Lipa, and their families refused to have anything to do with us. If we passed one of *those* cousins on the street, they would look straight ahead, as if we didn't exist. My mother instructed us to say hello when we met them, but we rarely did.

Several years after the fight started, when I was a young man of about 25, I decided — naïvely — that it was time to make peace in the family. I had recently married, and it pained me to no end that half of my mother's family had not even been invited to the wedding.

The court proceedings between Shula and Max had stalled due to some technicalities, and I resolved that it was high time to put this ridiculous feud to rest. I approached Rabbi Appelbaum, the *rav* of the shul where Opa had davened, and told him that I would like to make peace between the warring factions.

Rabbi Appelbaum smiled sadly. "You're wasting your time, Yossi," he said, shaking his head. "There is no way to bring *shalom* to your family. If you're looking for ways to inflict needless pain upon yourself, I can suggest some easier ways to accomplish that."

Not one to be easily deterred, I spent an entire year running from one relative to another, trying to reconcile each angry aunt, uncle, and cousin with the particular individuals against whom he or she nursed a grudge. During this process, I kept meticulous notes, and at one point I even created a spreadsheet of who said what about whom and what each one wanted to see happen. By that time, however, the issue was no longer the will or the inheritance, but rather the layers upon layers of resentment that had accrued since Opa's death.

What complicated matters even further was that most of my relatives categorically denied the existence of any *machlokes*, claiming that they harbored no hard feelings toward the others — even as their mouths continued to spew venom at the opposition.

"I have nothing against So-and-so," one cousin told me very seriously. "But you should really tell your wife to stop shopping in his store. Everyone knows he's a crook."

Other cousins made it very clear that they considered my peacemaking attempts annoying and meddlesome and said they were causing unwarranted pain to their parents. Realizing that I was becoming persona non grata, I finally gave up.

Rabbi Appelbaum was right, after all, I told myself sadly. *There really is no way.*

A while later, the *tzaros* started. Uncle Lipa, who was in perfect health, died of a sudden heart attack at the age of 61. Within a couple of years, Aunt Gertie passed away as well, succumbing to a rare but virulent strain of the flu when she was just shy of her 60th birthday. Shortly afterward, my mother contracted lung cancer — although neither she nor anyone in our family smoked — and she died a few months later, at the age of 64.

Before long, the only siblings of my mother's left alive were Max and Shula, the principal combatants. But don't think they were spared the destroyer's ax. The *tzaros* were simply dispersed among their spouses, children, and grandchildren. The number of deaths, divorces, older singles, and off-the-*derech* kids in those two families was staggering; the neighborhood gossips would cluck their tongues as they contemplated the bad *mazel* that haunted these families. "You'd think they had a curse hanging over them," one astute yenta commented.

The court battle over Opa's estate ended three years ago, with no apparent victor, but the *machlokes* continued unabated.

About a year ago, Shula's 48-year-old daughter, Chana, was involved in a major car accident. She emerged with only minor cuts and bruises, but was badly shaken.

Less than a week later, her 42-year-old brother, Barry, contracted meningitis and fell into a coma. "He's done," the doctors pronounced. "There's nothing that can be done for him."

The day Barry was admitted to the hospital, his children circulated an e-mail asking the extended family to say *Tehillim* for him. I replied to that group e-mail by writing, "You're wasting your time. The only thing that can save your father is if everyone in this family lays down their arms."

My inbox quickly swelled with responses from across my family that ranged from the indignant to the downright nasty.

"After what So-and-so did to me, there can never be peace," one cousin wrote.

"Who do you think you are to mix into our business?" another demanded.

"Enough is enough," I wrote back. "Barry isn't sick from meningitis; he's sick from *machlokes*, the same sickness that killed so many others in our family."

After consulting with *da'as Torah*, I drafted a *shtar mechilah* and sent a copy to every one of my 33 cousins. The *shtar* read as follows:

> *We agree to be mochel with a complete mechilah all those who ultimately undersign this document for any past grievances done to us, including, but not limited to, lashon hara, embarrassment, false accusations, revenge, false suspicion, hurtful words, apathy, and emotional pain. In exchange, we ask those who undersign to please grant us full mechilah as well in order that we are all forgiven for our sins both in this world and the next.*
>
> *We declare that we deeply regret the personal wrongdoings and family separation that has transpired over the past 20 years, whether or not we were directly or indirectly the cause. We genuinely want to make an effort to mend relationships to the best of our abilities.*
>
> *We offer our assurances that we will make a conscious effort to eradicate feelings of animosity, hatred, and resentment from our hearts, and from this day forward we will refrain to the best of our abilities from speaking or accepting lashon hara about any of the undersigned.*
>
> *As a declaration of shalom we are agreeing to make a strong effort to invite all of the undersigned to our future simchahs and to greet them respectfully when encountering them in the street, at a simchah, or anywhere else.*

Over the next few days, I spoke with every one of my cousins and convinced them to sign. "Barry's going to die if you don't sign," I warned the more intransigent ones.

"Don't talk like that, Yossi!" they admonished me. "You're opening a mouth to the Satan!"

"The Satan already has all the ammunition he needs against this family," I retorted.

My cousins had all the reasons in the world not to sign.

"There never was a *machlokes* to begin with," one of them claimed, "so signing this document is admitting to a falsehood."

"I can't sign because it is a violation of *kibbud av*," argued another.

"Revealing who does and who does not sign constitutes *lashon hara*, and I want no part of it," insisted a third.

My favorite argument was "What you're doing amounts to extortion, and true peace can't come about in such a fashion."

At first, Shula ordered her children not to sign my *shtar mechilah*, so I took a morning off from work and paid her a special visit. "Auntie Shula," I said, "forgive me for speaking this way, but you have a daughter who was just in a car accident and a son who's in a coma. How much more do you need before you make up with Max and the rest of the family?"

"That has nothing to do with anything," she insisted hotly.

Upon the advice of my *rav*, I focused my efforts after that on making peace between the cousins. After much cajoling and lobbying, I managed to get every one of my cousins to sign the *shtar mechilah*.

When the *shtar* bore all 33 signatures, Barry's daughter Etty brought it into her father's hospital room and read it aloud at his bedside. "This is all being done as a *zechus* for you to have a *refuah sheleimah*," she told her unconscious father.

As she was reading the agreement, a doctor ran into the room. "What's going on in here?" he asked. "The monitors outside show that your father's brain activity just started to normalize."

To the amazement of the medical staff, Barry's condition improved steadily from that moment, and he subsequently emerged from his coma and recovered.

This is no fairy tale, I assure you.

I never dreamed it would happen, but after Barry returned home from the hospital, Shula decided to visit Max — after not speaking to him for 25 years — and ask him for *mechilah*. Astonishingly, he forgave her!

The *shtar mechilah* between the cousins was signed about a year ago, and I am happy to report that in the past year every branch of our family has seen *yeshuos*. A bunch of older single girls have gotten engaged, and a couple that was childless for 13 years is now expecting a baby.

When I tell this story, it seems so clear that all the *tzaros* in the family were linked to the *machlokes* over Opa's will and that the subsequent *yeshuos* were linked to the termination of that *machlokes*, but considering that the events I've just described took place over a span of 25 years, the causal relationship could easily have been missed or denied. Thankfully, the correlation between the *shtar mechilah* and the incredible *yeshuos* that we have been witnessing one after another has not been lost upon my family.

I thought long and hard about whether to share my family's story. What made me decide to go ahead and tell the story in this forum was the hope that my story will inspire other people who have seen similar splits in their own families and have despaired of ever bringing *shalom* between their warring relatives.

I have instructed my children to bury me after 120 years with a copy of the *shtar mechilah*, because I consider it one of the greatest accomplishments of my life. In the past, I used to shed tears when I thought about the pain that our family's *machlokes* must have brought upon the *neshamos* of Opa and Oma. To have survived the Holocaust and then toiled to build a family, only to have that family senselessly torn apart — what a tragedy!

To me, the most frightening part of the story is that the aunts and uncle who died prematurely were not the ones most intensely involved in the *machlokes*. When my sister once commented that my mother had died of *machlokes*, not of lung cancer, my brother observed that there were others who were far more involved in the fight, and yet they were fine. "So how can you blame her death on *machlokes*?" he asked pointedly.

But the truth is that it doesn't make a difference how involved any particular person was. *Machlokes* is like a fire, and fire burns everything in its path: good or bad, right or wrong, innocent or guilty. Once the destroyer is let loose, the only way to rein him in is by erecting a firewall of peace and forgiveness.

Postscript:

"That story was wild," someone wrote to me about this story. *"It couldn't have been true."*

I'll let the following letter to the editor speak for the story's veracity:

> *Yasher ko'ach for this article! Let me tell you — if you have any machlokes in your family and you don't try to do something, you are as guilty as the ones involved. Machlokes is a fire that usually strikes the innocent ones. The Satan leaves the people who are the cause of the machlokes alone, since he's enjoying it too much, and the arrows shoot out among the rest of the family. I know this very well, since I was one of the cousins in this story.*
>
> *Yes, my mother, a"h, died of "machlokes" — lung cancer at 64. She never was involved in the machlokes, and I even took her to be menachem avel her sister when her sister's husband died of heart problems. She cried many tears over her family issues, but was not strong enough to do anything about it. She kept quiet. Unfortunately, the Satan hit her as well. Before she died, she told one of my siblings to make sure there was peace in our family.*
>
> *Don't just sit there! Try! Try with all your ko'ach to bring some sort of peace in your family. Hashem will surely shower on your own family berachah and only good in return. Hatzlachah rabbah!*
>
> *Signed,*
>
> *Opa's einekel*

Against the Odds

My daughter Devora *a"h* was diagnosed at a young age with a rare Jewish genetic disease, familial dysautonomia (known as FD). As a child, she spent a lot of time in a New York area hospital.

Having grown up in a small community where everyone knows everyone else, she never developed the "I'll-let-you-mind-your-business-if-you-let-me-mind-mine" attitude that characterizes so many big-city natives. Despite her illness, she loved to visit the hospital's Bikur Cholim room and see if there was anything she could do to make the people who needed its services more comfortable.

"If you're hungry, the fridge is stocked with all kinds of food," she'd tell people. Or, "If you want to lie down, there are recliners available." She was invigorated by her efforts to ease the plight of other patients and their families.

Any time she met the relative of a patient in the Bikur Cholim room, she would ask them for the patient's full Hebrew name so we could daven for him. At times, people were reluctant to provide this information, maybe because they were suspicious of strangers, sick thirteen-year-old girls included.

But sometimes there was more to this reluctance.

No one wants to see their loved ones suffer. Why prolong their time in this world? Why not just let them go?

But when you're the parent of a child with a chronic disease, you develop a keen appreciation for the value of life. You understand that with all the pain that life can entail, the gift of having a *neshamah* connected to the body is meaningful in a way that transcends even the most challenging physical circumstances. So as long as Hashem gives us life, we continue to daven and hope that the suffering will subside, allowing the light of the *neshamah* to shine more brightly.

This concept was one that we discussed openly with our young daughter, and it shaped her attitude to life in general and to her illness in particular.

We were walking into the Bikur Cholim room one evening, when we spotted a *frum* thirtyish fellow sitting at a table typing furiously on a laptop computer.

"*Shalom aleichem,*" I said, extending my hand to him. "Yale Butler."

He politely accepted the proffered handshake and returned my greeting.

"Who do you have here in the hospital?" I asked him.

"My father," he replied. "He's had the *machalah* for a while, and now he has some serious complications."

"What's his name?" Devora piped up.

He sighed. "You don't need my father's name."

"Sure we do!" she exclaimed. "We want to daven for him."

"Nah," he said. "He's at the end of the line. It doesn't look like he'll make it out of the hospital. Nothing you can say will help. But thanks anyway."

"What do you mean?" I asked. "The Ribbono shel Olam is a *Kol Yachol*! He can do anything at any time!"

I felt a bit preachy saying this, but since this belief had been front and center in my mind ever since Devora's diagnosis more than a decade earlier, the words just popped out of my mouth.

"That's true," he agreed. "But I don't think He's going to do anything here."

"You have to have *bitachon*," Devora said somberly. "We can't ever stop hoping."

It's hard to say no to a young girl in a wheelchair wearing hospital pajamas. "O.K.," he capitulated. "His name is Yisrael ben Ita."

We shmoozed a little more, and I learned that his father was not that old, only in his late 70's. The cancer had spread throughout his body, however, and there was nothing the medical community could offer by way of treatment.

"My father always hated hospitals," the man told us. "He keeps begging us to take him home. But there's no way the doctors will let him go in his condition. They told us to be prepared for the worst."

As I sat down next to him, I recalled the doctor's dire prediction, made over 10 years ago when Devora was first diagnosed.

"Four to nine years maximum," the doctor said. "Medical science has no cure."

We sought a second opinion, not from another doctor, but from the Klausenberger Rebbe *zt"l*. He gave us a *berachah* that we would be *zocheh* to walk Devora to the *chuppah*. Noting the puzzled look on my face, the Rebbe asked me, "What's bothering you?"

"Rebbe," I said, "the doctors say that the nine-year maximum has been proven by science!"

"The doctors don't know enough science," the Rebbe said emphatically. "It will take them a few years. By then, they will know more science."

True to the Rebbe's word, Devora outlived the doctor's prediction. (We would indeed have the *zechus* to walk her under the *chuppah* with her wonderful *chassan*. But that's a story unto itself.)

The next night, I was wheeling Devora into the Bikur Cholim room when we saw the same fellow sitting there at the table in front of a laptop computer. Or *was* it the same fellow? Something about him was different.

"That guy looks like the man we saw yesterday," Devora whispered to me. "Maybe it's his brother."

I greeted the fellow with a hearty *shalom aleichem*, and when he looked up at me with no flicker of recognition in his eyes, I realized that Devora was right — this was probably the brother of the man we had met yesterday.

"What brings you here?" I asked him.

"My father's not well," he answered. Worry lines creased his forehead.

"What's your father's name?" Devora asked. "We'd like to daven for him."

The man smiled. "That's very kind of you," he replied, "but my father's in a bad way, really sick. We've done our *tefillos* already."

"*HaKadosh Baruch Hu* is *Kol Yachol*," I said, glancing involuntarily at my daughter.

The man's expression softened. "My father's name is Yisrael —"

"Ben Ita?" Devora interrupted.

His eyes widened. "How did you know?"

"We met your brother here yesterday," she explained. "We've already been davening for your father, and we hope you don't mind if we continue."

"It's a free country," he said with a shrug, and turned back to his computer.

As I pushed Devora's wheelchair out of the Bikur Cholim room, she turned around to meet my gaze.

"I don't understand," she said. "Why don't these people want to daven for their father? Don't they want him to live?"

I didn't know what to say. Should I tell her that it was hard for them to see their father suffering?

"I don't know," I answered. "They're obviously going through a very hard time."

"Well, I'm going to daven very hard for Yisrael ben Ita," she declared, "even if his own sons have already given up."

Two days later, when we entered the Bikur Cholim room again, we noticed a thin, pale, elderly man with a cane, dressed in a white shirt, dark vest, and dark pants, sitting in an armchair.

After giving him my trademark *shalom aleichem*, I asked him whom he had in the hospital.

"Who do I have here?" he asked. "Me!"

"Oh," I said. "You don't look like a patient. What's your name?"

"Yisrael Feuerstein," he replied.

"I haven't seen you around here before," I said. "Are you an outpatient?"

He chuckled. "Well, I was in the ICU earlier this week, but yesterday they put me into a regular room, and today they're letting me go home, even though they thought I'd never make it out of here alive. So, yes, I guess you could say I'm an outpatient, *baruch Hashem!*"

Devora was seated across from where I was standing, a bit behind Mr. Feuerstein's armchair, and I could see the expression of intense curiosity on her face.

"Can I ask him what his mother's name is?" she whispered to me.

I nodded.

She moved up her wheelchair a bit. "Was your mother's name Ita?" she asked the old man.

"Actually, yes," he replied, looking surprised.

"We've been davening for you," she said.

Mr. Feuerstein smiled broadly. "It worked!" he said. "*Shkoyach!*"

My eyes moved from Mr. Feuerstein to Devora and then back to Mr. Feuerstein. How much longer would he live? How long would she live?

Where there is life, there is hope, I mused. *Our job isn't to predict the future, but rather to make the most of the time and energies Hashem gives us. And part of that is davening, no matter how bleak the situation looks.*

Just then the door to the Bikur Cholim room swung open, and a man rushed in. I recognized him as Mr. Feuerstein's son, although I wasn't sure whether it was the one we had seen two nights earlier or the one we had seen three nights earlier.

"Daddy," he said, "I signed the discharge papers. We need to leave right away. I'm parked illegally outside."

Devora turned in her wheelchair and looked the younger Mr. Feuerstein straight in the eye. "*Yisrael ben Ita li'refuah sheleimah,*" she intoned.

The man spun around. "Yes," he admitted. "You taught me an important lesson in *bitachon*. Hashem *is Kol Yachol*. You were right."

Postscript:

This story was actually the catalyst for this entire book. I spoke to Rabbi Yale Butler about a year after the story was published, and he told me that it had brought great comfort and chizuk to many people who knew Devora, a"h, some of whom were distant from Judaism.

Rabbi Butler is the one who urged me to compile my LifeLines stories into a book, but I gave him a list of reasons why I thought it wasn't feasible. He handily shot down each of my reasons and gave me a slew of creative ideas for turning this book into a reality.

I guess you could say I got a taste of the same inspired determination that Rabbi Butler and Devora brought to the Feuerstein family.

Alone in
the Water

Port Graham Bay, Alaska
 Situated about 30 miles from Homer, Alaska, Port Graham Bay is home to a large salmon cannery that dates back to the early 1900's. As a young man, I spent my winters studying psychology at the University of Alaska Fairbanks, and my summers fishing for salmon in southwest Alaska and selling them to the cannery.

Each morning, I'd head out on the bay in my skiff, which was basically a large motorized rowboat, and spread my fishing nets. After bringing my day's catch to the cannery, I'd head back to the campsite where the other fishermen slept. We lived in a small log cabin with a woodstove for heating and cooking. We had no phone and no running water; we drank water from the nearby mountain streams. Once a month we ventured into Homer to buy supplies.

One day, as I was steering my skiff into the bay, a large boat sped by, setting off a wake. (A wake is a track of waves left by an object moving through the water.) Thinking that I could jump the waves in my skiff, I continued my foray into the bay. I jumped the first wave, but when I reached the second, I miscalculated its speed. My skiff rammed directly into the wave and capsized, plunging me into the water.

When I came to the surface, I could see my skiff bobbing in the water. Treading water, I estimated that it would take me 10 to 15 minutes to swim back to shore. But then I'd lose my skiff, and I'd be embarrassed to face the other fishermen. I opted, therefore, to swim further into the bay and climb back into my skiff, which was spinning in large circles in the water.

It would take me about 12 minutes to reach my skiff, I estimated, but I was a strong swimmer, having spent a considerable amount of time in the lakes and rivers around Fairbanks during the summers of my youth. Fortunately, the water in the bay was not too cold, and I thought I could reach my skiff safely.

After swimming for some time, though, I felt myself becoming drowsy. I knew what that meant: hypothermia. My younger brother Joey had once contracted hypothermia and had fallen asleep in the snow. Luckily, someone found him and rescued him before it was too late.

By now, I was already a full half-hour from shore and only about six minutes from my skiff. I felt the strength ebbing from my limbs. My blood was being pulled out of my arms and legs toward the core of my body, where warmth was most needed.

Fighting exhaustion, I continued swimming. Now I was only 20 feet from the skiff. A few more strokes and I'd be there.

But I couldn't do it. My limbs were limp. My body was cold and so, so tired. If I could only close my eyes and rest for a few minutes...

No! a voice inside me screamed. *Fall asleep, Stan, and you die!*

I tossed my head, trying to shake some energy into myself. I knew that the first rule of survival in a dangerous situation is don't panic. Yet here I was, alone in the water, lacking the strength to pull myself into my skiff, my body becoming colder and colder. It was hopeless. I started to panic.

Suddenly, a memory came to me. I was about 5, or maybe 7 years old. My parents wrapped me in a warm parka, hat, scarf, and mittens, led me outside into the 50-degree-below Alaskan winter, and drove to services at the local church. My parents were devout Catholics, and belief in a Higher Power had been instilled in me from early childhood. I had stopped attending church services in my teenage years, however, and religion had long ceased to be a factor in my life. But now, as I felt my body succumbing to hypothermia, I knew with certainty that G-d existed.

For the first time in many years, I started to pray.

As I begged G-d for mercy, something strange happened. Everything around me — the water, the shore, the trees in the distance, the sky — seemed to lock into place. All sound went still, and all motion ceased. I was viewing my surroundings as I would a photograph, perceiving an image of reality that was separate and removed from me. Then the photograph began moving upward and away, like a curtain, revealing a white light behind it. The white light came closer and closer, until it enveloped me, and I felt all of my fear evaporating.

This entire scene then reversed itself: the white light receded, the photograph returned, the sound and motion turned back on, and the water, the shore, the trees, and the sky resumed full animation. I was still in mortal danger, but I felt completely at peace, secure in the knowledge that I was cradled in G-d's Hands.

And then I saw the skiff. It wasn't my skiff; it was a skiff driven by two teenage fishermen. They had seen my empty boat, and, suspecting an accident, they had decided to look around for its owner. When they spotted me, they steered their skiff in my direction, hauled me on board, and rushed me to shore. From there, they ordered a bush plane to fly me to the nearest hospital in Homer.

The hospital released me the same day, and the next day I was back on the bay fishing. But my life would never be the same. My experience in the water, reaching out to G-d and finding Him, propelled me to search for Him in the crannies of everyday life as well.

At the time, I knew nothing of Judaism. I had never even met a Jew. Seeking a greater connection to the G-d Who had saved me from certain death, I turned my attention to the arts, martial arts, and sports.

While still studying at the university, I met a lovely girl named Enid who was studying maternal behavior in sea otters. She was very spiritual, but not religious. At the time, I had no idea she was Jewish, but I think that what attracted me to her was her Jewish *neshamah*. We didn't start dating then; it was only a few years later, when our paths crossed again, that we began to see each other seriously.

We married and settled in a picturesque home in the middle of the forest, where moose roamed freely in the yard and snow covered the ground and trees nine months of the year. We had three little boys, the last of whom had Down syndrome and required open-heart surgery as an infant. When he survived the surgery, we adopted another child with Down syndrome so that our son would have a constant friend and companion.

Alaska was hardly the ideal place to raise our two children with Down syndrome. Even forgetting one's mittens could be life-threatening in that frigid climate, so we began to seek other living options. My wife, who had attended Jewish schools in her youth, half-jokingly raised the possibility of moving to a kibbutz in Israel, thinking this would be a good long-term arrangement for our special-needs children. I took this suggestion seriously and traveled to Israel on a pilot trip in 1994. Not only did I fall in love with Israel, I also wanted to convert.

We were a nonreligious, intermarried couple when we made *aliyah*, and the reality of life in Israel was a shock on many levels. Our first rude awakening was the shattering of our dreams about the idyllic kibbutz lifestyle: no kibbutz wanted us with our two special-needs children. "We have enough problems of our own," they told us.

Another major adjustment was exchanging our spacious two-story home in the forest for a tiny two-bedroom apartment in an 80-unit apartment building that served as an absorption center for new immigrants. Yet the power of our quest for spirituality propelled us through the obstacles we faced, and we persevered in our decision to make a life for ourselves in Israel.

With time, I came to realize that Torah Judaism was the path of truth. Wishing to learn more, I joined a yeshivah, and after some time I approached the local *beis din* and asked to convert. Seeing that I was sincere, the *beis din* agreed to convert me after a specified study period. During that time, Chaya (formerly Enid) and I were not allowed to live together as husband and wife.

My conversion took place on a Thursday, the day before Shavuos, and on Sunday, Chaya and I celebrated our Jewish wedding.

Becoming a Jew was, in a sense, the culmination of the process that had begun so many years earlier, when I left the religion of my birth, reconnected to Hashem in the icy Alaskan waters, and began to seek the truth.

Eighteen years have passed since my conversion, yet the process that began in the water is by no means over. In my daily davening, I continually seek to achieve the feeling of absolute peace and security that I experienced back in Port Graham Bay. I must admit that I have never managed to recapture the feeling of being utterly enveloped in Hashem's presence. Despite my efforts to focus on my *tefillos*, I often find my mind wandering and my heart listless. Yet ever since I experienced that one-time gift of total connection to Hashem, my goal in life has been to rebuild that connection through my every action.

There is no treading water in Judaism; being a Jew means being in a constant state of striving for closeness to Hashem. To this day, I envision myself alone in the cold waters of the bay, and I remind myself: *Fall asleep spiritually, and you die.*

Postscript:

Chaya, the wife of this story's narrator, makes only a brief appearance in this story. But she is definitely worthy of a story of her own — and perhaps more than one. She has adopted four children with Down syndrome, in addition to her own six children. She also donated a kidney to a Yom Kippur War veteran, despite the protestations of many of her relatives and friends.

I actually wrote about her kidney donation in a LifeLines piece entitled "Blood Relatives." That story (which isn't included in this book) described how, from the moment Chaya was introduced to the possibility of kidney donation, she davened that she be given the opportunity to perform this mitzvah.

"You're a mother of 10 children," people told her. "How can you even think of this? What if you yourself need a kidney one day?"

"If I or someone in my family needed a kidney," she replied, "I'd want someone to step up to the plate and donate one. But if I wouldn't be willing to donate my kidney to someone else, how can I expect another person to do that for me or my kid?"

Did any readers imagine that this woman was the wife of the narrator of "Alone in the Water"? I doubt it. But when Hashem rescued Stan (now Yisrael) from the frigid Alaskan waters of Port Graham Bay, He was setting in motion a process that would eventually lead to Yisrael and Chaya building a home of incredible chesed together.

What a Lucky Boy

I'm a really big boy now. I turned 7 in the summer, and now I'm in the second grade. We're learning *Chumash Bereishis*, and we just started *Parashas Chayei Sarah*.

My rebbi this year is Rabbi Meisels, and he's a really nice rebbi. He smiles a lot, and he gives good prizes.

Before Succos, Rabbi Meisels made a contest. He gave out a chart with stickers to put on for davening, learning, and good behavior, and he said that whoever brings the chart back filled with stickers after Yom Tov was going to get a special prize.

I made sure to daven and behave good so I could get stickers, and I asked my mommy before Yom Tov if she could learn *Chumash* with me, but she said she was too busy packing to go away, and anyway it's better to learn *Chumash* with Tatty.

Tatty doesn't live with us, so I can't always learn with him, but my mommy said that over Yom Tov I would have a lot of time to learn with him. Afterward, when I was out of the room, she told Aunt Dassy that *he* could do some homework with his kid once in a while, not only buy pizza and ice cream.

I was going to tell Mommy that Tatty doesn't only buy pizza and ice cream — he sometimes makes barbecues and buys presents, too — but I decided not to tell her that because I didn't want her to get upset and start crying. A lot of times when I say things about Tatty she gets upset, especially when I tell her that I miss him and I want to see him during the week, not only on Sunday.

Since Mommy's *chasunah*, before last Pesach, she doesn't cry as much. I guess it's because now she has an *abba* to make *Kiddush* and go to work and come home and talk to her. This new *abba* — his real name is Yaakov, but I'm not allowed to call him that — has three kids, Elana, Yoni, and Ashi, and they come to us every other Shabbos now because their *ima* has custody.

I know what "custody" means. It means that the mommy gets to take care of the kids the whole week and do all the laundry and the cooking, and the *tatty* gets to take the kids out on weekends and spoil them rotten. See? I really do know. Yoni and Ashi didn't know what it means, 'cause they're younger than me, but I told them. I even know what "visitation" is; it's like a visit, but you need an invitation from a judge because otherwise you can't go.

I'm a very lucky boy, because I already have a mountain bike with 12 gears and a sports watch and Rollerblades. All my friends wish their *tattys* would give them these things, too. My best friend, Dovid, told his mommy that he wants to have a *tatty* and an *abba* just like me, but she said that one *tatty* is more than enough, thank you.

Dovid told me that he was going to his *zeidy* and *bubby* in Montreal for the first days of Succos and coming home for the second days. Before Succos, I asked Mommy if we could build a *succah*, too, like Dovid, and she said, "No, sweetie, not this year. This year you have so many *zeidie*s and *bubbie*s and families who want to see you! Isn't that nice?"

She was smiling, but her eyes looked sad. Maybe she also wants to have her own *succah*.

Dovid said I was lucky, because I got to go to four different places for Succos. On *erev Succos*, my *tatty* drove in from Lakewood to pick me up, and he took me to Zeidy and Bubby Tepperman in Flatbush for the first days. I was happy that his other kids, Devora and Chanale, weren't there, because they're girls and they always run to Shoshi and tell her I'm bothering them, even when they're the ones who start up. (Shoshi's their mother — they call her Mommy, but I'm allowed to call her Shoshi. Probably because Tatty doesn't have "custody," like Mommy.) Then Shoshi tells my *tatty* that I misbehaved, and he makes me say I'm sorry to Devora and Chanale even though it's their fault.

I did some of my *Chumash* with Tatty on Yom Tov, but we didn't finish, and Tatty said he would do the rest with me the day after Succos.

Mommy and Abba came after *Havdalah* to pick me up because they said we had to drive through the night to Cleveland to pay a *chol hamo'ed* visit to Grandma and Grandpa. That's Abba's parents. I was never in their house before, but I once heard Mommy tell someone that they're very proper people. I didn't know what proper people were, but I thought it had something to do with not making noise.

In Zeidy and Bubby Tepperman's house, I was allowed to make all the noise I wanted. When Abba drove up in his minivan to get me, I told Tatty that I wanted to stay in Bubby's house, and I sat down on the floor and started crying, so Tatty had to carry me outside. But I'm big and strong already, so I kicked and screamed until Tatty had to put me down, and then I ran back into the house. Finally Abba came to the door and told me that if I come nicely, he'd buy me a new game for my Xbox.

I don't think Tatty was too happy about that, because he doesn't want me to have an Xbox, but he didn't say anything about it. He just gave me a big hug and a kiss, and his throat made a funny noise — you know, like when a car drives through snow? And he said, "You're my big boy. Remember to be good."

It was squishy in the minivan, and Ashi kept kicking me, so I kicked him back. Mommy told me to leave Ashi alone, and then she told Abba that I always come back nuts after visitation. I stopped kicking after that.

We stayed in Cleveland for two days. Grandma kept calling me "dearie" and Grandpa kept calling me "young man," even though I told them a hundred times that my name was Moishy. I tried not to make noise, but it wasn't my fault that the big vase in the front hall — they call it a "*foyay*" — fell over when I bumped into it and broke into a thousand pieces. Now I know what proper people are.

I was hoping that we could go home after Cleveland, but Mommy reminded me that we had no *succah*. "Besides," she said, "don't you want to see Zeidy and Bubby Perkowski? We haven't seen them since Pesach!"

Zeidy and Bubby Perkowski are Mommy's parents, and they live in Long Island. I think it's called Long Island because it takes a long time to get there, especially from Cleveland. I usually like going to visit Zeidy and Bubby Perkowski, but this time I had to share a room with Yoni and Ashi, and they kept saying that this *zeidy* and *bubby* are old and not fun at all, so I had to punch them a few times.

Mommy kept asking me why I was so hyper, and she told Bubby that she didn't know what in the world *his* parents did to me the first days. Then she started crying and said why does everything have to be so complercated.

Elana, Yoni, and Ashi got to go home to their *ima* after Simchas Torah, but Mommy said that Tatty had visitation on Isru Chag, and he was going to pick me up the next morning from Long Island.

In the morning, Tatty came and told me that he had a surprise for me. "We're going to visit Shoshi's family in Boro Park," he said.

I told him that I needed to finish my *Chumash*, and he said, "Yes, yes, of course we'll finish your *Chumash*. Just get in the car."

This time Devora and Chanale were with us, and they kept jumping up and down because they were so excited to see their Saba and Savta. I told them that Saba and Savta are silly names for grandparents, and Chanale started to cry, and Tatty said that he's going to get into an accident if I don't shape up.

I don't think Shoshi really wanted to have me coming along, because while I was playing outside in the backyard I heard her telling Savta — that's her mother — that she hates Sundays. She didn't say that it was because Tatty had visitation, but I figured it out myself.

I played in the backyard most of the day, and then Tatty told me that he was going to take me out for pizza. I reminded him that we still needed to do *Chumash*, and he smacked his forehead and said, "Oh, gosh, I forgot all about it, and we don't have time now. You'll have to do it with your mother. Otherwise you'll come home late and she won't be happy."

I didn't say anything to Mommy about the *Chumash* that night when I came home, because I didn't want her to tell me that Tatty was supposed to do it with me. Just to be safe, I waited until the next morning to tell her that I needed to bring back my chart to Rabbi Meisels.

She didn't know where my chart was, and I said I wasn't going to school without it, and she said oh yes, I was, and I said I was going to be the only kid in the class who didn't bring back the chart, and she said I should go to school and she would track down the chart and I could bring it back tomorrow and please don't throw a tantrum, so I went to school.

When I came home from school, Mommy said she had spent the whole day on the phone trying to find my chart — she even called Bubby Tepperman! — but no one seemed to know where it was. "I'll write Rabbi Meisels a note," she said.

The next day, Mommy wrote me a note that said that I had davened and behaved and learned my *Chumash*, but I didn't give it to Rabbi Meisels because I knew it wasn't true. I didn't learn all the *Chumash*, and I didn't behave good on Yom Tov.

Even though I didn't give Rabbi Meisels the note, he gave me the big shiny whistle that everyone else in the class got, except Yudi, who also didn't bring back his chart but his parents live together so it's not okay for him to lose his chart. I told Mommy that Rabbi Meisels gave me the whistle even though I lost my chart, and she said, "What a lucky boy you are!"

I really am a lucky boy, right?

Postscript:

Was this story extreme? Or did it just uncover the tip of the iceberg? It depends who you ask.

This is a letter from one reader, who thought the story should not have been printed:

> The only message I took away was a very bleak, sad, and depressing one. What was the purpose of this story — to scare away parents from getting a divorce? I think everyone knows that not all children of divorce end up in such a sorry state, even if divorce inevitably does, indeed, take its toll on children and their parents. I would be curious to find out what readers thought of this story, as I would hope that such a dismal story should not be necessary to convince parents not to get divorced (if that was the message), and that such a story is depressing and unfair to those parents and children who are, unfortunately, in such a situation.
>
> *Anonymous*

Others, including the letter writer below, felt differently:

> In response to Anonymous, who expressed dismay over "What a Lucky Boy":
>
> There is not the slightest doubt in my mind that you are not a child of divorce. No child of divorce could have written such a letter. Because the story presented was not anywhere near a worst-case scenario — one that is nevertheless quite common — in which parents actively pit children against each other. ("You want a new bike? Tell your father. He still hasn't paid for your health insurance.") On the contrary, it was an excellent depiction of what is "normal" for a child of divorce.
>
> Children of divorce are thrown into a sad, difficult, and lifelong situation, generally with no say whatsoever in the matter. For starters, it is more common than not for a divorced parent to complain about the ex's methods of child-rearing, as the mother in the story did. Even if they do not do so to their children, it is a rare individual who is scrupulous not to complain within his child's earshot, and an even rarer one who does not speak negatively about his ex-spouse at all.

As divorce becomes, tragically, more and more common, more and more children live in situations where they are split between two homes. It is standard for children of divorce to spend one night a week and every other weekend with the noncustodial parent. Do they want to? Not necessarily. But no one asks them.

What happens when Tatty has custody for Shabbos, and the children are too young to stay home while he goes to shul? Does his daughter get left by a neighbor? Shlepped to shul where she sits and waits for him? Left by the strangers who were kind enough to agree to host them for the meal? All these things happen regularly.

And does anyone ask these children if they want to spend every other weekend in a different place? Or one night a week for that matter? What happens when Chani has a big test on Thursday and really would rather not go out for two hours with Tatty on Wednesday night? Some fathers are big enough to put their children's needs first, but, generally speaking, courts recognize parents' "right" to have that time with their children, not children's "right" to decide how to spend their time.

Anyone with school-aged children knows the difficulty of keeping track of all their papers, charts, supplies, uniforms, etc. Can you imagine adding to these difficulties that of moving back and forth between two residences and two guardians? What about the following incredibly common scenario: Child is invited to a get-together at another child's house. But it will be on the Shabbos when his father has custody, and father is not willing to give up his week. So negotiations ensue to change Shabbosos. Mother doesn't want to miss her Shabbos with her child either, but father reasons that she has him most of the week so she should give in. Or, even worse, mother has already made plans to go away that week and doesn't want to lose out on her freedom and so will not switch weeks.

In such a child's life, everything, everything becomes a negotiation. He tells his mother he needs new pants. Let your father pay for them. He wants to go away for Shabbos to a friend. No, not on my week, go on Mommy's week.

One last comment, though any child of divorce knows that I could go on for pages: You say that "everyone knows that not all children of divorce end up in such a sorry state." I found this comment interesting as the story does not tell us where the child "ends up." Yes, many children of divorce go on to become effective adults and parents, though in the process, without exception, they face challenges unique to the realities of divorce. But the story does not address what happens later in life; it only gives a glimpse into what reality looks like for a child whose life is split in half.

Such stories are indeed necessary. For one thing, I have found that teachers and rebbeim, despite their best intentions and well-meaning efforts to be understanding of children in these situations, still do not understand what these children go through. More importantly, though, many of those who divorce nowadays do not clearly understand what the repercussions are for the children.

I do not mean to excoriate those who do get divorced; I know each case must be judged separately and the case for divorce is often strong. I also think that the general spiritual weakness of our time creates more situations where divorce is the unavoidable outcome. But I do still think that there are those who divorce more cavalierly than they might if they realized just how greatly and completely it affects the children. Moreover, even those who must divorce need a better understanding of the difficulties their children face constantly in their day-to-day lives.

Children are the innocent bystanders, the civilian casualties, of divorce. Kol hakavod for giving a voice to those who often don't have one.

In the next story, we hear from a "lucky child" who has since grown up — and considers himself truly lucky. That story is the true postscript to this one.

Lucky Parents, Lucky Children

Dear Lucky Boy,

Reading your story moved me to tears and brought back a flood of memories. You see, I was also a child of divorce, and I know exactly how it feels to be living with one parent and bumped around from one relative to another without anyone asking you how you feel about it.

I don't know anything about the circumstances of your parents' divorce, but from what you described, they seemed like basically healthy, stable people. I doubt that you ever experienced the cycle of escalating hostilities, abusive explosions, separation, and ultimate reconciliation that marked my parents' marriage. Often, after one of his explosions, my father would storm out of the house, returning a few days later to resume the cycle.

I loved my father, and I still love him. He isn't a monster; he actually has many good qualities that I admire to this day. But he suffered from a progressive mental illness that caused him to be depressed at times and fly into manic rages at other times. When I was very young, he didn't show any symptoms of this illness, but certain difficult events in his life triggered the onset of behaviors that were truly frightening. Life in my parents' home was beyond toxic. It was a living nightmare.

Some of the things my parents did when they were divorcing are high on the top-ten list of things that divorcing parents shouldn't do: involving children in the divorce proceedings, making them feel that they are to blame, and using them as pawns in a financial or custody battle. At one point, my father actually sat us down and told us why he and my mother were getting divorced, and why it was all our fault. On some level, we realized that he was ill and irrational, but that didn't make the experience any less painful.

My mother was basically a healthy person, but she was so consumed with her difficulties with my father that most of the time she couldn't focus on putting her children first. Initially, she was determined to make the marriage work, and she put all her energies into improving her *shalom bayis*. Later, when things got really bad, she was concerned with her own survival. Even after my parents separated permanently, it took years before the *get* was finalized, and the court battles and restraining orders continued for many years after that. I remember feeling so, so relieved when the divorce became official.

Several times since the divorce, my father has told me, "Shragi, you know how long I stayed married to your mother for your sake?"

There's no point in trying to explain anything to him, but what I wish I could say is, "Ta, you didn't do anyone a favor by staying together when you needed to get divorced."

Lucky Boy, you *are* lucky that your parents don't live together. *Frum* people don't usually get divorced over trivialities, and they generally try hard to make things work before heading to *beis din*. So I'm assuming that if your parents made the decision to split, they really did need to live apart. By divorcing, they gave you the opportunity to grow up in an environment that was at least stable, if not ideal.

I didn't have that opportunity, and I had plenty of reasons to fail in life. Had I gone off the *derech* or engaged in self-destructive behaviors or had a miserable marriage, I could have presented my dysfunctional background as an excuse. But then I would have continued to suffer, excuses and all.

Instead, when I was a young teenager I resolved that I was going to have a happy marriage, and I was going to be the best husband and father. True, I didn't have a good model of what a stable home looks like, but I had a leg up because I realized that my childhood home was not normal and that the behaviors I had witnessed as a child were pathological. That realization was the first step in my journey toward a successful marriage.

It wasn't enough just to reject what I had seen between my parents, though. I needed to find positive role models whose relationship and communication skills I could emulate. Going to yeshivah out of town gave me that opportunity. I became particularly close to one rebbi, to the point where I was practically a *ben bayis* in his house.

What I liked about my rebbi and his wife was that they were so *normal*. I didn't think of them as special, lofty individuals; I just saw them as healthy, happy human beings, the type of people I wanted to be like. I was a frequent Shabbos guest at several other families, and each time I visited them I observed their interactions and family dynamics and took mental note of what normal family situations look like. At that point, and later when I went to learn in Eretz Yisrael, I felt as though I was gathering puzzle pieces that I would one day use to build a marriage in place of the scattered shards of my own broken home.

Before I entered *shidduchim*, I sought out a skilled therapist with whom I could sort out my own emotional issues. I wanted to make sure that I wasn't going to be an abusive husband, and that I wasn't going to be attracted to a spouse who was abusive or otherwise unhealthy.

The therapist helped me tremendously, and after several months I felt ready to start going out. I was very nervous, and not altogether confident in my ability to be the wonderful husband I wanted to be, but Hashem was very kind to me. When I met my wife, Aliza,

I had no doubt that we would be able to build a beautiful home together. When my rebbi confirmed that Aliza was right for me, we became engaged and we've never looked back.

They say that children of divorce go one of two ways: either they get divorced themselves or they go on to build great marriages.

Aliza and I are in the second category. She's also a child of divorce, although her experience was a lot less dysfunctional; more like yours, Lucky Boy, than like mine. But she, too, was determined not to repeat her parents' mistakes, and she, too, worked on herself to eliminate the emotional baggage of her upbringing.

Today, I consider myself exceptionally lucky. Lucky to have a happy, close marriage, yes, but also lucky to come from the background I came from. I wouldn't wish a broken home on anyone, but for those who emerge from the experience intact, there is an exceptional sweetness in the feeling of having grown and fought to be where you are.

And now I have been blessed to watch a process that I certainly did not imagine or expect. My children are the second generation of lucky — genuinely lucky. They were born into a family in which they are surrounded by multiple variations of grandparents, great-grandparents, aunts, uncles, and cousins. My mother remarried a few years ago and had a baby, so my children even gained an uncle who is the same age as them. My father-in-law recently remarried as well, so my children have yet another grandmother. Since many of our relatives are unwilling or unable to be in the same room, my kids get to have a rotating circle of loved ones at every *chag*, party, and special occasion.

It is by no means simple, and Aliza and I have had to become experts in diplomacy, but all my children know is that they are surrounded by more *bubbie*s, *savta*s, and grandmas than they can count. The very same factors that at times made my childhood confusing and unsettling make theirs exciting and blessed. My children don't see our "broken" families; they see a giant puzzle made up of all the people who love and care about them.

So hang in there, Lucky Boy. Do the work you need to deal with whatever issues linger after the divorce (and trust me, there will be issues). Find a mentor, a *rav*, a therapist — all the people you need to help you prepare yourself to build the kind of family *you* want. But always know that with some effort and *siyatta d'Shmaya*, you can give yourself and your children the best of both worlds. The story does not have to end with the "Lucky Boy." That can be just the beginning.

Your friend,

A Lucky *Tatty*

A Listening Ear

The call, like so many others, begins with silence on the other end of the line. I wait patiently, hoping that this caller will not lose courage and hang up. Since the crisis hotline I volunteer for is anonymous, we have no way of tracking our callers, no way of determining how many times, on average, people call and hang up before actually taking the plunge and telling their stories.

"*Shalom*, Zichron Chana hotline," I repeat in a well-practiced tone that is compassionate and inviting while at the same time calm and businesslike.

"Yes, hello," comes the hesitant response from the woman at the other end of the line. "Um, I'm not sure this is a crisis…"

"It doesn't have to be a crisis," I assure her. "We're here to provide support and referrals for whatever the issue is."

"Okay," she says. Long pause. "Well, uh, it's my son. He's being bullied terribly in school and —" Choked sob.

"So you're saying that your son is being bullied." I repeat the information slowly, trying to buy time in which she can regain her composure and dignity. "It's happening in school, the bullying."

"Yes." A sniffle. "It's been going on for months. I keep begging the school to do something about it, and they keep promising me that it's going to be dealt with, but it's not!"

If she's talking about "I" and "me," not "we" and "us," there must not be a husband in the picture; this woman is either a single mother, or she's living with an emotionally absent husband.

"It's really hard to watch your child suffering this way."

"Oh, it's torture!" she whispers. And then the floodgates open, and the whole story comes pouring out: how she tried valiantly to hold her marriage together, how she was forced to fight for her *get*, how her young son suffered through the separation and subsequent custody battle, how the kids in school taunted him mercilessly because he had a lisp.

"Do you know how much I pay for his speech therapy?" she cries. "You think I can afford it? And then these bullies go and undo everything, killing his self-esteem and wiping out whatever progress he's made."

"Your son is lucky to have a mother who cares so much about him and is willing to go to bat for him," I say. "With all you've been through, you're still able to focus on his needs and make his emotional health a priority, despite the expense. That's really impressive."

Having undergone six months of intensive training before assuming my post at the hotline, I know a thing or two about how to listen and talk to a person in pain: *Make the caller feel safe. Reflect back what she said in different words to show her that you heard and understood her. Offer empathy. Build up her self-confidence by pointing out what she's doing right.*

But my real training in listening comes from somewhere else completely.

———◆———

I've been married for 15 years, and I have three wonderful children. My husband is a brilliant mathematician who earns a generous living and is known as a big *ba'al tzedakah*. We live in a beautiful house in a small *yishuv* near Yerushalayim, and I have the option of working if I feel like it or not working if I don't feel like it.

So for years I've been spearheading all sorts of volunteer *chesed* work in the community. I organize and cook meals for families of sick people and new mothers. I belong to the local *chevrah kaddisha*. I take in children from broken homes when they need a place to go. I answer calls at a hotline for English-speaking women and children in crisis. I often receive donations of money and food to distribute to needy people at my discretion, and I am asked to speak in schools and at women's events about topics related to my communal work.

In our community, I'm the address for people who need any sort of help, whether they know me or not. Abused children, divorcees, widows, people with mental problems — ever since I can remember, they've come to me for help and advice.

To them, my life seems perfect. They see me — always smiling, well dressed, and willing to help — and they think I've got it all.

What they don't know is that my husband, Efraim, has mild autism, is severely depressed, and takes heavy medication. I am his caretaker, his mother, his secretary, and his personal assistant, but he is not a husband, a partner, or a friend. Our relationship goes one way only: from me to him. He provides me with money — which I'm not minimizing — but nothing more than that.

We've been in counseling on and off since the third week of our marriage, I've read all the *frum* self-help books and then some, and I've worked on my *middos* over and over again, but to no avail. Our relationship has remained frozen, almost nonexistent.

It was only a few months ago that Efraim was diagnosed with Asperger's and mild autism. Then, finally, everything fell into place, and I started to understand why nothing I tried had any effect. There is no cure for his condition, no medication that can mitigate its effects, and no real treatment.

He does not have a relationship with me or with the children and is little more than a body in our house. He is not an active participant in any family activities: meals, conversations, vacations, even *simchahs*.

Our oldest child seems to be on the spectrum, too, and I am in the process of finding the right diagnosis and seeing whether there is any way to help him. Our second child has severe emotional issues that stem from lack of contact with his father, and our youngest child is constantly fighting with Efraim.

I make sure to do all my *chesed* work when the children are in school so that I can be there when they're home. Emotionally, I'm their only parent, and I need to be available for them. But who's available for me?

I've turned to several people for support, but they've reacted to my story with skepticism and disbelief. "You have such a good husband!" they say. "Look how much he does for the community! He was even honored at the yeshivah dinner last year!"

Or they tell me, "But you look so good! You always have a smile on your face! It can't be that bad. Why don't you try going for counseling?" Or, "Oh, all men are like that. You just have to get used to it."

One person I confided in met me the following week and said, "I saw you and your husband walking together the other day, and you looked great. I'm so happy to see that things are working out."

Hah. Has anyone ever mentioned that appearances are deceiving?

Why can't people just *listen*? Why do they think they have to have answers and solutions for every problem? Do they think that by denying or diminishing my pain it will go away?

People think they understand. But they don't. They've never been in my shoes. And the more they busy themselves giving answers and advice, the less they listen, and the less they understand.

It doesn't take that much to be a good listener. All you have to do is acknowledge what the person is expressing ("So you're saying that..."), empathize with their difficulty ("That's really hard"), and refrain from judging, lecturing, or giving helpful suggestions — unless you're specifically asked. Ultimately, the person in pain is the one who has to do the work; with all of your good intentions, you can't do it for him. All you can do is listen and really care and *daven*.

That's exactly what I do during my hotline shift, as well as with all of the suffering people who make their way to my door or call me with their tale of woe. I listen, I acknowledge, I empathize, I offer up a *tefillah* that Hashem should help them and put the right words in my mouth.

I make recommendations only when the person reaches a point where he or she is asking directly for them — unless the situation is a real emergency, in which case I immediately connect the caller with the appropriate crisis intervention resource. But most of the *tzaros* that come my way are chronic situations that ebb and flow, and most of what I do is try to build people up to enable them to cope on their own.

Today's caller belongs to the latter group. I listen patiently as she describes the details of the situation, responding with the occasional "mm-hmm" or cluck of the tongue.

"The rebbi and the principal keep telling me that they're dealing with the bullying," she continues, "but Reuven's still coming home every day in a horrible mood. He doesn't like when I ask him about it, but here and there he'll mutter something about what the kids said that day."

She's talking about the school again, which means the problem really is the school and not some other issue that she's afraid to bring up directly.

"O.K.," I say. *Let's summarize the problem.* "The issue here is that you're trying to help your son, but the school isn't cooperating."

"Yes!" she practically shouts. "I'm just a single mother, and they don't give a hoot what I say!"

"You feel that they don't take you seriously."

"Exactly! What on earth am I supposed to do?"

Now she's asking for ideas. That means I can cautiously start to give suggestions.

"Has the school ever given you a concrete plan for dealing with the bullying? Did they promise that they would do anything specific?"

"No," she says. "They just said they're dealing with it."

"Would you feel comfortable approaching them and asking them to sit down with you and work out a plan?"

"I don't know," she says, her voice breaking again. "My Hebrew's not too great, and I feel like a fool every time I talk to the principal. Besides, I'm not sure myself what should be done."

She doesn't feel comfortable. Back off and revert to empathy. "It's a tough situation," I agree.

"And the worst part is —" Her voice cracks. "I feel that a lot of this is my fault. It took me a long time to realize what was going on. And I should have dealt with his lisp a long time ago, but I thought — silly me — I thought it was cute."

"We all make mistakes," I soothe. "But Hashem runs the world, and whatever happens is part of his plan — even the mistakes. If this is how things played out, that's what was meant to happen. Now, we need to figure out what's the best way forward."

She sighs. "I wish I knew what that was!"

Time for another suggestion. "Would it be better for you if there was a professional involved between you and the school, someone who's comfortable in both languages and has experience with the Israeli school system?"

"I've thought of doing that," she says, "but I have no idea who to speak to. And how would I pay for such a thing?"

Let's praise that little bit of creative thinking. "Good for you for thinking of solutions." *We're on the right track.*

"I can give you the name of an English-speaking professional who specializes in dealing with bullying," I tell her. "And then we can talk about possible sources of funding."

We speak for another few minutes, and then the woman thanks me for the advice and resources I provided. "And thanks so much for listening," she adds. "If feels so good to know that someone understands."

"That's what we're here for," I say. "Feel free to call again anytime."

She probably thinks that my little bit of advice is what's going to help her, I muse in the lull between that call and the next. *She doesn't realize that what's really going to help her is the fact that I made her believe in her own ability to deal with the problem. Sure, I gave her some pointers and phone numbers, but she could have come up with those on her own. What she really needed was someone who would listen without judging, who would understand without lecturing, and who would encourage without criticizing.*

I consider myself fortunate. Fortunate to have been blessed with a family. Fortunate to have money to use and to give away to those in need. Fortunate to be able to contribute to the community in so many ways. Most of all, I feel fortunate that my own pain has taught me how to really listen.

Wherever I go, I listen. And because my ears and heart are open, and my mouth and cell phone are mostly closed, I hear many things. People's *tzaros*, yes, but a lot of other things, too.

Just recently, I visited Yerushalayim. When I passed through the Judean desert, near my home, I heard the songs of King David echoing through the desolate hills. When I walked the streets of the Holy City, I heard the houses, the stones, the pavement lamenting the city's spiritual devastation, its outward construction boom notwithstanding. When I sat on the Egged bus as it barreled past the Mount of Olives, I heard the whispered pleas of the holy dead rising Heavenward. And when I finally reached the Wailing Wall, I could practically hear it wailing, in all its broken glory: wailing for the Father Who has been distanced from His children, wailing for the senseless hatred that divides those children, and wailing for all the tragedies that have befallen our people and united us in pain.

Perhaps I was imagining it, but I thought I heard something else that day, too: the faraway clip-clop of an age-old donkey and a faint, thin voice calling out, "Today, if you will only listen!"

Postscript:

One of the aspects of writing LifeLines that gives me tremendous satisfaction is the ability to act as a "listening ear" to the people who tell me their stories. I'm not a therapist, or an adviser; my job is to listen and really understand what a person is going through, to the point that I can put myself in his shoes and write the story in his voice.

Many people have told me that the opportunity to tell their story and really be listened to was therapeutic, even cathartic. That means a lot to me.

Sometimes, however, it's clear to me that the person telling me their story is making a serious mistake: cutting off ties with a family member, adopting a disastrous parenting approach, moving to a community that's not right for him. That puts me in a dilemma: On the one hand, I consider these people my friends, since they open their hearts to me and share deeply personal experiences. On the other hand, our relationship is strictly professional, with them telling me their stories and me listening and writing them up.

Is it my job to just listen and be supportive, or is it my job to warn them that they may be about to run straight off a cliff?

What do you think?

Part of the Family

I was sitting and saying *Tehillim* outside the operating theater when finally, finally, the door opened and a doctor strode out.

I jumped up. "Do you know what's happening with my wife?"

He stopped in his tracks, looked me up and down, and then turned his face and hurried down the hospital corridor. My eyes followed him helplessly.

I didn't know what to think. It's confusing and scary enough to enter a hospital's delivery ward in anticipation of the birth of your first child, and a whole lot more confusing and scary when you hear all sorts of ominous beeps and buzzing and your wife is rushed for an emergency C-section, her life and the baby's life in imminent danger.

As a first-time father-to-be, your presence is tolerated by the medical staff as a necessary nuisance, and the gravity of what is transpiring awes you into meek submission. Feeling useless, you try your best to be unobtrusive, wishing you could help out in some way but knowing that davening is the safest and only thing you can do.

So I continued saying *Tehillim*, watching the door to the operating theater out of the corner of my eye. It was an eternal few minutes before a second doctor walked out.

"What's happening?" I accosted him.

"It's a boy," he stated flatly.

A boy. I was a father!

"And is everything O.K.?"

But he was already hurrying down the corridor, and he didn't hear my question.

Just then, I heard a ping from my cell phone. It was a text message from my mother, who knew we had gone to the hospital 36 hours earlier and was waiting anxiously for an update. "Am I a *bubby* yet?" she had written.

Excitedly, I texted my reply: "*Mazel tov*! It's a boy!"

Then I quickly texted the same message to my in-laws.

After that it was ping after ping, as my cell phone buzzed with *mazel tovs* from my siblings and Suri's, plus a barrage of questions from the delighted grandparents: Did you see the baby yet? How much does he weigh? Is he cute? Who does he look like? Can you call?

"Can't call from here," I typed back. "Don't know any details yet." Oh, how maddening it was not to know!

After what seemed like an eternity, the door to the OR opened again, and this time a woman emerged. I thought she was a nurse, but she introduced herself as a neonatologist.

"Your baby suffered severe oxygen deprivation and has little chance of survival," she informed me. "Even if he does make it, he will be horribly brain damaged."

She rattled off the prognosis as though she were reading a newspaper, and then disappeared back into the OR.

I was numb, hardly hearing, understanding, or believing what she said.

I was sitting there with my *Tehillim* again when in burst my parents, carrying a huge bunch of "It's a boy!" balloons. I squirmed as I apprised them of the baby's condition and watched their expressions turn from delirious joy to shock and apprehension.

Our baby's condition only became a reality to me when I was allowed into the NICU and saw him in an incubator, hooked up to a million tubes and machines. The nurses handed him to me, and I could see that he was a beautiful baby, even with all the tubes. *This is my son*, I thought. *Wow.*

While I was holding him, the machines suddenly started to beep one after the other, and then they all switched off. Feeling panicky, I looked down at the baby's bluish skin, and I knew.

The baby was taken from me, and a different neonatologist came over and gently confirmed that he was no longer with us.

I swallowed hard, struggling to digest the news and the implications. Nine months of waiting, culminating with 36 hours of *Tehillim* and limbo, and now, no baby. I wasn't a father, after all. Bye-bye, balloons, bye-bye *shalom zachar*, bye-bye *bris*, *upsheren*, bar mitzvah, wedding.

There wasn't even a *levayah* to attend. The *chevrah kaddisha* took away the baby, not telling me about anything that was being done. To this day, I don't know where my son is buried. The whole process was sterile and impersonal.

For me, that is.

Suri was a wreck. Physically overwrought from the birth, and stunned by the loss of the baby who was so much a part of her, she turned into a despondent, hypersensitive stranger. This was not the young, happy, vibrant wife I knew, the girl who occasionally descended into a grumpy mood but then sprang back to life after a few hours.

We were in different worlds. I was devastated, but ready to move on with life. She was completely traumatized. We were both so helpless, so frozen.

Instead of waking up to a baby late at night, I found myself lying awake listening to Suri weeping into her pillow, or going in and out of the room trying to find a comfortable position: first in her bed, then on the couch, then in her bed, then on a chair.

There was no *shivah*, so I didn't know what to do with myself. Should I go back to yeshivah as though nothing had happened? I would have wanted to do that, but was it right to leave Suri alone? For the first few days, my mother-in-law came to stay with us, taking care of the cooking and the laundry and matching Suri's tears two to one. But then we were on our own.

A few of Suri's friends visited in the week or two after the birth, and I used the opportunity to escape to yeshivah for a few hours. There were a few guys who came over to me to clear their throats and say that they were sorry to hear what had happened, and I appreciated their concern. But I equally appreciated the people who said nothing and gave me the opportunity to feel normal and get back into the *sugya* I was learning.

Suri, on the other hand, was crushed when people didn't acknowledge her loss. And woe unto the hapless friend or acquaintance who tried to foist *emunah* onto her.

One day, when I came home from yeshivah after a close friend of hers had visited, I found her completely hysterical.

"Aviva was here for two hours," she choked out, "and she didn't say a single word about what happened! Not a word! She was talking about all sorts of things, asking where we're going to be for Yom Tov, but nothing, nothing about this whole situation. Doesn't she care at *all*?"

"If she took off a morning from work to spend with you, she probably does care," I said.

I thought what I said was reasonable, but Suri apparently felt otherwise, because she dissolved into a fresh flood of sobs.

Each time I'd walk in the door, Suri would interrogate me: "Who did you see? What did they say?"

I'd hem and haw, feeling quite frustrated by the expectation that I come home every day bearing a new report of exactly who had said what about our loss and in exactly what tone of voice and did he really look distressed or was he just saying it to be nice. At some point, I coined the phrase "the sympathy detection squad" to describe the way Suri grilled me on any bit of sympathy or validation people would offer.

I could understand Suri's need for sympathy, even though I wasn't looking for it myself. What I could not understand at all was the way she got equally upset at the people who didn't offer any sympathy and at those who offered it in a way that wasn't exactly to her liking on that particular day. *This is totally irrational,* I thought. *Does she expect people to read her mind? How's anyone supposed to know what she wants them to say? She herself doesn't even know!*

Once, when I called her *bein hasedarim,* she was in a tizzy over something one of our neighbors had said. "Can you imagine?" she wailed. "I met her on the way into our building, and she started telling me all about her baby's antics, how he already knows how to roll over, how he's starting to eat solids. Doesn't she realize how hurtful that is for me? Our baby would have been doing the same things by now!"

"But, Suri," I protested, "you complained to me just a few days ago that your sister didn't tell you when her Malky started walking. And you told me a few times that you hate when people avoid talking to you about their babies, and you wish they would just act normal around you."

"This was different," she pouted. "Here she was going on and on about her baby. It was too much."

"Honestly, I don't get it," I said. "If they don't tell you about their babies, it's no good. If they do tell you about their babies, it's no good. If they act unnatural and stilted around you, it's no good. If they act natural and enthusiastic around you, it's no good. Do you realize that practically everyone you talk to insults you in some way because of something they said or didn't say?"

"You don't understand my pain," she whispered. "You just don't understand."

In a flash, I did understand. This wasn't about what anyone did or said. This was about a grieving mother looking for ways to express her pain. There simply weren't enough words to give voice to Suri's feelings of loss and grief, so she was pinning her pain onto the thoughtless or even innocuous statements people made, using every possible encounter as a vehicle on which to unload her emotional turmoil.

It didn't matter what people said or did; they were just the convenient train car stopping at her station and relieving her of some of the heavy emotional burden she was carrying. In fact, they were doing her a *favor* by allowing her grief to piggyback on whatever it was they happened to say. She wasn't upset at anyone. She just needed a fresh license every day to continue to feel pain.

I can give her this license, I suddenly realized. *Even if I can't fully relate to the pain she's going through, I can give her the space to talk about her pain in whatever shape it takes at that particular moment.*

From then on, I started to really listen. Not so much to the words she said, but to the pain that formed their backdrop. When she cried to me that someone had asked her if she had any kids, I nodded wordlessly, translating the ostensibly hurtful question into a statement of longing to cuddle her own baby, who was instead being cuddled by the cold earth.

Once I learned how to really listen, we were able to really talk. We talked about *emunah*, about the idea that everything that happens is for the good, about the challenge of assimilating that idea into the difficult events of your own life. We talked about what could have been, and then we told each other that no, it couldn't have been: even if we had known better, even if we had gone to a different hospital, even if the doctors had handled the situation differently.

Entering Suri's world helped me to access my own emotional world, and I discovered that although I had processed the experience primarily on an intellectual level, I still had plenty of grief to deal with and lots of questions. Of course a Jew doesn't ask why, but still: why? And why us? What were we supposed to be learning from this? It was difficult for me to daven, and no matter how hard I tried to muster *kavanah*, my *tefillos* remained hollow and frosty.

Suri had questions, too, and so we went to speak to my *rebbeim* and to *gedolim*. Some of the answers we heard gave us comfort, while others made us feel agitated. Some of the answers were satisfying to me and unsatisfying to Suri, while others were satisfying to her and not to me.

"This isn't working for me," Suri would often say after I told her something one of my *rebbeim* had said. So we'd talk through it, trying to figure out why she couldn't accept a particular point. We'd open *mussar sefarim* in search of explanations, discussing and debating hashkafic points until the wee hours of the night.

We talked about why the idea of our loss being a *tikkun* didn't comfort us, and we decided that it was because we weren't on the level to appreciate what was going on in the spiritual realm. That humbling realization was strangely comforting.

In general, though, the approach from which we drew the most *chizuk* was the thought that there was a glorious future lying ahead of us, and that our loss would become the foundation for a beautiful family, in much the same way a seed rots in order to bring forth life. "It's painful, but the pain is not for nothing." That became our motto.

I wrote down all of the answers we heard from the people we spoke to, and at different points down the line I went back to those written answers. To my surprise, I found that as time went on, some of the insights that had given me *chizuk* initially no longer satisfied me, and some of the approaches that I had initially been unable to accept now resonated strongly with me. *It's a process*, I realized. *Every day is different.*

The process wasn't only about focusing on our grief; we also tried to distract ourselves. I made a point of bringing home little treats for Suri almost every day: a single rose, an iced coffee, her favorite nosh, a new CD. We went out to eat, we went out shopping, we went for long walks. Just as we gave ourselves permission to mourn, we gave ourselves permission to move on and be happy.

This was our *avodah*, and it wasn't easy. It would have been easier for Suri to stay home and mope, and for me to closet myself in yeshivah, especially since Shmuel, the *bachur* I learned with for first *seder*, was annoyed with my erratic attendance and inability to focus. When I explained to him that it was important for me to be *mechazeik* my wife, he said, "The bottom line is, you're not coming to *seder*, and you're not being the *chavrusa* I need." I was torn, but I knew that I could always find a different *chavrusa*; a different wife I wasn't going to find. (After Shmuel got married, he called to ask me *mechilah*. I guess marriage gave him a different perspective.)

As time went on, I found myself experiencing spurts of grief, intermingled with periods of detachment from the loss. When someone in my yeshivah lost a baby to crib death, I felt myself reliving the death of our baby, and when I went to be *menachem avel*, I felt my own loss more intensely than ever before.

At the times when I felt the ache acutely, I found that my davening was vastly improved. It was as though being in touch with myself put me in touch with the *Ribbono shel Olam*, too. There were fluctuations, of course, and some days were better than others, but the pattern was clear: at the times when I was disconnected from my feelings, I wasn't able to have *kavanah* in davening, and when I allowed myself to feel, my davening gained depth and passion.

In the soil of our loss, our marriage has flourished. We were still a *shanah rishonah* couple when we buried our first child, but in the months that followed, our relationship became closer and stronger than many couples who have been married for years. And today, *baruch Hashem*, we are the parents of several beautiful little children, as well as a precious *bechor* in *Gan Eden* who is still very much a part of our family.

Postscript:

After this story was printed, I received the following request:

> *I work as a chaplain at a hospital in the United States. I thought that many of my colleagues might benefit from the LifeLines column from the issue prior to Shavuos regarding the woman who bore a baby that died right after birth. It spoke of a number of profound truths.*

We received a similar request from someone involved in a well-known organization that helps those struggling with infertility and pregnancy loss. We also received a letter to the editor from a woman in England who runs a program that helps parents and grandparents after a miscarriage, stillbirth, or infant loss.

It wasn't surprising to me that these people took an interest in the story. But I thought that the story's message was much broader than the specific circumstances it addressed.

It's hard to know exactly what to say — and what not to say — to a person in pain. Does the person want sympathy, or does he prefer not to be reminded of his tzarah? Sometimes, as in this story, whatever you do is wrong. And when the person suffering repeatedly rebuffs you — retreating when you show concern, or lashing out at you when you don't — the natural reaction is to distance yourself, just when he needs you the most.

It helps to know that the person's reaction is less about what we said or did and more about what he himself is experiencing. Instead of withdrawing in guilt and confusion, we can chalk up his reaction to pain and keep showing him that we're there for him no matter what.

Who's on First?

My husband, Chaim, and I made *aliyah* shortly after the birth of our first child, Yoni. Other than some distant relatives in Haifa and Carmiel, we had no family in Israel, but that didn't deter us from pursuing our dream of living in *Eretz HaKodesh*.

I was secretly happy about moving to Israel for a different reason. In *chutz la'aretz* we belonged to a small community where family ties are very tight, and where absolute obedience and loyalty to one's parents is expected. My husband would never say no to any request his father or mother made, and he would routinely drop everything to do their bidding. Many times, his allegiance to his parents came at my expense, and while I never dreamt of making an issue about it, I was glad that we were going to be moving far away.

Following Yoni's birth, before we moved to Israel, I had spent two weeks recuperating at my parents' house. During that time, the baby and I were showered with the adoring attention of both my parents and my younger siblings. The challenges of new motherhood were greatly alleviated by the comforts and pampering I enjoyed, and I don't remember lifting a finger the entire two weeks. It also helped that Yoni was a good-natured, placid baby who ate and slept when he was supposed to and didn't fuss much.

I gave birth to my second child, Avraham, a year and a half after we arrived in Israel. My parents were not able to come to Israel to help us, and I quickly realized that recuperating after a baby with no support system — and an active toddler to care for — is no picnic. What's more, Avraham was a screamer from day one, he didn't eat well, never slept, and cried around the clock. *And* Yoni came down with chicken pox two days after I came home from the hospital.

During this time, Chaim was very busy preparing for the arrival of his parents, who were supposed to land the day before the *brit milah*. First, he was busy searching for an available apartment near us that would meet my mother-in-law's exacting standards. Then he was busy setting up the apartment for them. And then, he was busy arranging a cell phone and other amenities for them.

I assumed that my in-laws would go directly to their apartment to rest after they landed, but instead they came to us to see the baby. Yoni was whining and looked awful with his chicken pox, and he clung to me tightly, refusing to even say hello to his grandparents.

I wasn't really up to having company, but no one asked me. Chaim and his parents sat in the living room and chatted, while I tended to Yoni and occasionally retreated to my bedroom to feed the baby.

At some point that afternoon, seeing that my in-laws were showing no signs of leaving, I went into the kitchen to prepare supper for them. The supper I prepared was presentable, but far from gourmet, and I was sure my mother-in-law would never have served such a supper to guests. I very badly wanted to make a good impression on my in-laws, especially since this was the first time we were having them over, and I felt quite embarrassed at my performance.

We had many other guests for the *Brit Yitzchak* (our community's version of a *vachnacht*) that evening, and I was busy on my feet for hours.

My in-laws stayed with us until after midnight. I was exhausted, but I didn't dream of going to sleep while they were in my apartment. Nor did I feel comfortable tackling the mess while I had company.

Finally, at about 12:30, Chaim accompanied his parents to their apartment. That was when I began to straighten up the house. I was hoping that Chaim would be back within a few minutes to dry dishes or hold the baby, who cried every time I put him down, but Chaim didn't return until 1:30 a.m., which was about when I finished cleaning up.

When I asked Chaim what had taken so long to accompany his parents, he became very upset. "I had to help them settle into their apartment," he said. "They just traveled 6,000 miles for our *simchah*, they're not familiar with the country, and we're the only ones they have here."

I absorbed his explanation wordlessly. I knew that my in-laws were planning to stay for three weeks, and I realized that I would just have to rise to the occasion and take care of them during that time. *I'll rest after they leave*, I told myself. Had I been a guest in my mother-in-law's house, I wouldn't have had to lift a finger. But since the tables were turned, and my in-laws were the guests, it was up to me to cater to them. And that was how I found myself serving three proper meals every day. After the *brit*, my in-laws came straight to our apartment, and the first thing I did was serve them lunch. No one seemed to find it unusual that I was on my feet — cooking, serving, and clearing — just eight days after giving birth, and it didn't occur to me to shirk these responsibilities or ask my guests to help out. Chaim was waiting on his parents hand and foot, and he expected me to follow his example and put aside my own needs in favor of theirs.

In the meantime, I was becoming increasingly frustrated with my two babies. Both Yoni and Avraham were demanding attention constantly. How could I take care of them if I was busy making sure my in-laws were comfortable? At times, especially in the middle of the night when both Yoni and Avraham were crying, I would break down in tears, angry at the babies for not letting me rest.

There was no way I could rest during the day, with Yoni still sick, Avraham recuperating from his *brit*, and my in-laws around. My mother-in-law occasionally held Avraham, but when he cried she invariably told me that he was hungry and handed him back to me to feed. I clenched my teeth each time she did that, resenting being told when to feed my baby. I ended up just holding him myself. Besides, it wasn't as if I could take a nap when she was holding him; what would she do if he really was hungry?

Each time my in-laws left our apartment, my mother-in-law would say something to the effect of "You really should be resting more, you know. Go lie down."

I never quite knew how to respond. I couldn't exactly say, "Well, if someone would offer to watch Yoni and Avraham, I might be able to rest." Instead I said, "It's O.K., I'm fine."

Chaim would look relieved when I said that, and he would invariably proceed to rush out with his parents for an indeterminate amount of time. There was always some errand or another to run for them: "My parents weren't happy with the night-light I bought them, so I had to go to a few stores to find the type they wanted."

I blamed myself for not being capable enough to take care of two babies on my own while keeping the house in tip-top shape, serving well-balanced meals, and preparing elegant Shabbat fare. Whenever I complained, Chaim would look at me disapprovingly, as though he considered me a failure for being unable to fulfill my basic duties as a wife, mother, and hostess.

I knew that I was pushing myself too hard, and that I needed to be taking better care of myself, but I didn't see that I had a choice. No one was offering to help me, and Chaim was too busy with his parents to be attentive to my needs. I looked forward to the day when my in-laws would leave and I could go back to being a human being. But in the meantime, I could not afford that luxury.

One Friday afternoon, Chaim was out with his father, and my mother-in-law walked in as I was washing the floor. She was aghast. "Why are you washing floors, right after birth?" she demanded. "You should have a cleaning lady do that."

I was about to tell her that Chaim usually did the floors on *erev Shabbat*, but I thought better of it. She wouldn't like the idea of Chaim washing floors any better than the idea of me washing floors. And I was embarrassed to tell her that we couldn't afford a cleaning lady.

Instead I said, "It's really no big deal. I don't mind it at all."

"To each his own," she said with a shrug, as she gingerly tiptoed across the wet floor and seated herself on the couch.

Somehow I managed to keep juggling everything that had to be done — until my in-laws left. Then I fell apart. I stopped getting dressed, I stopped cooking, I let the house go to shambles. I took care of Yoni and Avraham in a detached way, as if in a daze. And when Chaim would say something about the house going to pieces, I would either start sobbing or yell at him unintelligibly.

One day, after a particularly angry exchange, Chaim decided that there was something very wrong with me. "I think you have postpartum depression," he said. His tone was accusing, not sympathetic.

"Maybe," I said helplessly.

Chaim made me call an organization that helped women with postpartum depression, and they referred me to a psychologist who specialized in PPD. Feeling like a total loser, I made an appointment with Dr. Rosman, the psychologist.

"Dr. Rosman would like your husband to accompany you for the first appointment," the secretary chirped.

When we sat down in Dr. Rosman's office, I didn't know what to say, and I looked to Chaim to begin talking. He described how moody I was, how I would often break down in tears for no apparent reason, and I would yell at him almost maniacally when he had done nothing wrong.

Dr. Rosman nodded gravely as Chaim spoke, taking copious notes on a sheet of paper. Then he turned to me and asked me to describe what my life had been like since the baby's birth.

I told him about Yoni's chicken pox, about Avraham's crying spells, and about my in-laws' extended visit. I told him how difficult it had been for me to juggle all of my roles and how hard it had been to please everyone.

Dr. Rosman listened intently. Finally, when I finished speaking, he looked Chaim squarely in the eye and said, "Your wife does not have postpartum depression. She has been stretched beyond the limits of human capability, and what you're seeing now is the inevitable result."

Turning to me, he said, "You have to know that you're not a superwoman, and you have to learn to recognize and respect your own needs. You need rest, you need help in the house and with the kids, and you need emotional support. If the people around you do not appreciate or legitimize those needs, you have to make them aware of your needs and insist that they be respected. A person shouldn't live for himself, but only if your physical and emotional needs are met will you be able to fill the needs of others."

Then he looked back at Chaim. "It's wonderful that you're so devoted to your parents," he said. "But after a man gets married, his first obligation is to his wife. If she needs help — and every woman in the world needs lots of help after birth — it's your responsibility to be there for her, even if it means that your parents have to manage on their own during their visit. Her needs have to be your top priority."

We were both a bit stunned by Dr. Rosman's diagnosis, and it took us some time to absorb what he was saying. But I'm happy to say that the lesson he taught us has made a huge difference in our marriage. Chaim's a good, caring person, and once he internalized Dr. Rosman's words, he made a dramatic shift in his priorities and began directing his primary attention to my needs instead of those of others. As for me, I began learning to identify my own needs and ask for the assistance and support I required without feeling guilty or incompetent.

My respect for my own needs, coupled with Chaim's recognition that I come first no matter what, has completely changed our lives. I only wish that the two of us had learned these lessons back in our *chattan* and *kallah* classes, instead of learning the hard way.

Postscript:

Here's an update from the narrator, three years after this story was printed:

We are doing great; we have four beautiful children, and are still living in Israel. The second my husband learned what was right and wrong, our marriage just became something amazing. As for my in-laws, my mother-in-law adores me, as does my father-in-law. They feel that my husband married an amazing girl. I am so thankful to my therapist for the simple knowledge he gave us.

Interesting that her in-laws adore her, no? If you think about it, though, it's not surprising. No one likes a doormat. When people establish healthy limits, they earn a lot more respect from the people around them than if they allow those people to trample all over them.

Respect is the foundation for any healthy relationship. But in order to win the respect of others, a person needs to have self-respect first.

Part 2

חַיִּים שֶׁל טוֹבָה, חַיִּים שֶׁל בְּרָכָה

A Life of Goodness,
a Life of Blessing

A Forest Grows in Brooklyn

They say that being a girl in *shidduchim* is like being lost in a desert, and being a boy in *shidduchim* is like being lost in a forest. I can see why being lost in a desert might be more painful, more lonesome, and more desperate, but being lost in a forest is a lot more confusing and overwhelming.

The fact of the matter is, there are lot more "good" girls out there than "good" boys. Maybe it's because it's easier to be a good girl than a good boy: you don't have to learn three *sedarim* a day, get up in time for *zeman krias Shema* every single day, and never miss davening Shacharis, Minchah, and Ma'ariv with a *minyan*, no matter where you are. Or maybe it's because girls are generally gentler, more disciplined, and inclined to do the right thing, unlike boys, whose nature is more aggressive.

I may not have been *the* top guy in my *shiur*, but just being a solid learner and a *mentch* made me a prime catch in *shidduchim*.

Add to that the fact that I come from a nice, *balebatish* family, plus I cut a decent appearance, plus I actually speak a decent English, and you get this equation: one good boy equals hundreds of girls being *redt*. I know it sounds obnoxious, but thems the breaks.

I don't expect any girls out there to pity me, but the reality is that when you're looking to marry one person, hundreds of names are no better than a handful. Not only was my mother on the phone day and night with would-be *shadchanim*, but wherever she went, she was inundated with suggestions. It seemed everyone thought that I'd be just *perfect* for this friend or that relative.

Much as we appreciated these well-meaning suggestions, there came a point when my mother dreaded picking up the phone or venturing out to a *simchah*.

"I know I should muster a thank-you when people *redt* a *shidduch*, but it's all I can do not to scream!" she said, sighing. "How on earth am I supposed to check out all these girls? They all have the most wonderful *middos*, they're all intelligent and accomplished and have great personalities, not to mention *simchas hachaim*. Where on earth do I start?"

Since my mother's name is Sara Esther, the easiest place to start was by weeding out any girl whose name was Sara or Esther, or any permutation thereof, in whole or in part. That effectively eliminated a good 10 percent of *shidduchim* — even the ones whose proponents assured us that "she's not called Sara, it's just a second name, no one knows she has that name, you don't even have to put it on the invitation."

Next to be ruled out was any girl who lived outside the tristate area. We were being *redt* lots of good girls from Chicago, Baltimore, Toronto, Los Angeles, and elsewhere — with promises that they would come in for every date, that they would make the wedding in New York, that they would support me for 10 years, even buy me a house — but why schlep out to *yehupitz* when there were so many wonderful girls right here in Brooklyn? My parents even thought twice before saying yes to girls from Monsey, Lakewood, or the Five Towns. Nothing against these girls, of course, but all things being equal, you sooner say yes to a *shidduch* that's in your own backyard.

Even with these criteria in place, the decision of whom I should go out with was made with equal doses of "eeny, meeny, miny, moe" and "the squeaky wheel gets the oil." When my mother could find no compelling — or even not-so-compelling — reason to say no to a *shidduch, and* the *shadchan* gave her no rest, she'd reluctantly give a yes. "I don't know why this one is better than the other dozen I'm looking into," she'd say. "But her aunt's been calling me every day, and I needed to get her off my back already."

Needless to say, going into a date this way doesn't engender a great deal of enthusiasm. At the end of the day, the girl you're meeting is just a human being with imperfections, idiosyncrasies, and moments of weakness, and the thought that there are hundreds of other, potentially better candidates out there makes it hard to believe that *this* is the one. Maybe the next one will be better? Maybe number 281 on the list will be better?

In this way, I went out with girl after girl — once, twice, three times, even eight times — methodically making my way down the list. And the longer I was in *shidduchim,* the longer the list became. There was always a reason to say no: the girl was too forceful or too meek, too sophisticated or too simple, too serious or too flighty. There were also plenty of times when the girl said no, which stung, but it was easier in a way than having to agonize over whether to end the *shidduch.*

Each time a *shidduch* ended, there was always another girl waiting in the wings. "I told Mrs. Taback that her sister-in-law's cousin would be next," I heard my mother telling my father one evening as I was getting ready to meet the girl du jour. When I came home later that evening and told my mother that the date had been a nonstarter, she looked almost relieved. "So I can get back to Mrs. Taback with a yes," she half-asked, half-stated.

I groaned. "Ma, I need a break! I've gone out with three girls in the last month alone!"

"Fine, I'll tell her to wait a week or two. But not more — she's driving me crazy!"

One Shabbos, we were sitting around after the *seudah* and my father mentioned that there was a new receptionist at the busy medical clinic where he worked as an ophthalmologist.

"They never ask me to interview the secretaries," he said. "That's Dr. Lederman's job, he's the HR guy. But Lederman was out this week, and I was the oldest doctor around, so Mrs. Coleman, the office manager, tells me, 'Do me a favor and interview this girl. I think she'll make a good receptionist, but I want one of the doctors to meet her and see if you think she'll be able to deal with difficult patients.'

"I don't know the first thing about interviewing, but everyone in the office knows you don't say no to Mrs. Coleman. So I say sure, no problem, and I sit down to interview this girl, even though I'm probably more nervous than she is. But she comes in and introduces herself very naturally — 'I'm Esther Malka Sussman from St. Louis' — and the whole interview goes so smoothly."

"Did you hire her?" my mother asked.

"I sure did. I was really impressed with her: so refined, so mature, so responsible, so unspoiled. Her parents are in *chinuch*, and she needs to work to pay her way through school. She's enrolled in a master's degree program here in Brooklyn, and she's living with her aunt and uncle. I asked her if it's hard for her to be away from her family, and you know what she answered? She said, 'I think it's harder for my parents.' That's the kind of girl you want your son to marry, you know what I mean?"

I felt my ears growing hot. Even after being in *shidduchim* for close to three years, it was uncomfortable to hear a prospective *shidduch* being discussed in front of me. Not that this was *shidduch* material: the girl's name was Esther, she was from out of town, and her parents were obviously not the *balebatish* type. But still.

As it happened, Mrs. Coleman went on vacation the following week, and my mother went into the office a few times to do some paperwork for my father. Working alongside the new receptionist, she, too, came home with glowing reports.

"This girl, she's different from the girls you've been dating, I can't explain it. In another league somehow. Too bad the name's Esther. Otherwise I'd consider having someone *redt* it."

"But, Ma," I pointed out, "she's from St. Louis! You can't get more out of town than that."

"Yeah," she agreed. "Can you imagine *us* doing a *shidduch* with a St. Louis family? And from what I understand, they can't scrape two pennies together."

She sighed. "It's really a shame, though, because she's exactly what you need."

For the next few months, Esther Malka Sussman continued working in my father's office, and I continued going out with girls who boasted the right first names, zip codes, and pedigrees. Until, one day, Mrs. Coleman marched into my father's office and said, "Dr. Markowitz, what are you waiting for? One day this Esther Malka is going to get engaged, and then you'll kick yourself for not snapping her up. And don't start giving me all the silly reasons why it's not *tzugepast*; if there was ever a girl for your Dovid, she's the one, and I don't care if her father hasn't bought himself a new hat in 20 years and her mother uses plastic tablecloths at every meal!"

Everyone knows you don't say no to Mrs. Coleman — everyone except Esther Malka Sussman. My parents asked a *she'eilah* and were told it's no problem for my mother to have a daughter-in-law named Esther Malka, so they told Mrs. Coleman to go ahead and *redt* the *shidduch* to Esther Malka's parents. But when Esther Malka heard about it, she walked into Mrs. Coleman's office and said, "I appreciate your thinking of me, and this does sound like a wonderful *shidduch*, but I don't feel that it's fair to put Dr. Markowitz in such an awkward position. He was kind enough to hire me, and I can't compromise our professional relationship by making him embarrassed to meet me at work because I'm going out with his son."

"Listen, sweetheart," Mrs. Coleman said, peering over her reading glasses, "*I'm* the office manager here, so *I'll* be the one to decide whether any professional relationships are being compromised. And don't think you can say no, because I already convinced your parents — not that they needed much convincing, they said they just had to run it by you — and just this morning I told Dr. Markowitz that you're interested in meeting his son."

Esther Malka was livid. "You agreed to the *shidduch* without getting a yes from me?" she asked Mrs. Coleman incredulously. "That alone is a reason for me not to go on the *shidduch*. But since I don't want to hurt Dr. Markowitz, I'll meet his son. Once."

A Forest Grows in Brooklyn | 85

Unlike so many of the girls with whom I had gone out previously, Esther Malka did not seem to feel inordinately privileged to have landed a date with me. Which made things interesting, quite different from my usual first dates.

At the time, I didn't know that Esther Malka had agreed to go out with me only once; I was sure that we'd go out a second time. So I was shocked to hear Mrs. Coleman's evasive answer when I asked her to set up a second date. Mrs. Coleman didn't *do* evasive, and if she wasn't giving a straight answer, it meant that Esther Malka could not be strong-armed into giving a yes.

Rabbi and Mrs. Sussman convinced their daughter to give it a second try, Mrs. Coleman's maneuvering notwithstanding. Esther Malka was still a bit standoffish on the date, however, and although I did see why my parents thought we'd be compatible, I felt ill at ease, and so did she.

Nevertheless, we both agreed to a third date. But there was a string of legal holidays coming up, and Esther Malka was going home for the week.

"You know," my mother mused, "you should really fly out to St. Louis to meet her."

I couldn't believe what I was hearing. "Go out to St. Louis during the *zeman*?" I wondered. "Ma, you're the one who wasn't happy if I had to drive out to *Monsey* for a date!"

"You're right," she admitted. "But somehow, because I know Esther Malka, I think of her as my own daughter, not as some random name in my *shidduch* notebook. I wouldn't want my daughter to have to go out in a different city, far away from me, so I think it's only fair her to meet her on her home turf, and take her out from her parents' house, where she feels comfortable."

In St. Louis, *I* felt uncomfortable. Not knowing my way around, I was completely at the mercy of Esther Malka and her parents. I was planning to rent a car and stay in a hotel, but when I spoke to Esther Malka on the phone, she told me not to bother.

"I'll pick you up from the airport, and my parents have an extra car that they'll be happy to lend you. You can stay with my neighbors, the Krasnows; they have a huge basement, and they love having guests."

When I landed in St. Louis, Esther Malka drove me to the Krasnows. "There's Minchah at 5," she told me. "I'll leave you the car so you can get there and maybe take a spin around St. Louis, and then you can come over to my parents' for supper before we go out."

"It's fine," I protested feebly. "I brought along food. I can take care of myself."

"Of course you can take care of yourself," she agreed. "But you're our guest, so this is our pleasure. How often do you think boys come out here?"

Not often, I supposed. For the first time, I found myself understanding what it must be like for a girl to be dating in a foreign city, far away from her family. Even if Esther Malka knew her way around New York better than I knew my way around St. Louis, the feeling of being a stranger in a strange land — a desert, to boot — must have made *shidduchim* so, so hard for her.

Having stepped out of my regular environment, I no longer felt like Mr. Prime Catch whose list of names could have filled an entire phonebook. I was just a visitor who didn't know anyone and was grateful for the hospitality of the Sussmans and the Krasnows.

And Esther Malka was no longer the polished, professional medical secretary, or the master's degree student pursuing a profitable career. She was just a nice girl from a nice family, plastic tablecloths and all.

When we went out on our third date, with me driving her parents' car and her directing me to the nearest hotel lounge, it didn't feel like a date at all. It was just the two of us talking and getting to know each other. I had ventured out of my forest to meet a lonely desert traveler, and suddenly, we found ourselves in an oasis.

It's been a few years since then, but we're still talking and getting to know each other, over the din of a bunch of rowdy kids.

Postscript:

In response to this story, a reader wrote:

> *I was deeply touched by the article because I live out of town myself, and as an amateur shadchante, I experience this scene*

too many times. *The finest, most accomplished girls are being rejected simply because they are from "out of town." How my heart aches for them. I wish more young men and their families would have the open-mindedness to follow along the path of that young man in the story. They might be pleasantly surprised at the hidden treasures they would discover along the way.*

Shidduchim, we know, are as difficult as the splitting of the sea. During the shidduch process, people often have to stretch themselves beyond their comfort zone, move past their self-imposed boundaries and limitations, and jump into a situation that is unfamiliar and unexpected. And that's true whether a person is lost in a desert or a forest.

If shidduchim were a commercial enterprise, then establishing geographic restrictions in order to filter suggestions might be a good idea. But a shidduch isn't a business deal; it's a supernatural event, a convergence of two disparate lives, a reunion of two half-souls of undetermined geographic proximity.

The bas kol that declares "Bas ploni l'ploni" doesn't specify location. If we want the sea to split for us, maybe we have to be prepared to cross it.

From Mourning to Joy

On July 26, 1970, the 22nd day of Tammuz, 20-year-old Neil Gross and 18-year-old Elaine Queller — both of Middle Village in Queens, New York — were married in a Conservative ceremony at the Electchester Jewish Center in Queens. Four years later, they had a daughter, Amy — me — who was followed by a son, Steven. By then, my parents had settled in Bensalem, Pennsylvania, where they have lived ever since.

My parents lived the American dream: a house, two children, two cars, working dad, and stay-at-home mom. Okay, so we didn't have a puppy or a white picket fence (ours was metal), but it was close enough.

Our life was blessedly ordinary. In the morning, Daddy would make Mommy a coffee and bring it to her. When my brother and I would come home from school, the dinner table would be set, with a quarter of a melon or a half of a grapefruit (already sectioned for us, with a maraschino cherry in the center) sitting at each place.

Then it was time to wait for Daddy to come home. When we heard Daddy's car rumble into the driveway, my mother would hurry to the mirror to make sure she looked her best. "No telling Daddy any bad news until after he has dinner," she'd remind us.

The four of us would eat together and discuss what had happened to each of us during the day. My father would then head to the den, where he would watch Dan Rather report the news, while my mother cleaned up from dinner. Weekends were variations of that, with occasional restaurant outings, softball games, and get-togethers with family and friends.

My mother had memories of going to shul with her grandmother and wondering why Grandma Sadie always kept a pot of food on the stovetop all day Saturday, but her parents had assured her that those things were just ancient holdovers from Austria and Poland. My father's exposure to Judaism was even thinner, almost non-existent.

I guess being Jewish was on my parents' radar screen to some degree, though, because when I entered the third grade, my parents decided it was time to join a Conservative synagogue and enroll me in the congregation's afternoon Hebrew school. Most of the kids there hated the routine, but I loved every minute of it.

Mrs. Geltzer at the Hebrew school taught me to read Hebrew and talked a lot about Shabbat. She let each child take a turn bringing home the "Shabbat Box," which contained candles, grape juice, and challah, so that we could perform these rituals on Friday night with our families.

I still remember the week it was my turn to be the Shabbat Child and bring home the box. I lit the candles and said the prayer, while my mother peered over my shoulder, beaming with pride. "Good Shabbos," she said to me once I uncovered my eyes.

"We say, '*Shabbat Shalom*,'" I corrected her.

With time, we became more committed Conservative Jews, joining first the Friday-night services and then the Saturday-morning services as well. When I came home from Hebrew School at the age of 10, after a stimulating discussion about *kashrut*, I asked my mother why we didn't keep kosher. She looked at me and said, "I don't know."

Within a few weeks, my parents were taking classes with the rabbi, and he was helping us *kasher* our home. From then on, we kept very strict *kashrut* in the house. (We still allowed ourselves to frequent *treif* restaurants and eat pepperoni pizza on paper plates in the backyard. Apparently, we were very concerned about our dishes going to Heaven!)

Right after Rosh HaShanah, the year I was 11, I asked my father, "Daddy, why don't we have a *succah*?" The next thing I knew, my father was at the hardware store buying four-by-fours, rolls of canvas, and other materials to build our first tiny *succah*. Shortly afterward, I was bat mitzvahed, and I proudly read from the Torah while wrapped in my pink tallit.

I joined the United Synagogue Youth, went to Camp Ramah, and attended Hebrew high school. If I learned about something Jewish, I wanted to do it and experience it, and my marvelous parents went right along with it, either joining me or cheering me on in the background.

I chose to attend University of Maryland for a number of reasons, among them the active campus Hillel. My first Friday night there, I excitedly made my way to Shabbat services. Such diversity! In addition to the vibrant Conservative *minyan* that I attended, there were Orthodox, Reform, and Reconstructionist sit-on-the-floor-guitar-playing services all going on at the same time. The Shabbat dinner was lively and spirited, with an abundance of traditional foods and singing. I met a few really nice people and had some great conversations.

As I walked back to my dorm that night, I couldn't help but feel that I was in the prime of my Jewish life, and I went to sleep happily dreaming of the four amazing years of Jewish experiences ahead of me.

The next morning I slept a bit late, and by the time I reached the Hillel House for Shabbat morning services, it was already 10:30. I was expecting to find a large crowd in attendance, but to my surprise, there were only a few guys sitting around, waiting for more males to make up a *minyan* so they could start.

Where was everyone? Sleeping, I quickly learned. Apparently, the Jews at the University of Maryland circa 1992 participated in the feel-good Jewish stuff, but when it came down to getting out of bed on a Saturday morning to pray, they left that to the handful of religious students on campus. To say that I was disappointed is an understatement.

When I returned to the Hillel House on Monday morning, I noticed a sign advertising a class on the weekly *parashah* with Rabbi Tzvi Teitelbaum that evening. I decided to attend the class, but I didn't understand most of it. Rabbi Teitelbaum kept talking about Moshe Rabbeinu and Avraham Avinu, which I found very interesting, since I hadn't known that Moses and Abraham had last names. I went up to Rabbi Teitelbaum after the class to introduce myself and ask him a couple of questions, and before I knew it, he invited me to his house for Shabbos. I was happy not to have to repeat the previous week's experience at the Hillel House, so I accepted.

That Friday, I bought a bottle of wine and headed to the Teitelbaums' house for a Shabbos that changed my life forever. The Conservative movement had taken me as far as it could, but when push came to shove, it was as empty as the *minyan* on Shabbos morning at the Hillel House. Not so what I saw at the Teitelbaums.

When Mrs. Teitelbaum, surrounded by her adorable daughters, entered the dining room to *bentch licht*, I felt something stir inside me. The beautifully set table, the delicious food, the stimulating discussions at the table, the insightful *divrei Torah* that connected the *parashah* to real life, and the rousing *zemiros* — I wanted to be connected to all that. I couldn't wait for Shabbos to come again.

With time, I developed close ties with the Teitelbaums, as well as with members of the *frum* community in the White Oak neighborhood of Silver Spring, Maryland, which was then under the leadership of Rabbi Kalman Winter, *z"l*.

I naïvely thought that my parents would be happy that I was progressing in my Jewish observance, just as they had been enthusiastic when I had expressed interest in various observances in the past.

Boy, was I wrong.

My parents began to complain that I was spending an awful lot of time off campus, and not at the fraternity or sorority scene where college students typically hang out. "Who are these people you're going to for Shabbat?" they would ask suspiciously.

My parents were livid when they discovered that I wanted to keep Shabbos "the real way," and not the way we had done it when I was growing up. One week, when I was home for Shabbos, I wished my mother "good Shabbos" after she lit candles.

"I used to say 'good Shabbos,'" she retorted angrily, "but that wasn't good enough for you. Now '*Shabbat Shalom*' isn't good enough for you?" The meal started with icy silence and ended with screaming and tears.

These arguments went on for months. Many phone calls turned into shouting matches and ended up with all of us crying. Even conversations that had nothing to do with religion ended up there.

It was an awful year and a half for all of us, culminating with the final blow of my dropping out of college and going off to Israel for a year to learn in EYAHT. I spoke to my parents once a week on Sundays, which was a big luxury 20 years ago. But those conversations yielded dividends. Because the minutes were so precious, we spent the time carefully, not yelling or crying. Slowly, my parents started to take an interest in what I was doing, while I kept tabs on the news at home, including the fortunes of the Philadelphia Phillies and Eagles. At the end of my year, my parents came to visit me, and they spent an authentic Shabbos in Har Nof.

Finally, they started to understand what had attracted me to this unfamiliar and radical lifestyle. And I started to understand that it wasn't that they were anti-Torah per se; they were just terrified of losing me and fearful that the religious thing would drive a wedge between us. My father had dreams of walking me down the aisle in our Conservative synagogue, and my mother was hoping that one day her grandchildren would spend weekends with her. They thought that my *frumkeit* was a rejection of them, of their values, and of the life lessons that they had diligently instilled in me.

What neither they nor I realized at the time was that their lessons had seeped through me like hot water seeps through a tea bag. In the process of becoming *frum*, I had learned how to be a Jew, but growing up in their home, I had learned how to be a *mentch*. From my parents, I absorbed the precious lessons of love, devotion, respect, and admiration, lessons that eventually formed the foundation of my own marriage.

My husband, Shmuel, and I adhered to a few guiding principles that we learned early on from exceptional people who acted as mentors to us.

"Don't try to be *mekarev* your family," they told us. "It's not your job. Simply live each day with good *middos*, respect, and love for them. Torah can sell itself when it's obvious that your choices in life are a direct result of your *mitzvah* observance."

We were also advised to avail ourselves of whatever leniencies we could in order to avoid imposing our religious demands on our non-*frum* family members. In response to our concern that our children would get confused, we were told, "If you conduct yourselves with *seichel* and according to *da'as Torah*, then your kids won't be confused at all. On the contrary, they will learn from you how to treat people respectfully."

We went to great lengths to honor and respect my parents. And they, in turn, learned to respect our way of life. It wasn't one experience, or two, or 20 that led to their change of perspective. It was a collection of many Shabbosos and *Yamim Tovim* spent with our family and the amazing people of our community in Silver Spring. It was seeing the way *frum* Jews care for each other. It was the outpouring of *chesed* that enveloped us after the birth of our quadruplets: volunteers, meals, financial assistance, everything. It was the feeling of never being judged negatively for saying the wrong thing, or wearing pants, or not covering hair, or wearing a different yarmulke.

Originally, my parents had disliked the Teitelbaums, whom they viewed as evil and cultlike, but after attending my Shabbos *sheva berachos* — which was held at the Teitelbaums' home — they began to see what had drawn me to this special family. Two and a half years of resentment melted away during that Shabbos, and from then on a beautiful relationship began to blossom between my parents and the Teitelbaums. Eventually, without any pressure from us, my parents embarked on their own journey to *mitzvah* observance.

The first major step occurred during Elul a number of years ago, when Rabbi Teitelbaum asked my father, "What *mitzvah* are you taking on this year? It's important to go into Rosh HaShanah with a commitment to grow in some way."

My father told Rabbi Teitelbaum that he wasn't sure what he was planning to take on, so Rabbi Teitelbaum suggested that he start putting on *tefillin*, which he did. Shortly afterward, a member of the Bensalem *kollel* knocked on my parents' door and invited my father to learn *Mishnayos* with him. That small *seder* led to others, which eventually turned into a commitment to being *kovei'a ittim*. My mother progressed at her own pace, studying *hilchos Shabbos* and then moving on to *shemiras halashon*.

One thing that began to sadden my mother as her knowledge of *Yiddishkeit* expanded was the fact that her wedding had been on 22 Tammuz, during the Three Weeks. From the time she learned that this had been a contravention of halachah, she would express regret every year on her anniversary.

"Ma," I would soothe her, "you and Daddy weren't *frum*, and you didn't know any better. Your marriage is still fine!"

Yet even with all of these reassurances, the topic continued to surface every year as my parents' anniversary approached. This year was no different, except that my mother took it a bit farther than usual. "Which rabbi would have married us during the Three Weeks?" she demanded. "Shouldn't he have known better? I am going to check my *kesubah* to see who signed it."

She went to retrieve her *kesubah*. She thought she had kept it in the safe, but when she looked there, she couldn't find it. She and my father searched for the *kesubah* high and low, combing through every paper in the house, but it was gone.

My mother called me in a panic. "What are we going to do? We lost the *kesubah*!"

"Don't worry, Ma," I said. "You just have to get another one written. Call your *rav* and find out what to do." (I still pinch myself when I suggest to my parents to ask a *she'eilah* and they do just that rather than launch into an argument about people being able to think for themselves, and why does a rabbi have to tell you what to do, etc.)

They called Rabbi Travitsky, the *rav* of their shul, who asked a lot of questions about their wedding. It emerged that besides the problem of the missing *kesubah*, there was also a problem with the *kiddushin*: the *eidim* had been relatives of my father. What's more, there had been no *frum* people at the wedding who could even have acted as *eidim*. My parents were certain that there were no *frum* people on the guest list. Besides, which *frum* person would attend a wedding during the Three Weeks?

Rabbi Travitsky went to speak to a noted *posek* in Lakewood, and the resulting *psak* proved that my mother's longtime fears were well founded: their *kiddushin* had been invalid! Rabbi Travitsky explained to my father that a new *kiddushin* ceremony was required and that it should be held as soon as possible.

By this time, my parents were far enough along their journey to happily rectify their invalid *kiddushin*.

My father received the *psak* from Rabbi Travitsky on Friday, July 18, and my husband and I discussed the ramifications with my parents while they were driving from Bensalem to spend Shabbos with us in Silver Spring.

After a few phone calls back and forth, it was decided that the "*chasunah*" would be scheduled for *motza'ei Shabbos* in Silver Spring. We laughed a lot that Shabbos about Bubby and Zeidy getting married after Shabbos, to the point that our youngest son started to get confused.

After *Havdalah*, we all headed to the home of our *rav*, Rabbi Reingold, for the "*chasunah*." He wrote a new *kesubah* and then officiated over the *kiddushin*.

My husband and I, along with our children, had the *zechus* of watching my father saying, "*Harei at mekudeshes li*," and my mother receiving her ring and *kesubah* from my father. It was by far the most moving wedding I had ever attended.

There are no coincidences in Hashem's world. The date of my parents' new *kiddushin* was 22 Tammuz, exactly 44 years after their wedding at the Conservative synagogue. As for my mother's fears about the wedding taking place during the Three Weeks, we received a *psak* that it was preferable to hold the *kiddushin* immediately, before the Nine Days began.

This date, while occurring during such a sad time on the Jewish calendar, obviously had some significance for my parents. Just as this time of mourning turned into a time of joy for our family, may it turn into a time of rejoicing for all of *Klal Yisrael*, with the coming of the *geulah*.

Postscript:

What was it about the day of 22 Tammuz that held special significance for this couple? Could it really be that a day of national mourning deserves the distinction of serving — twice — as a wedding anniversary for one particular husband and wife?

Here's a fascinating letter from a reader that may shed light on this mystery:

> *Regarding the wedding held on 22 Tammuz, I think the family would like to know that among chassidim, especially Karlin-Stolin, 22 Tammuz is a very special day, and they make the berachah of shehecheyanu on that day even though it's in the middle of the Three Weeks. It is the yahrtzeit of Rav Shlomo of Karlin, who was killed by a Cossack during Mussaf, in middle of Kesser; it is said that he had the neshamah of Mashiach ben Yosef.*
>
> *Many other chassidic dynasties also consider it a day of mazel, and if they have to start a new business in the Three Weeks, they do so on this day. The previous Stoliner Rebbe used to say that if not for the fact that people would not understand, he would allow chasunahs to be held on this day. He also pointed out that from 17 Tammuz through 9 Av there are actually 22 days — one more day than three weeks — which might refer to this day being excluded.*

Barley Flour

I was one of the forgotten 35-year-old girls who fell through the cracks waiting for my *bashert*. Why I was not married by 22, like most of my classmates, was anyone's guess — and everyone's guess: I was too intellectual, too picky, had commitment issues, too sophisticated, wasn't sophisticated enough…

The preponderance of varied and even opposing explanations for my still-single status led me to suspect that none of these explanations were on target, even as I valiantly tried to contort myself into a version of me that people would deem more marriageable.

My single status would have been a mystery, if not for the fact that so many bright, kindhearted, pretty, talented older girls like me were also single. And I might have stayed single forever had I not met *him*. It was a wonderful day when I met him, because he gave me a whole new perspective on how to approach *shidduchim*.

He was Rabbi Mann, a high-school rebbi who had made a number of *shidduchim*, mostly for older singles or people with medical or cosmetic issues. I met his wife, Leah, at a *shiur* in our community, and she finagled me into eating a Shabbos meal at their house. After the meal, when the Mann kids had left the table, the conversation turned to *shidduchim*, as it invariably does when there is an older single in the room.

"I have a theory about older singles and *shidduchim*," Rabbi Mann remarked.

"And what's that?" I asked.

"I only share it with people who are able to hear it," Rabbi Mann said. "Some people get very upset when they hear my theory, so I'm careful about who I tell it to."

Now my curiosity was piqued. "I'll try not to get upset," I said. "Can I hear the theory?"

"Okay," he said, "here goes. My theory is based on a story in the Gemara, a story you've probably heard.

"During the time of the *Churban*, there was severe hunger in Yerushalayim, and the wealthy Marta bas Baisus sent a servant to purchase fine flour from the market. By the time the servant arrived at the market, there was no fine flour to be had, so he returned to Marta and said, 'There's no fine flour, but there is white bread.' She told him to bring her that, but by the time he reached the market, the white bread was gone, too. He came back and reported, 'The white bread is gone, but there is coarse bread.' She sent him back to the market to buy the coarse bread, but by then there was only barley flour, and he returned to Marta and duly reported that only barley flour remained. Marta decided to go to the marketplace herself to see what was available, but she died before she reached the marketplace.

"This story is the story of older singles," Rabbi Mann continued. "Marta is a girl in *shidduchim*, and the servant is the *shadchan*. Marta didn't read the situation right; by the time she lowered her expectations enough to obtain food to eat, it was too late. She didn't quite grasp that she was living in a time of famine."

Rabbi Mann pushed his chair back from the table. "When a young girl enters *shidduchim*, she can, and should, look for the best of everything: *middos*, learning, family, personality. This is Plan A, the 'fine-flour' approach. Plan A lasts for a certain number of years.

"After that, a girl has to draw a line in the sand and realize that it's time for Plan B: barley flour. In Plan B, all that matters is that the boy is stable and committed to living according to halachah, and that the couple has some degree of compatibility. Nothing, but nothing else makes a difference: not marital history, not moderate medical issues, not family, not religious background, *nothing*. It's a famine! You either take what's available or you starve."

Rabbi Mann let out a long sigh. "Unfortunately, schools don't teach the girls anything about Plan B, parents don't usually suggest it, and many girls cling to Plan A well into their late 20's and beyond. The *shadchanim* dutifully follow orders, and try valiantly to locate the right type of boy, but as girls wait anxiously for the right one and slowly, slowly lower their expectations, all the good boys disappear.

"So that's my theory," Rabbi Mann concluded. "Lots of people don't like it, and some people even find it insulting. But I know a few older girls who took what I told them to heart and went on to build beautiful Jewish homes. Not exactly the homes they had originally envisioned, but beautiful homes nonetheless."

I listened silently to what he was saying, trying to digest the import of his words. I was feeling quite agitated, but since I had said that I'd try not to get upset, I forced myself to respond calmly. "So what you're suggesting," I said, "is that an older girl should just settle for anyone and take whatever she can get?"

"I'm not suggesting that anyone settle," Rabbi Mann clarified. "I'm suggesting that people broaden their horizons to include possibilities that don't fit into the Plan A, fine-flour mode. There are many wonderful boys out there who are kind, honest, and dependable and who would make terrific husbands and fathers. They may have no *yichus* to speak of, they may have moderate medical issues, they may have learning disabilities, their appearance might be compromised, they may be divorced. Or they may be *ba'alei teshuvah* who can't learn Gemara but are fine, *ehrliche* Yidden nonetheless.

"A girl who is serious about building a *Torahdik* family can do it even with a 'barley-flour' husband, and she can go on to raise children who are true *bnei Torah*. But without flour, you can't bake bread at all."

I argued, I resisted, I fought Rabbi Mann fiercely. But he stuck to his guns, telling me that the *Yiddishkeit* in the home is dependent mostly upon the woman and not the man.

"There is at least one *gadol* today whose righteous mother married a fellow who was far less observant," he said. "They produced a family of great *yirei Shamayim*."

While I certainly could not stomach marrying someone who wasn't *frum*, I got the point. I took a deep breath and let go of the Plan A helium balloon.

I contacted the *shadchanim* I knew, most of whom had long given up hope on me, and I apprised them of my new, abbreviated wish list: a boy who lives according to halachah and is eager to grow in his *Yiddishkeit*.

"Family background is not an issue," I told the *shadchanim*. "Actually, nothing else is an issue."

I was quite surprised to discover how many nice boys there are out there who are interested in marrying a Bais Yaakov girl and are looking to grow. All these boys want, I learned, is a good girl who will say yes to them despite their background and whatever baggage they bring to the table.

From then on, I would agree to a brief, but immediate meeting with any boy who met my minimal criteria. A few of the boys were obviously incompatible, but because I hadn't wasted that many hours, there was no harm done. Sometimes, I agreed to go out with a boy even though I doubted that anything would come of it, and I was usually right — except once, when I agreed to go out with Nathan, a recent *ba'al teshuvah*.

Nathan was a couple of years younger than me, and also a few inches shorter than me. He worked as a salesman for a software manufacturing company, and during his travels he had been invited to spend Shabbos at the homes of Jewish families in many different cities. Eventually he had decided to become observant. But he still couldn't read Hebrew fluently.

I could hardly imagine myself marrying a guy who couldn't pronounce the letter *chaf*, but I reminded myself that my new marriage criteria didn't include the ability to pronounce a *chaf*, and I agreed to meet him despite his status as a newly minted *ba'al teshuvah*.

There was nothing remotely yeshivish about Nathan — which wasn't surprising, considering that the only yeshivah he had ever studied in was the local branch of Ohr Somayach. Yet beneath the striped shirts and crocheted black *kippah*, I could see that he was deeply committed to *Yiddishkeit* and that he truly desired to advance in his learning and build a Torah home. He was someone I could respect, if not for his scholarship, then for his sincerity.

My parents were stunned when I announced my intention to marry Nathan. I think it was harder for them to get past the Plan A paradigm than it was for me, and even now, some time after my wedding, they are still struggling to come to grips with my choice. As for my Hungarian *bubby*, I doubt she'll ever recover from the shock and shame of having a grandson-in-law whose mother showed up to our *vort* in a *straw hat*.

"In the middle of the winter," Bubby lamented. "If she would have at least put some velvet on it…"

The reactions of people outside the family were mixed. Many people tried to hide their pity, but I suspect that some of the older singles who came to my wedding actually envied me. "You're so brave," my friend Shira, 37, whispered in my ear.

I'm married to a man who can barely make *Kiddush*, never mind learn a *Tosafos*, and I have no doubt that there will be significant challenges ahead. But I now have a loving husband, someone with whom I can finally look forward to building a family. Together, we are working to create a home for the *Shechinah* and lay the foundations for the next generation of *bnei Torah*.

Postscript:

The original version of the story said this:

"Plan A lasts for a certain number of years — I'd say until the age of 25. After that, a girl has to draw a line in the sand and realize that it's time for Plan B: barley flour."

The printed version of the story said this:

"Plan A lasts for a certain number of years. After that, a girl has to draw a line in the sand and realize that it's time for Plan B: barley flour."

Did you spot the difference? The printed version is missing the words "I'd say until the age of 25." What happened?

After the story was finalized, having been reviewed by a number of wise people, "Rabbi Mann" sent me this e-mail:

> *I suggest that the quote "I'd say until the age of 25" be removed. It appears that this suggestion may have a Heaven-sent component. Two weeks ago, a 28-year-old girl became a kallah. The chassan, 24 years old, began dating not that long ago. On the morning before this great l'chaim, the girl's mother asked her daughter for mechilah for trying to convince her to lower her standards and give up on marrying a ben Torah. The boy is my son.*

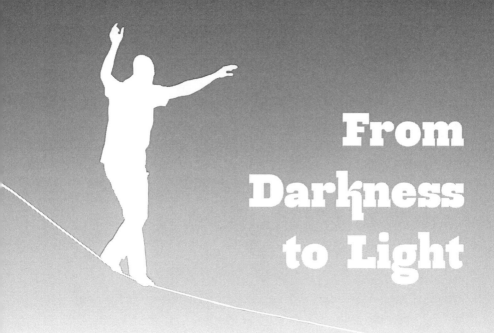

From Darkness to Light

At the ripe old age of 21, I found myself in *shidduchim*. For the second time.

If you think the *shidduch* scene is tough, try going into it after you've given a *get*. On the second round, every candidate is automatically suspect, and in place of the innocent excitement of the first round there's this guarded distrust. When you're sitting in a hotel lounge and you see your date trying to size you up — *Creep? Loser?* — it's all you can do not to ask for the bill right then and there.

Even so, once you've been married, even if the experience was painful, you don't want to be alone. And that's why I agreed to meet one eligible woman after another. I didn't get very far with any of them until, at the age of 27, I met Esty.

Esty was a lovely young divorcee who seemed like a good candidate for marriage. The first three or four dates went well, and I was starting to get my hopes up. But then we hit a brick wall. We had exhausted all the mundane topics you discuss during your initial meetings, but somehow things weren't progressing to the next level.

At around that same time, a friend of mine happened to mention that there was a kabbalist visiting from Eretz Yisrael who possessed tremendous powers and had helped many people. "I was having a hard time with my business about a year ago," my friend said, "and this *mekubal* told me exactly what was going to happen and what I should do. His predictions came true to the letter, and because I followed his advice, my business was saved."

I had never heard of this kabbalist, but when I asked a few people about him, they said he was a known *mekubal* and that he was "scary."

What *hashgachah*! I needed advice in how to move this *shidduch* forward, and this *mekubal* sounded like the perfect person. He would be staying in our city until the next week, so I hurried to make an appointment with his *gabbai* for that Thursday night. If only I'd known...

When I came for my appointment, I was surprised to see that the *gabbai*, Yishai, was a young, clean-shaven Israeli. I had expected him to have a long white beard, like the *gabbaim* of other Rebbes — but then I reminded myself that this was a *mekubal*, not a regular Rebbe, and that the rules were different.

"The Rebbe takes a minimum *pidyon* of 10 times *chai*," the *gabbai* told me.

I smacked my forehead in consternation. How could I have forgotten to bring a *pidyon*?

"Can I bring the money next time?" I asked. "I don't have that much cash with me. Or can I give a check?"

"The *shefa* doesn't come down without a *pidyon*," the *gabbai* replied. "A check doesn't have the same *hashpa'ah*."

I dashed out and ran to the nearest ATM, praying that the *mekubal* would still be seeing people when I returned. Thankfully, there were still a few people waiting in line ahead of me when I returned.

Finally, it was my chance to enter the kabbalist's chamber. The room, I noticed, was dimly lit by a single 20-watt bulb, but the *mekubal* seemed to glow with otherworldly radiance. He was holding a tiny, yellowing volume close to his face, and when he looked up from the volume I felt myself tremble under his gaze.

He glanced at my *kvittel*, on which I had written my name and the words "*zivug hagun.*" What he said then left me shaken.

"You have already met your *zivug,*" he intoned in a rich, classical Hebrew. "There will be an upturn, followed by a downturn, and in Shevat, there will a *mazel tov.* Hold on, and don't let this *shidduch* slip through your fingers. Your mother will be opposed, but do not pay heed to her objections."

The next thing I knew, the *gabbai* was ushering me out of the *mekubal's* chamber. Dazed, I stumbled out of the house, picturing myself standing under the *chuppah* with Esty, my *bashert.*

The *mekubal* said it would take until Shevat… two full months. But I had waited this long, I could wait a little longer.

My next date with Esty was Sunday afternoon, and from the get-go, I sensed that we had turned a corner. Apparently, Esty felt the same way, because she confided to me that before things became serious, she needed to speak to her *rebbetzin.*

"Sounds like a good idea," I agreed. I figured that this *rebbetzin* must be Esty's mentor or adviser, and I was hoping that she would be the one to give Esty the push she needed.

"Is this a *rebbetzin* you're close to?" I asked, just to keep the conversation moving in a meaningful direction.

"Well…" Esty hesitated. "I've never actually met her. But she knows everything about me. The way it works is, you send her your name, your mother's name, and your date of birth, and she's able to see all sorts of things about your past, present, and future."

That sounded a bit strange to me, but after my own experience with the *mekubal*, I found it easier to relate to the idea that there were holy people out there who knew things that the rest of us didn't. The *mekubal's* words were coming true right before my eyes; this was unquestionably an upturn.

"I have an appointment with the *rebbetzin* at 6 o'clock," Esty added, glancing down at her watch.

"Oh," I said. It was 5 o'clock, and I understood that Esty meant that we should be heading home. I was a bit disappointed, because the date was going so well, but I reassured myself that it was in my best interests for Esty to speak to the *rebbetzin*.

There was some unexpected traffic on the way home, and Esty started to get antsy. "If I miss my appointment, I'll have to wait a few weeks for another slot," she said anxiously. "And I'll lose my $85."

"She takes $85 for a missed appointment?" I asked incredulously.

"It's $85 whether you keep the appointment or not," Esty explained. "I already sent in a check, because her secretary insists on advance payment."

"Wow," I marveled. Inwardly, though, I was a bit skeptical. A *pidyon* for a Rebbe, yes, but for a *rebbetzin*?

As I dropped Esty off at her house — at precisely 5:58 — I asked her if I could call her the next day to arrange another date.

"Sure," she said before dashing out of the car.

When I spoke to Esty the next day, I could tell right away that there was something wrong. After making some small talk, I ventured to ask, "How did your talk with the *rebbetzin* go?"

"It went well," she hemmed.

"So," I said, "what did she have to say?"

"She said that you're a kindhearted, *ehrliche* person and that you'll make a devoted husband and father."

What a relief! So the *rebbetzin* really did know! But why did I detect an edge in Esty's voice?

"Did she say anything else?" I asked. "You seem concerned about something."

"Actually..." Esty's voice trailed off.

"It's important that we be open with each other," I assured her. "You don't have to feel uncomfortable sharing your misgivings."

"Um, I don't think I should be telling you this."

"It would be a big favor to me if you did," I said lightly, "because then I'll save myself the $85!"

"Well, if you really want to know. . . She said that you suffer from depression. And that you have an anger issue. And that you're not so reliable financially. And that you daven late."

I was stunned. It was true that for a period after my divorce I had been depressed — who wouldn't be? — but I had gone for counseling and had worked hard to regain my *simchas hachaim.* And it was true that my income wasn't stable, since I worked as a commission-only salesman. But I did have money in the bank, and I was considered a fairly successful salesman. Davening late? Well, I come from a *chassidish* background, and I make sure to daven with a *minyan* three times a day, even if the *minyanim* do start later than those in a *litvishe* shul.

The one thing I couldn't make sense of at all was the anger issue. I'm the most even-tempered guy you ever met. When was the last time I had gotten angry at someone? A few years ago, when some bar-mitzvah-age boys were taunting a kid with Down syndrome in shul?

I felt so... misunderstood, so reduced to a pile of data that, even if true, needed to be seen in context. *Don't listen to this lady,* I wanted to beg Esty. *She's telling you things that can be said about anyone. It's all a matter of perspective, of how you view the total person.*

Instead I said, "That's very interesting. Would you like me to explain what I think she means with those descriptions?"

"It's okay," Esty responded politely. "I have to turn this over in my head a little. I'll let the *shadchan* know if I want to go forward."

I couldn't believe what I was hearing. But then, as the phone clicked dead in my ear, I had a vision of the *mekubal* telling me, *There will be an upturn, followed by a downturn.* Of course! This was the downturn he had foreseen. Heartened, I resolved to sit tight and wait for the *shadchan* to get back to me. At most, it would be two months.

In the meantime, though, I was feeling quite disappointed, so I decided to go back to the *mekubal* for some *chizuk.* It was Monday, and he was leaving for Israel the following day, so maybe, just maybe, the *gabbai* would let me in again.

"*Pidyon,*" Yishai said softly.

Again? "Can I give something smaller this time?" I asked.

Yishai looked horrified. "For the Rebbe? People give a hundred times *chai*! Less than ten times *chai* doesn't work."

Embarrassed, I pulled out my wallet and handed Yishai two $100 bills.

This time, when I entered the kabbalist's chamber, I didn't remain silent as I had the last time. "Rebbe!" I cried out. "There was an upturn, but now... now she heard all sorts of things about me, many of them not even true, and she's having second thoughts. What should I do?"

"I told you there will be a downturn," he murmured. "Do not give up. Do not listen to those who tell you to meet others. You will wait, and she will come back. In Shevat you will say *mazel tov*."

The next two months were torture. I waited and waited for the phone call from the *shadchan*, but there was no call. Shevat came and went with no *mazel tov*.

I couldn't go to the *mekubal*, because he wasn't in the country. When I called up Yishai overseas and asked if I could speak to the *mekubal* on the phone, he explained that that wasn't done. "But the Rebbe said I'd have a *mazel tov* in Shevat," I lamented, "and there hasn't been one!"

"Did he say this Shevat?" Yishai asked.

My heart fell. Could it be that the *mekubal* had meant next year Shevat? How could I possibly wait that long?

"All good things come with patience," Yishai said sagely. "The Rebbe will be back in your city in four months' time. *Savlanut*."

I resigned myself to waiting for Esty. In the meantime, my mother started to nudge me about this *shidduch* and that *shidduch*. "Ma," I said, "I met the right one. It's only a question of time."

"You're not getting any younger," she pointed out. "It's unhealthy to sit around and wait."

Once again, the kabbalist's words came back to me with stunning clarity. *Your mother will be opposed, but do not pay heed to her objections.*

"I'm sorry, Ma," I said softly. "I have to do what I feel is right."

The *mekubal* would come to our community three times a year for about two weeks at a time, and each time he came, I'd go to see him several times, to warm myself with his holiness and draw *chizuk* from his insightful words. It never ceased to amaze me how he was able to home in on exactly what was going on in my life: "There are many *kelipos* chasing you, but you are rising above them," he would say, just at a time when I felt myself challenged by depression. Or he'd say, "There will be a big *simchah* in your family," right before my sister had twins.

On one visit, the *mekubal* told me, inexplicably, that I should grab the piece of real estate that was available for me to buy. I saw this as out-and-out *ruach hakodesh*, because just the previous week a fellow in the neighborhood had told me about an investment property that he said was a "steal." I had dismissed the offer at the time, because I couldn't commit to paying a mortgage. But now that the kabbalist had spoken — without my breathing a word about the property! — I understood that I was meant to buy it.

"I can't afford the mortgage," I told him.

"It will be okay," the *mekubal* assured me. "I see a lot of money in your future." A bubble of joy rose through me. I had never dreamt of being rich, but the promise of a financially secure future was tremendously comforting and would no doubt be a boon to my *shidduch* profile.

I purchased the property, my fingers tingling with delight as I signed the papers.

I used up all my savings on the down payment, but I managed to conjure up the cash for the first few mortgage payments. After that, however, it became more and more difficult to come up with the money, and I had to borrow from several kind friends to keep up with the payments.

The next time the *mekubal* came to town, I confided to him how stressed I felt over the property, but he kept telling me to have faith. "The property value will go up, and then you will sell it," he promised.

I left his chamber feeling buoyed, as I always did after basking in his presence.

But in the months that followed, I defaulted on a few consecutive payments, and the bank threatened to foreclose on the property. Unable to consult with the *mekubal*, who was in Israel, I decided to sell the property in a short sale so that I could at least repay my creditors and settle with the bank. I did this with a sinking feeling in my heart, because I knew that the *mekubal* would probably have advised against it. But what choice was there?

The next time the *mekubal* came to town, my conscience weighed heavily on me when I went to see him. Not only had I sold the property without his blessing, but I had barely a penny to my name, and could not offer my usual *pidyon* of $180. "I can give $18 dollars," I told Yishai abashedly, "but even that is hard for me right now."

Yishai's face hardened. "With no *pidyon*, one doesn't see the Rebbe."

"But I've been coming here for two years!" I protested. "Can't you let me in with a token *pidyon*, just this once?"

Yishai pointed to the full waiting room. "There are many people waiting to see the Rebbe," he said. "Come back when you have the money."

I stumbled out of the house, feeling utterly broken. My life was going nowhere: no wife, no property, not a penny to my name. And now, not even a Rebbe! How I yearned just to see the radiance of his face. But no — I was destined to be enveloped in utter darkness.

I turned my gaze upward to Hashem. "Save me from this darkness!" I begged.

At least Hashem listens to me for free, I reflected glumly.

And then the anger started to well up inside me. *Over the past two years*, I thought, *I've visited this mekubal at least fifteen times, forking over close to $3,000 for his advice — which has gotten me nowhere, and worse. And now, when I can't afford the $180, he won't even see me at all. What kind of Rebbe is he?*

He's just after my money. . .

It was a sickening realization, but one whose truth was so glaring that I couldn't dismiss it. I had found it strange that Esty's *rebbetzin* took $85 for a phone call, but I had never questioned the mandatory $180 "*pidyon*" of my "Rebbe."

Come to think of it, what made him a Rebbe? For that matter, was he a *mekubal* at all? I had never heard anyone extol his scholarship, his *ahavas Yisrael*, or his *tzidkus* — all anyone ever said about him was that he knew things, that he had scary powers.

Wait! A shepherd is only a shepherd if he has a flock. Other than Yishai, and a gaggle of suckers willing to shell out cash to hear some heebie-jeebie predictions, what *chassidim* did the Rebbe have?

What was even more disturbing, I suddenly realized, was the way this *"mekubal"* misused whatever knowledge he had, stringing people along with unsubstantiated promises that sowed incalculable misery in their wake.

This kabbalist was — dare I admit it to myself? — nothing more than a talented con artist. And worse than the money he had bilked me of, both directly and through his investment advice, was the way he had raised my hopes and caused me to waste two years of my life pining for a girl who was just a pawn in the hands of another unscrupulous stargazer.

Esty and I really *were* a good *shidduch*: two people so blinded by pain, so unsure of our own worth, and so hungry for security that we virtually signed away our lives to money-hungry charlatans.

I'm not waiting for Esty anymore, although I hope for her sake that she's escaped from the clutches of that evil woman. And no, I'm not a *mekubal*, but now that I've broken free of the forces of darkness, I'm starting to see light in my future.

Postscript:

Careful readers may have noticed that this story did not give any details about the narrator's divorce or about his ex-wife. That wasn't by accident.

In the process of interviewing the narrator, I asked him questions about his background and his life experiences up to the point where the story begins so that I could get a feeling for who he was. He was happy to answer my questions — until I asked him about his divorce.

"I've never said anything bad about my ex-wife to anyone," he said, "and I don't plan to start now." This, despite the fact that in the aftermath of the divorce, damaging rumors had been spread about him.

After his divorce, he searched for a shiduch for many years. "People who are going through a hard time are vulnerable," he explained to me. "Ideal prey for these unscrupulous 'mekubalim'."

Why do people go to "mekubalim" – whose credentials as serious students of kabbalah are generally very weak, and sometimes non-existent – as opposed to rabbanim or gedolim? Probably because, in their desperation for a yeshuah, they are looking for a miraculous cure, a quick fix, a guaranteed recipe for salvation from someone who knows what's going on in the mystical spheres.

We Jews are enjoined, however, to eschew the heebie-jeebie stuff — "Tamim tihyeh im Hashem Elokecha" — and instead follow the Torah's age-old prescriptions for blessing. But those prescriptions typically involve lots of hard work and patience, which is why it is often tempting to take shortcuts. Hence the popularity of so-called mekubalim and the spiritual magic potions that they peddle.

A couple of years after this story was published, the narrator wrote to me that he had gotten engaged. I don't know what the zechus for his shidduch was, but I couldn't help but think about his refusal to speak negatively about his ex-wife. Refraining from mudslinging is not as easy as going to see someone with "powers" — indeed, it's a tough path to choose — but it might just be a powerful prescription for a yeshuah.

Dayeinu

It was a lovely evening, that gathering for childless women, full of *chizuk* and support and inspiration. Lovely, that is, until a fortyish woman whose name tag read "Chana" asked me the Question: "How long are you married?"

I hadn't realized, before signing up for the event, that almost all the other women in attendance would be senior members of the infertility club, married far longer than my measly three years.

"*Three years?*" Chana half-shrieked when she heard my barely audible answer. "You're just a baby yourself!"

Maybe I *was* a baby compared to Chana and all the other veterans there. But did that make my lack of a baby any less real, my *nisayon* any less intense?

———◆———

Going into marriage, I knew that I might have some fertility issues, and so, shortly before our first anniversary, I went to see a doctor. She prescribed a mild medication, and when that medication didn't achieve the desired result, she recommended that I see a specialist in Manhattan.

That was our official welcome to the world of infertility: a world in which your life revolves around your failure to achieve parenthood.

It wasn't that I was desperate to be a mother. I was honestly quite terrified of having a baby and somewhat relieved when my first few pregnancy tests came back negative. As the third of four children — the other three of whom were boys — I had not grown up with babies, nor was I particularly drawn to young children. I could never understand why some of my friends went gaga anytime they saw an infant. To me, babies seemed like a frightening responsibility.

Motherhood was scary to me for another reason, too. My own mother was an anxious, moody person, and living in our house was like living in a fire station: you never knew when the alarm would be triggered, sending Mommy into a tizzy. As a child, I was secretly afraid that one day my father would say, "Enough is enough," and then our family would fall apart.

I wanted to think that I could be that calm, smiling mother I had so badly wished for as a child, but I very much doubted that I'd be able to maintain my composure when faced with the frustrations of motherhood. *Who are you fooling?* I'd scoff whenever I caught myself daydreaming about cradling a baby in my arms. *You'll just go to pieces, that's all.*

Still, when everyone around you is pushing a baby carriage or proudly sporting maternity clothing, you start to feel distinctly out of place. Even as you tell yourself that you're not ready to be a parent, your maternal instinct kicks you in the gut and you almost feel like snatching your neighbor's sleeping infant out of his bassinet.

Most of the time I dismissed this yearning for a baby as completely irrational, telling myself over and over again that if I wasn't expecting yet, it meant that Hashem didn't consider it the right time for Shmuel and me to become parents.

No one suspected that I was already taking fertility medication a year after my wedding, and so they didn't openly pity me or censor their conversations around me. I prided myself on my ability to remain completely at ease during discussions that revolved around morning sickness, colic, or diaper prices.

You're only 22, I'd remind myself. *And you've been married only a year.*

The medication I was taking didn't know that, though. The fertility specialist I saw had prescribed a "first-stage" medication that wasn't supposed to interfere terribly with my life, but the moderately uncomfortable side effects I experienced, coupled with the regular tests and ultrasounds I had to undergo, turned infertility into an ominous shadow that followed me everywhere.

For a while, Shmuel and I decided to take a break from the stresses of fertility treatment and try a more natural approach that involved a strict diet and exercise regimen. The diet was restrictive and frustrating, though, so after a few months I gave it up and resumed the treatment cycle: medication, hold your breath, tests, disappointment, medication.

To avoid becoming dragged down with each cycle of treatment, I tried not to think about it too much. I had a life, thank you very much; I was putting in a full day of work as a speech therapist, in addition to running my little household and working to build a marriage.

It was funny, the marriage part. Shmuel and I were a great couple, and we really understood each other right from the start. I couldn't think of a single serious issue that stood between us. Yet at times we would argue over minor things, and those arguments escalated into huge confrontations that involved gallons of tears and frightening decibel levels.

All this could start just because of an innocent comment. "The chicken could use some more time in the oven," Shmuel might say.

"I put it in the oven the minute I came home from work at the highest temperature it could handle," I'd defend myself. "Would you want me to burn it to a crisp?"

"No, of course not," he'd protest. "I didn't mean —"

"I don't know what you meant, but do you realize that I worked hard to make supper for you, and all you have to say is that the chicken is underdone? Don't you care about me *at all*?"

And so on and so forth, until we both started to believe that it had been a mistake to marry each other in the first place, and the specter of divorce hung between us like a thick fog. When you grow up thinking that your parents are on the verge of divorce, you can't help but assume that your own marriage is similarly doomed. And that lack of confidence becomes a self-fulfilling prophecy.

It didn't help that Shmuel's father had died when he was a teenager, which had seriously disrupted the stability of his family. Each time our own relationship seemed unsteady, we were both gripped with the same terror that our marriage was about to unravel.

Many times, when I found myself dissolving into tears at the slightest provocation, I'd think to myself, *I'm just like my mother.* I remembered how an open cabinet door in the kitchen could spark a tirade about how inconsiderate people in the house were, and how she could make my father feel like two cents if he forgot to leave cash in her wallet. "You never think about me," she'd sob. At first, my father would look bewildered and helpless, but eventually he'd either start to shout back or storm out in a huff.

These interactions had been scary to watch, but it was even scarier to watch eerily similar interactions taking place between Shmuel and me. At those times, I'd think to myself that I was being punished, that the reason Hashem was not giving us children was because we couldn't get along and be good parents.

All along, I assumed that our *shalom bayis* issues were *our* problem, having something to do with the synthesis of our respective personalities. That changed at around the time of our second anniversary.

We went away for a few days to celebrate, but our whole vacation turned into a monstrous fight over some things we had forgotten to pack. Forty-eight hours into this fracas, I started to think morbid thoughts about the purpose of life, and I doubted if I even wanted to be alive. That's when I realized that the problem wasn't *us*, but *me*.

As soon as we got home, I made some discreet inquiries into therapists, and I scheduled an appointment with a therapist named Sari, who came highly recommended. I arrived at my first appointment prepared to tackle my inability to deal with conflict, to rehash the experience of growing up in a home where there was constant fighting, and to point out the similarities between myself and my mother.

But after asking me a few basic questions, Sari steered the conversation in a completely different direction. "You say you're married two years, and you're having some fertility issues," she said slowly.

I nodded. "But my *shalom bayis* problems have nothing to do with infertility," I assured her. "We never argue about anything related to having children, and I'm totally O.K. around my friends who are expecting or already have kids."

Sari didn't buy that. "Infertility affects women in all sorts of ways," she explained, "not all of which are conscious. Our self-image, as women, is inextricably linked with our ability to bear children, and whether or not a childless woman spends her time pining for a baby, her every interaction is shaped by her perception of herself as someone who hasn't validated her existence."

I sat up very straight in the plush armchair opposite Sari. "I don't think that's true in my case," I said. "I really do believe that Hashem will give me children at the right time, and I'm fine with waiting a little longer. It's only been two years, you know, and I'm really happy with my life and my job. It's just the *shalom bayis* issues that are giving me trouble."

"It may seem that way," Sari agreed. "But think of it this way. If someone would tell you she's tired, she has a headache, she's cold, she's lethargic, and, oh, by the way she hasn't eaten anything in two days, you'd tell her that her problem is that she needs food. She might protest that she doesn't feel hungry — and at that point, she might not even realize how hungry she is — but until you've addressed the underlying lack of food, it's pointless to treat the other symptoms."

"So what are you saying?" I asked testily. "That I should have a baby and all my problems will go out the window? Poof, just like that?"

"No, no, that's not what I'm saying at all. What I'm trying to say is that I can teach you all sorts of communication techniques and conflict-reducing strategies, but as long as you don't feel whole as a human being, we're not going to accomplish anything. First, we need you to start valuing yourself for who you are, independent of your ability to bring forth life, and then we can tackle the other issues that right now seem to be the real problems."

I left that appointment feeling confused and misunderstood. In the days that followed, however, I mulled over what Sari had said, and slowly it began to make sense. I thought back to my teenage years, when I had been a popular, confident, and academically successful student, and I compared the way I had viewed myself then to the way I saw myself now.

Back then, even if my home life was turbulent, I had seen myself as an accomplished person; now, even if I was a sought-after, accomplished speech therapist and a pretty decent wife, I never felt good about myself. I couldn't overlook even the most mildly negative word Shmuel uttered, because it reinforced my own negative impression of myself and brought forth a stream of self-recriminations and angst, which I then turned against Shmuel.

"Your husband's behavior is just a catalyst, an excuse for you to hold up a mirror to yourself and project your own self-hatred onto him," Sari explained at our next meeting. "You agree that objectively nothing he's doing or saying is so terrible. So the problem is the way you're reacting, and your way of reacting is a reflection of how you feel about yourself."

Sari put me through an evaluation that indicated that I was suffering from depression, and she referred me to a psychiatrist, who prescribed an antidepressant that was compatible with the fertility medication I was taking. Sari also began cognitive behavior therapy with me and got me to read several books that contained an approach to coping with infertility through mental relaxation techniques.

In the meantime, I decided to try acupuncture treatments. Previously I had thought that alternative therapies and conventional medicine were an either-or proposition: you had to commit to one track completely, at the expense of the other. Now, however, my goal wasn't only to bear a child; it was to boost my physical and mental well-being while continuing the fertility treatments. It was O.K. if the acupuncture didn't help with fertility, as long as it helped me feel good about myself and remain pleasant to be around.

At around the same time, I switched to a different doctor, who started me on painful injections. The combination of therapy and acupuncture is what kept me sane through these difficult treatments, and while I didn't see a dramatic turnaround in my personality and *shalom bayis* yet, both Shmuel and I realized that I was on a much better emotional path.

We decided, at that point, that because the treatments were interfering with my work schedule, and because my work environment was also a source of stress, I should end my workday in midafternoon, instead of working 9 to 5. The extra hours of downtime in the day did wonders for my overall mood, as well as for my *shalom bayis*.

With our third anniversary on the horizon, I decided to attend an evening of inspiration and support for childless women. When I registered, no one asked me how long I had been married, nor did anyone inform me that most of the women who would be attending had been married for 10, 20, even 30 years. I felt that I needed *chizuk* in order to continue functioning well despite the *nisayon* of infertility, and it didn't occur to me that my presence might be painful to those who had been dealing with this challenge for decades.

I found the evening uplifting and enjoyable, until that Chana person burst my balloon by reducing my three-year struggle to worthlessness. Infertility, it seemed, only counted when you were in the big leagues. If you couldn't put up the numbers, you didn't qualify for the club.

After that casual interaction with Chana, I was heartbroken. Later in the evening, when I met another middle-aged woman whose name tag said "Libby," I was already on guard. In answer to her question of how long I was married, I carefully said, "There was some sort of mix-up. I'm married only three years, but no one told me that this event wasn't for me."

"Oh," she said knowingly. "I remember that time. I think it was the hardest time of all. I didn't have any tools yet to cope with infertility, and I was on a constant roller coaster of hope and disappointment. I was such a mess back then; I didn't know who to talk to or what to think, and I didn't know yet that you can have a life even if you don't have kids. Good for you for taking care of yourself and coming here instead of suffering alone."

I looked at this woman in awe. She had to have been at least 50; she looked as though she could be my mother. Yet here she was, approving of my participation in an event for the infertile and making me feel so understood.

You have a choice, I told myself after that brief conversation. *You can be one of the Chanas of the world, who wear their suffering as a shield that cuts themselves off from the people around them, or you can be one of the Libbys of the world, whose suffering opens their hearts and allows them to connect meaningfully to others.*

The difference, I realized, was in the work you do on yourself. If parenthood is your one and only objective in your struggle with fertility, then each negative result will make you more bitter, more difficult, more unapproachable. But if your objective is to build yourself as a human being — parent or otherwise — then the disappointing results will be painful, but not devastating to your personality and relationships.

As I left the gathering, I reflected on the many improvements I had made in my life ever since I had officially entered the infertility club two years earlier. I had learned to feel good about myself and value the unique contribution I could bring to the world each day, and that made me feel more secure in my marriage. I had stopped going to pieces when Shmuel expressed disapproval or frustration, because I no longer interpreted his words as a confirmation that I was a total failure.

While undergoing fertility treatments, I had become a more complete person, a happier wife, and a better potential mother. When and whether I'd be entrusted with a baby, only Hashem knew, but I was no longer tormented by the worry that I'd become a replica of my own mother.

This is really the end of my story. As we say on Pesach, *dayeinu*: just the fact that I've come so far as a person is enough of a happy ending, and enough of a reason to rejoice and give thanks to Hashem. Yet after sharing so much about myself, I feel that it's only fair to let you in on the good news and tell you that I just found out that I am expecting.

I could have waited until after I gave birth to tell my story. But that would be missing the point. *Dayeinu.*

Postscript:

The couple in this story was blessed with an adorable baby girl. But what happened then? Did the normal difficulties of caring for an infant become easier in the light of their complex journey to parenthood, or were these difficulties exacerbated by the expectation that having a baby would bring joy and delight?

I spoke to the narrator of this story about a year after her baby was born, and this is what she said:

> *My baby was in the NICU for a few days after she was born, and when we finally brought her home, she was extremely colicky for about six months. She also had issues with feeding and weight gain. It was really hard.*
>
> *But I was prepared. When I was married for about a year and a half, I read a Mishpacha article about a mother of twins who felt terribly guilty when she found it hard to cope with her long-awaited babies. Eventually she learned that it was O.K. for it to be hard, and the fact that it's hard doesn't mean you're not grateful for what you have.*
>
> *That message stuck with me and comforted me when I was up for hours rocking, feeding, and singing to my screaming baby.*
>
> *At the same time, I have to say that the appreciation I feel as a result of waiting for this baby goes a long way. It's not that I never find things challenging; it's that I'm so inherently delighted to have my daughter that the challenges don't bother me the way they probably would have had I not waited.*
>
> *My husband and I are not naturally baby people. At the beginning, we were nervous about changing diapers, afraid*

to give the baby a bath. But you should see the joy in my husband's eyes when he holds the baby, a joy that I'm sure is reflected in my eyes, too. We would not be that way if we hadn't had to work for this.

Overwhelming Simchah

Has it ever happened to you that you wait and wait for a bus, and after an interminably long wait, three of the same buses pull up one after another?

That's what happened to me with the *shidduchim* of my three oldest children. We belong to a *chassidish* community in Canada where the norm is for both boys and girls to marry at 18 or 19. (Yes, our children are mature enough at that age to get married and stay married — happily, most of the time. And no, we don't have a *shidduch* crisis. But that's a separate topic altogether.)

So when my oldest son Sruli reached the age of 22 without meeting his *bashert*, everyone felt very sorry for us, especially because our 21-year-old son Meilech was waiting right behind him. In our *chassidish* circles, it's practically unheard of for a younger sibling to marry before an older one.

My own classmates, most of whom were grandmothers by the time they were 40, divided the *sefer Tehillim* among themselves as a *zechus* for my Sruli, the *eltere bachur*, to find his proper *zivug*. When I gratefully informed them that Sruli had finally gotten engaged, I asked them to please continue davening, this time for Meilech.

A few short weeks after we celebrated the *vort* of Sruli and his *kallah*, Etty, in New York, we drove to New York again for Meilich's *vort*. Not wanting to make Meilich wait longer than necessary, we scheduled his wedding for two weeks after Sruli's. Knowing that I'd be in New York from before Sruli's wedding until after Meilech's *sheva berachos*, I took a three-week leave of absence from my job as a reading specialist in a girls' school.

Since Sruli was getting married on a Sunday, we made his *aufruf* in Canada a full week before, so that we'd have time to travel to New York for the wedding. The next Shabbos, we made a small *aufruf* for him in New York and celebrated his wedding the next day.

During that week, a *shadchan* from England named Rabbi Paler called with a *shidduch* for my daughter Raizy, who had just turned 18. "Please," I begged him, "I can't think about this until after my next son's wedding."

But my husband, Lazer, was not as quick to dismiss the *shadchan*. He had learned with the boy's father in Eretz Yisrael, and the thought of making a *shidduch* with his old friend was quite appealing to him, especially since the boy, Sender Bornstein, had a sterling reputation.

"Lazer," I moaned, "we have a week of *sheva berachos* coming up, then another *aufruf*, then another *chasunah*, then another week of *sheva berachos*. I have no *ko'ach* to deal with another *shidduch* now! Can't it wait until we get back home? And besides, a boy from England? Traveling back and forth to New York was hard enough!"

"We won't have to travel at all, Mirel," Lazer assured me. "We have the girl this time. But if we're here in New York anyway, why don't we go ask Rav Shimshon what to do?"

Lazer had learned under Rav Shimshon Glick in his youth and had maintained close ties with him. Reluctantly, I agreed to go see Rav Shimshon.

"Do you have any objections to the *shidduch*?" Rav Shimshon asked me.

"I don't know much about the boy," I answered, "but from what I've heard, I can't say I *object* to the *shidduch*. It's just that I can't focus on it right now. I need to breathe a bit!"

"*Shidduchim* is a very serious matter," the *rav* said soberly. "I understand that this is a hectic time for you, but passing up a *shidduch* with no valid reason is something you may regret for the rest of your life. If a *shidduch* came up, you can't neglect it."

In between Sruli's *sheva berachos*, Lazer and I made inquiries into the boy, and Lazer told Rabbi Paler that we were interested. After that, I was free to focus on the current and upcoming *simchahs*.

At some point during the nonstop festivities, I started to feel like that cartoon character whose head is turning so rapidly from side to side that it starts to spin. At Meilich's wedding, the mother of Etty, my first daughter-in-law, sat down beside me, and I began shmoozing with her. Then I realized that my other *mechuteiniste*, the mother of *tonight's kallah*, Yidis, was standing behind me.

Help! I thought. *This is the old mechuteiniste! I'm supposed to be sitting next to my new mechuteiniste!*

On Shabbos *sheva berachos*, my daughter-in-law Etty met me outside shul and said, "I'll meet you after davening, and we'll walk to the hall together."

A short while later, my brand-new daughter-in-law, Yidis, met me and said, "I'll walk with you to the hall after davening, O.K.?"

When davening was over, I walked to the hall flanked by Etty and Yidis, not knowing how to divide my attention: If I gave the newer *kallah* more attention, would the first daughter-in-law be insulted? If I gave the first daughter-in-law more attention, or divided my attention equally between the two, would the newer *kallah* be insulted? This *was* her Shabbos *sheva berachos*, after all.

Until now, I had been pining for a daughter-in-law, and now that I had two, I didn't know where to put myself or which one to tend to first. It was like giving birth to twins after waiting for a child for years: I was overwhelmed with joy and gratitude for the double *simchah*, but I was also overwhelmed, period.

We drove back home on a Thursday. In the car, I turned around to my five unmarried children and said, "Okay, kids, no more shopping for the next *year*! Not a hat, not a hair bow, not even a shoelace. I've had it!" The kids nodded obligingly.

When we arrived home, I left all the suitcases unopened and collapsed into my bed. After five straight weeks of *simchahs* — an *aufruf* in Canada, an *aufruf* in New York, a wedding, *sheva berachos*, another *aufruf*, wedding, and *sheva berachos* — I was looking forward to resting up over the weekend before returning to work.

Apparently, however, rest was not destined for me, because on Friday morning Rabbi Paler called from England to tell us that the Bornsteins were interested in meeting Raizy. "They'll be arriving Tuesday morning and leaving Wednesday night," he informed me.

"*They*?" I asked.

"Yes, the boy and his parents," Rabbi Paler said matter-of-factly. I felt numb. "Oh."

When I told Raizy that the boy's parents were coming along with him and leaving the following day, she went pale. "You mean...you mean...I *have* to get engaged to him? In one day?"

"No," I said firmly. "You have a choice. Don't be intimidated by the fact that his parents are coming. You can say no, and you don't have to decide after the first meeting either."

On Tuesday morning, there was still a pile of passports sitting on my dining-room table, and the house was strewn with open, partially unpacked suitcases. My house was in no shape to host a prospective *chassan* or *mechutanim*, so I arranged for Raizy and Sender to meet in the home of my neighbors, the Kesslers, who were away for the week. They would sit in a side room, while Lazer and I would talk to his parents in the dining room.

Lazer and Mr. Bornstein had a great time reconnecting and reminiscing, and Mrs. Bornstein and I hit it off as well. Yet in my mind, I couldn't imagine them becoming my *mechutanim* — certainly not now. I soothed myself with the thought that Raizy was young, and she would surely take her time getting engaged to Sender, if at all.

But Raizy surprised me by expressing her readiness to go ahead after that one meeting.

"Maybe meet him a second time," I suggested, my heart pounding with terror at the prospect of having to arrange a *vort* before the Bornsteins flew back to England.

"I don't think it's necessary," she said calmly. "I can see that he's a really good boy, and we felt very comfortable with each other. They're leaving tomorrow, so why wait?"

We drank *l'chaim* and agreed that the *vort* would take place at 8 o'clock that night in a nearby hall.

That was when I snapped. I had been in *simchah* mode continuously from the time of Sruli's first *aufruf* five weeks earlier, and blessed as these long-awaited *simchah*s were, I felt drained both physically and emotionally. There was no way I could handle another *simchah* now.

I called my younger sister Breindy, who lives a few blocks away from me and has a houseful of little children. "Breindy," I said, "I need your help."

"Mirel," she said in alarm, "you sound terrible! Is everything okay?"

"Everything's fine," I said flatly. "Raizy's becoming a *kallah*. I'm making a *vort* tonight. The *mechutanim* will probably come over to my house at some point. I can't do this."

"*Mazel tov!*" she exclaimed. "I'm coming right over."

Minutes later, Breindy was in my house, rapidly pulling things off the table. As I watched her put the passports inside my breakfront drawer and stash the phone books away in my front closet, my mind screamed out to her that no, the passports went upstairs in the safe and the phone books belonged on the shelf above the telephones. But my mouth would not obey me. I just stood there, frozen and speechless, as though I was watching a film and could not communicate with the characters I saw on the screen.

"Where do you keep your *simchah* tablecloths?" Breindy asked, interrupting my reverie.

"I...don't...have...any...tablecloths," I said in a dazed voice, even as I willed my arm to point to the linen closet, where I had at least six matching tablecloths that would be suitable for the occasion. But my arm remained frozen to my side.

I watched as Raizy started making phone calls: to the grocery to order drinks, to the bakery to order cakes, to a local *gemach* to order tablecloths (because I supposedly had none).

"What are you wearing to the *vort*?" Breindy asked Raizy.

"I don't know," Raizy said. "I guess I can wear the outfit I wore to the two *aufruf*s."

"No," Breindy said. "I saw what you wore to the *aufruf*s, and that wasn't suitable for a *kallah*. You need a new dress for your *vort*. Come with me, we're going shopping. Mirel, you'll finish up the arrangements for the *vort*?"

I nodded through my haze.

They came home two hours later carrying a beautiful dress for Raizy and found me sitting at the table in my dressing gown, holding a cup of coffee in my hand and staring into space. Boxes holding all sorts of deliveries were stacked up outside the door, unopened.

"I don't believe this!" Breindy exclaimed. "Nothing's been done since we left, and it's only three hours to the *vort*! Mirel, you go get yourself fixed up, I'll take care of getting the stuff over to the hall."

Raizy just stood there, dismayed. Finally, she spoke up in a small voice. "Ma, do you have anything to serve the Bornsteins for supper? We should offer them something to eat before the *vort*, no?"

"You're pressuring me," I said thickly. "Stop it!"

Lucky for me, in addition to my wonderful sister, I also have a few very good friends. When they called the house and found out from Raizy what was going on, they sprang into action. My friend Leah, who's a semiprofessional party planner, spent most of the afternoon and evening at the hall setting up the tables. When she finally finished, she raced over to my house to style my *sheitel* and do my makeup.

As she spun around, brandishing a hair iron and then a fistful of makeup brushes, I leaned back in the chair and closed my eyes. "Oh, Leah," I said, "I'm so tired."

A few minutes later, my cell phone buzzed, and I looked down and saw a text message: "The tables are ready. Love, Dina."

I texted back: "What tables? And who are you?"

I should mention that Dina is my closest friend.

After Leah had made me look my best, I wandered out to the living room and plopped myself on the couch. Raizy, the *kallah*, was standing in the kitchen, an apron over her beautiful new dress, piping chocolate onto a platter of petit fours. "Ma," she begged, "can you help me finish these?"

"Raizy," I groaned, "I'm too tired for this. Please, not now." With that, I reached out and took one of Raizy's beautiful petit fours from the tray and sampled it, making a gap in her neat arrangement. Raizy looked as though she was about to cry.

At that moment, the phone rang. It was Mrs. Sommers, the principal of the school where I work, and she was in the midst of arranging an order for first-grade reading textbooks. She had no idea that Raizy was engaged, and she had pushed off the book order until after my two weddings, so she was anxious to finish up with it already. "Do you think we should stick with the Dick and Jane series?" she asked. "Or is it time to switch to a different system?"

For the next 20 minutes, I stood there in the kitchen giving Mrs. Sommers a detailed analysis of the different reading programs available and advising her which books to order. Raizy stared at me, mouth agape, as if to say, "Ma, you're too tired to help me with the petit fours, you can't lift a finger for my *vort*, and you can stand there talking animatedly to your principal about Dick and Jane?"

How could I explain to her that Dick and Jane was an escape, a welcome return to my decades-old routine and comfort zone? I didn't even understand it myself.

That night at the *vort*, I smiled politely at my family and friends and graciously accepted people's good wishes. I was on a different planet, though. At one point, I turned to my aunt Fraidel and whispered, "Why is everyone so happy? I just wish I could crawl into bed."

I was the same way throughout the engagement. If Raizy so much as dared mention something about shopping for housewares, I'd snap at her, "Stop pressuring me!"

I should mention that ordinarily I'm a top-notch *balebusta*, very capable and *geshikt*. Yet I couldn't bear the thought of calling caterers or photographers or musicians, let alone accompanying Raizy to the *sheitel macher*.

My "no shopping for a year" pronouncement quickly bit the dust, however, because Sruli and Meilech had gotten married in the winter, while Raizy was getting married in the summer. The velvet gowns my younger girls had worn to the first two weddings were not seasonally appropriate, and within a few months of Raizy's engagement, the boys' suits were already short at the wrists and ankles. Every one of the children needed to be outfitted again from head to toe, hair bows and shoelaces included. With the little ones, I had no choice but to shlep around town shopping, but I flatly refused to go anywhere with Raizy. "It's too much for me!" I'd tell her. "I can't!"

To her credit, she didn't complain. She went shopping with her friends or with her aunts. As I watched her take care of all the preparations for her own wedding, I didn't feel even a twinge of guilt or pity. I was just too tired. So, so tired.

In the year and a half after Raizy's wedding, I had plenty of time to rest. So when it was her younger sister Simi's turn to get engaged, I was all revved up for another *simchah*. The day of the *vort*, my friend Dina called to offer her assistance. "Can I speak to Simi?" she asked. "I need to discuss the bakery order with her."

"Why do you need Simi?" I responded. "You can talk to me."

"Uh, Mirel," Dina said, "you don't do this kind of thing. Remember Raizy's *vort*?"

"Of course I do this kind of thing!" I said indignantly. "I was just *simchah*ed out when Raizy got engaged, and I wasn't ready for another *mazel tov*. Or maybe I was just lazy then, I don't know. But now I'm totally fine. I already placed the bakery order, the tables are all set up, and the *kallah*'s having her hair done as we speak."

At Simi's *vort*, I reveled in my status as mother of the *kallah*, shedding tears of joy and thanking Hashem every few minutes for bringing me to this point. But then I spotted Raizy, and I saw right away that something was amiss.

Of course, I told myself. *She's remembering her own vort and thinking about how you weren't there for her.* Now, in retrospect, I felt horribly guilty for abandoning her, the 18-year-old *kallah*. I could only imagine how hard it must have been for her to navigate the intensely emotional engagement period on her own.

I accompanied Simi to every gown and *sheitel* appointment and enthusiastically shopped with her for linens, kitchen supplies, and clothing. Raizy wasn't there to see all this, but she knew that Simi's experience differed vastly from her own, and every time I spoke to her, I could hear in her voice that she was deeply hurt by this blatant show of favoritism.

I didn't know what to say to her. How could I explain that no, I didn't love Simi more, it was just that when Raizy had become a *kallah*, I had been in a different zone?

I wrote a long letter to a leading *frum* psychologist, chronicling the four *shidduchim* of my children and asking him to shed some light on what had gone wrong with me at *shidduch* number three.

"You seem to have been suffering from a form of post-traumatic stress disorder," he wrote back. "PTSD is usually associated with catastrophic or tragic events, but it can be triggered by any major stress, including that of a *simchah*. It's actually quite common for people to go numb and enter a state of near-paralysis when marrying off a child."

So that was it. I hadn't been lazy or uncaring or selfish when I had washed my hands of Raizy's *vort* and wedding preparations. I had been in a state of mild trauma.

And because I had so eagerly awaited the day when I, too, could make a *chasunah*, the stress of the two back-to-back weddings had been entirely unanticipated and had knocked me out like a tidal wave.

But how could I explain that to Raizy? Could she ever understand? Would she ever forgive me?

Can you, Raizy?

Postscript:

"All matters of the world, whether good or bad, are nisyonos for a person — poverty on one hand and wealth on the other…tranquility on one hand and suffering on the other" (Mesilas Yesharim, Ch. 1).

The narrator of "Overwhelming Simchah" was fortunate enough to be granted a nisayon of "wealth": she married off three children in the span of several months. Yet the fact that countless people would give anything to be in her shoes didn't make her nisayon any less intense.

In the previous story, we met a young woman who struggled with infertility, a nisayon of poverty. Her struggle was dismissed by a veteran member of the same club, on the grounds that she hadn't suffered long enough for her nisayon to count. "My nisayon is harder than yours," the thinking went, "so you have no right to complain."

In LifeLines, we discuss challenges of poverty alongside challenges of wealth, with the understanding that every person's nisayon is real and deserving of respect and validation.

Part 3

חַיִּים שֶׁל פַּרְנָסָה...
חַיִּים שֶׁל עֹשֶׁר וְכָבוֹד

A Life of Sustenance...
a Life of Wealth and Honor

Fighting Fire with Fire

We were sitting down, my husband Moshe and I, going through our finances item by item and finding places to cut so that we could manage to balance our monthly budget, when we came to the category called "insurance."

Between life insurance, supplemental medical insurance, and home-owner's insurance, this item was huge. Well, we weren't getting rid of our life insurance, nor were we touching the extra medical insurance, which had already served us in good stead when one of our daughters needed emergency abdominal surgery. But the home-owner's insurance, according to Israeli law, we no longer needed it since we had recently finished paying off the mortgage on our apartment.

The cost was only about a hundred shekels a month, but every agurah adds up, especially in a large family like ours, *kein ayin hara*, so home-owner's insurance was one of the things we decided to cut.

Which, in hindsight, makes no sense. Or maybe it does make sense. Maybe that, too, was part of Hashem's plan.

The morning of Yom HaAtzma'ut, Israel's Independence Day, was more or less a regular day for our family. The boys had yeshivah, and since our girls go to private schools, they had school as well. Our two preschoolers didn't have *gan*, and one of our older sons had the day off from work. Moshe was also off from his job as a special-ed teacher and had taken the opportunity to travel to Meron to daven.

At about 10 a.m., after getting the older kids out to school, putting the baby in for her nap, and settling the preschoolers on the porch with some toys, I went to my room to rest for half an hour. With Moshe gone, I had stayed up late working on the book I was typesetting, and I needed to recharge my batteries before sitting back down at the computer. My older son had returned from Shacharis, and since he didn't have to go to work, he had also decided to lie down.

As I dozed, I started to hear crackling sounds. I jumped out of bed, left the room, and saw that the crackling sounds were coming from the bedroom where our four younger boys sleep. The room was empty, but the bottom bunk bed was on fire.

"Get up!" I shouted to my son. "There's a fire in the house!"

I ran to the porch, where the two preschoolers were playing quietly, and told them to go downstairs and leave the building. They immediately complied, even though they normally wouldn't have been comfortable leaving the house by themselves.

In the meantime, my son had rushed to the bathroom and was filling up a pail of water in the sink. I filled up another pail from the bathtub, and then we both threw our water into the bedroom, which was now a conflagration of smoke and flames. The heat coming from the room was so intense already that my eyelashes and my son's hair were singed.

Not realizing how quickly the fire was spreading, I ran to my room to call the fire department. "Is everyone out of the house?" they asked.

"Yes, my son and I are leaving right now," I answered, before pushing the door to my room shut.

By the time I'd hung up, grabbed my cell phone, and left the room, the hallway was filled with smoke. But there was still about 18 inches of smoke-free space on the floor, so I bent all the way down and crawled out of the house.

My son, in the meantime, had grabbed the baby from her crib in the room adjacent to his and had crawled down the hall as well. It was a miracle that he remembered the baby, because when the fire department had asked me if anyone was still in the house, I had completely forgotten about her. We had actually moved the baby out of my bedroom just a few days earlier, and by the time I reached the front door and remembered her, my bedroom was completely inaccessible. Had she still been in there…

We were fortunate to get out alive and unharmed. As I closed the front door of my apartment, knowing that all 13 of my children were safe, I looked Heavenward and said, "Hashem, thank You for saving my family — now please save the *sefarim*. Everything else I don't care about."

By the time the fire trucks arrived 12 minutes later, the temperature inside the apartment was over 600 degrees Fahrenheit (300 degrees Celsius) and the firefighters couldn't enter the apartment. They broke windows to allow the smoke and heat to escape, and only afterward could they begin extinguishing the fire from inside. Thankfully, we live on the top floor of our four-story building, and since heat and fire travel upward, the flames didn't spread to any of the other apartments.

It took the firefighters over an hour to put out the blaze. Then it was time to assess the damage.

The boys' room was totaled. The aluminum window frames had melted away. The spare freezer in that room had disappeared except for the cooling element at the bottom. The heating pipes had melted into one large mass. The floor was covered with over four feet of debris.

In the bathroom/laundry room next door, the ceramic tiles had popped off the wall, the sink had cracked, and the washer and dryer had melted.

The kitchen was the room farthest from the boys' room, but

even there the countertops had cracked from the heat, and the Formica cabinets had splintered and warped.

All of the contents of our apartment were covered with an oily soot. The room that had suffered the least damage was my room, since I had closed that door when I left. Our important documents, including my *kesubah*, emerged intact. And somehow, inexplicably, my husband's *sefarim* were spared.

In the meantime, the outpouring of *chesed* in our community of Ramat Shlomo was beginning. A woman I didn't know called to say that she had saved her children's old clothing rather than giving it away to a *gemach*, because she had always bought expensive clothing and she had been waiting to give it to someone who would really appreciate and enjoy it. I headed over to her house immediately to assemble new wardrobes for my younger kids. A few people told me that they'd arrange new clothing for us because "you deserve it" (whatever that means), but I assured them that we were used to wearing hand-me-downs from relatives and *gemachim*; I rarely bought new clothing.

A friend arranged vouchers for us at a neighborhood clothing store, where I picked out socks, pajamas, and other basic items. Another friend held a clothing drive, gathering gently used items in all of my children's sizes and depositing everything in someone's home. We were invited to come by whenever we wanted to pick out and try on what we needed. "People are waiting in line to fill your needs," we were told. "All you have to do is ask."

But we didn't even have to ask.

My mother's quilting group in Beitar went on fast production to replace the "Bubby blankets" that my mother had lovingly sewn for the children over the past few years.

My son's teacher began collecting household items through an e-mail campaign. She compiled lists of people's "extra" items, from beds and closets to milk pitchers, hooks, and silverware. My son's preschool teacher, besides offering her support and assistance, implemented an innovative and thought-out plan to ensure that my little boy didn't walk away from the experience with any scars.

A family in the neighborhood invited us to move into their furnished basement until we found a suitable rental. Friends from the local Nshei offered to arrange meals for us, but they didn't have to make a single phone call: so many people called offering to send us meals that after booking meals for three full weeks, they started a waiting list. Even now, the meals are still arriving at our door daily. A friend recently complained to me that she wanted to make dinner for us a second time, but was told that not everyone who had called had had a chance to send us a meal for the first time!

The day after the fire, when everyone had left to work, yeshivah, school, and *gan*, I headed back to our apartment. As I climbed the stairs, I heard voices upstairs in the stairwell. When I reached the final flight of stairs, the voices fell silent. I saw five *rabbanim* and *askanim* from the neighborhood standing outside my door, all with long faces.

Why are they so somber? I thought. *They look like they're in a shivah house.*

"*Rabbosai*," I said uneasily, "no one died here!"

"We want you to know that we are with you in your *tza'ar*," one of them replied.

"What *tza'ar*?" I exclaimed. "Nobody was hurt! It's just a house! There was nothing here that we can't live without. Even the things that are not replaceable — the pictures, the kids' report cards — we can live without them. *Hodu laShem ki tov!*"

One of these *askanim*, who is involved with a major *tzedakah* organization, assured us that we would be receiving a large grant from the organization. We were relieved to know that at least a large chunk of the cost of the impending renovations would be covered.

The next day, however, the *askan* abashedly informed us that the organization's board had reviewed our case and had placed us at the very bottom of their priority list, behind all the many families who were coping with illness and bereavement, *lo aleinu*. We were on our own.

In Ramat Shlomo, in Yerushalayim, in my home community of Baltimore, and within my husband's and my parents' families, people began collecting money for us to renovate our apartment. The momentum of this fund-raising campaign spread quickly to all four corners of the world, and before we knew it, money was coming in from as far away as South Africa, Canada, England, and even China.

At first, Moshe and I were extremely uncomfortable accepting contributions. We had always worked hard to support ourselves and to be givers, doing *chesed* for others with our limited means. The idea of funds being raised on our behalf was repugnant to us, and we were ashamed to have to stretch out our hands and accept people's contributions. But what choice did we have?

Seeing my distress, my neighbor attempted to put me at ease. "Hashem wants *Klal Yisrael* to be there for each other," he explained. "You don't have to look at this as *tzedakah*; look at it as a form of community insurance. It's not just insurance for you, it's insurance for the entire *kehillah*, because the *chesed* and *achdus* that you are engendering is earning *shemirah* for all of us."

Moshe and I wanted the children to realize that being beneficiaries of *chesed* comes with responsibility rather than entitlement. We called a family meeting, and we talked about the different messages that Hashem had sent us through the fire and its aftermath. We made a list of the many manifestations of *hashgachah pratis* we had experienced, from the fact that no one was hurt down to the fact that my daughter had left her notebooks in school the day before.

"If we are to be the recipients of all this *chesed* and *achdus*," we told the children, "then Hashem is going to be extremely *medakdeik* with us in our own interactions. We can't just be the conduit for other people's *zechusim*. We have to work on our own *bein adam l'chaveiro* as well."

We had just moved into a short-term rental, and our living quarters were quite cramped. On Shabbos we had to borrow chairs so that everyone could squish around the small table, and every night we spread mattresses end to end across the floor of the apartment. The lack of space and privacy was hardly conducive to everyone remaining gracious at all times, but we reminded the kids that we had to be careful to maintain *shalom* in the house because that was what would allow the flow of *berachah* to continue. It became a family project to work on *savlanus* and *vatranus*, with even the little ones reminding each other to be *mevater* and keep an even keel.

All this time we were busy trying to make our house livable again. An experienced interior designer offered her services pro bono, helping me plan for the unexpected renovations that I'd now have to oversee.

After days of sorting through the rubble and trying to salvage whatever we could, we brought in a contractor to give an estimate for the renovations. But as time went on and more and more damage was uncovered, the estimate kept ballooning. It turned out that all the electrical wiring and plumbing in the apartment had to be replaced, which meant that all the flooring had to be torn up and the interior walls taken down.

Difficult as it was to know that we were dependent upon the generosity of others, I tried not to worry about how we would manage to pay for everything. But there was one memorable day when I was sorely challenged. That morning, the contractor informed me that the entire house was going to need new flooring. Shortly afterward, an organization that was helping us requested a copy of the fire department's official report. When I called the fire department to request the report, they told me it would only be sent to us after we paid their fee, which amounted to tens of thousands of shekels. I had been told that since the fire wasn't our fault, the fire department's services should be free, but apparently that's not the way it works.

My heart fell. *How are we going to put together this money?* I wondered. I sat down and said a *perek* of *Tehillim*, and then I said, "Okay, Hashem, You've been helping us deal with this until now. So now there's more for You to deal with."

In general, we tried to take the same attitude toward recovering from the fire as we had always taken toward our finances. Well-meaning people had often asked us, "How do you support such a large family on your meager salaries? How are you going to marry off your children?"

Our standard response to these questions was "Hashem takes care of everything. When it comes to marrying off our children, He'll take care of that, too."

Now, on top of taking care of our family and helping us marry off our children when the time comes, Hashem is also putting our house back together for us. He put us in this situation, and He's helping us through it. He's not scared off by a bill of $200,000, even if we are sometimes.

Many people have tried to comfort me by telling me that it says somewhere that after a fire you get rich. I have to admit that after hearing this over and over again, it starts becoming tiresome, and it's an effort to smile at the person and say, "Really? That's so interesting," especially since we still don't know how we are going to cover the huge debt caused by the fire. But then someone put an original spin on this aphorism.

"Chana," she said to me, "my father had a fire in his house years ago. He used to say, 'You know why you get rich after a fire? Because before the fire you say, 'I need this,' 'I don't have that,' and after the fire you say, '*Baruch Hashem,* I still have this…and that… and that!'"

If before the fire paying the bills had been an ongoing struggle, after the fire we kept talking about how lucky we were that no one ended up in the burn unit — or worse, *chas v'shalom*. Every item retrieved from our sooty apartment was new cause for delight. After we cleared the mountain of debris from the boys' room, I spotted a rubber doorstop at the bottom of the pile, still white and pristine. "Look," I said to my daughter, who was with me at the time. "Hashem picked this doorstop to survive."

Just as that little doorstop made us feel Hashem's love and concern, we feel people's love and concern with each and every contribution. Even the smallest donation is, to us, a sign that someone is sharing in our *nisayon* and helping us rebuild.

In the days after the fire, I was thinking that we were going to have an awfully long list of people to send *mishlo'ach manos* to next Purim. But by now, I've realized that I won't even be able to send thank-you e-mails to everyone who has helped us, let alone *mishlo'ach manos*, because I don't know who most of them are! It's truly humbling to be so indebted to so many people, and the least we can do is show our overwhelming *hakaras hatov* to all the people who have offered their support and assistance.

So to all of you who are reading this and have in some way assisted in our rebuilding campaign, I say thank you from the bottom of my heart. May Hashem repay you richly, and may you be *zocheh* to always be on the giving end.

We're scheduled to move back into our apartment before Tishah B'Av, but I can't imagine moving into a newly renovated house if Hashem's House is still lying in ruin. How can our personal *galus* end if Hashem and *Am Yisrael* are still in *galus*?

Perhaps the fire of *chesed* and *achdus* that's burning so brightly on behalf of my family will douse the flames of *sinas chinam* and bring down the fiery Beis HaMikdash of the future.

Postscript:

Nowhere in this article was there an appeal for financial assistance. The narrator's goal in telling her story was to express public hakaras hatov, because, as she said, there were so many people involved in helping her family after the fire, she couldn't possibly thank each one personally.

Yet the lack of an appeal did not stop caring readers from galvanizing to help this family. In fact, one reader took it upon herself to fund-raise for the family by sending a letter to people she knew and enclosing a copy of this story along with it.

Her campaign reminded me of a different LifeLines story, "At Your Door," about a woman who goes collecting door to door in Yerushalayim to support her family, marry off her children, and pay off the staggering debts her husband incurred as a result of a business deal that soured. The purpose of that story (which didn't make it into this book) was to highlight this woman's inspiring character, but a number of kindhearted readers wrote in afterward asking how they could donate money to her. One reader actually sent an anonymous donation of $5000!

Mi k'amcha Yisrael!

Outsourced

"Hi, Rina, good morning."

It's Mrs. Kepler at the door, handing me 9-month-old Asher. She's rushing off to work, and her hastily applied makeup can't quite hide the shadows under her eyes that belie a chronic shortage of sleep.

"I couldn't find his pacifier this morning," she tells me as she fumbles through her purse for her cell phone, which just started to ring. "I looked all over the place for it, but then I had to leave."

A warning bell goes off in my head. Asher used to have a spare pacifier in my house, but Mrs. Kepler took it back last week, when she couldn't find any in her own house. And Asher *needs* his pacifier.

"How will he go to sleep without a pacifier?" I ask, trying to sound nonchalant.

But Mrs. Kepler is already answering the call on her cell phone. Covering the mouthpiece, she says, "Oh, I don't know, you'll figure it out. So sorry!"

With that, she trips down the steps, leaving me to wonder how exactly Asher is going to cope today.

Asher's pacifier is not the first thing I've had to figure out this morning. At 8:30 sharp the doorbell rang, and a breathless Mrs. Yaroslawski presented me with 11-month-old Sarale, who was whimpering in her stroller.

"She hasn't eaten anything yet today," Mrs. Yaroslawski said apologetically. "I just decided to wean her, and she's giving me a really hard time eating solids. Maybe you'll have an easier time feeding her."

"Oh," I said. "Did you bring her a bottle just in case?"

"Nah," she said. "The pumping business is getting too much for me."

"What about formula?" I persisted.

"I don't want her to get hooked on formula now," she responded. "She's almost a year old. She has to learn to eat food, that's all."

She glanced at her watch. "Oh, my, I'm going to miss my car pool. I must get going. Thanks, Rina, you're the best."

Rounding out my "figure-it-out" list for the morning is 14-month-old Eliezer Barnett, whose father drops him off at 8:40, toting his tallis bag in one hand and pushing a double stroller with the other. Beside Eliezer in the stroller sits his 2-year-old brother, Naftali, who is on his way to being dropped off at a playgroup two blocks away.

When I lift Eliezer out of the stroller, I immediately feel that he is soaked. I'm about to ask Mr. Barnett — or is it Rabbi? — whether his wife sent a change of clothing, but he's clearly in a rush to get to Shacharis, and I don't want to hold him up.

I sigh. Mrs. Barnett, I know, has to be out of the house by 7:30 every morning, leaving her husband to care for the two little ones. She's a very put-together young woman, and she'd be horrified to know that most mornings her adorable Eliezer comes to me wearing the same diaper she put him to sleep in. I've thought many times about telling her to please make sure that Eliezer's diaper is changed before he comes to me, but I don't want to cause any friction between her and her husband. As it is, that couple is clearly under a lot of stress, and finding a clean stretchie for a fourteen-month-old shouldn't be too big a deal. I'll figure it out.

Thankfully, there are no issues today with 5-month-old Leah Prager, who is peacefully gurgling in her infant seat. But 16-month-old Moishy Ganz isn't here yet. His mother can go into her accounting office whenever she feels like it, and there is no predicting when she might drop Moishy off.

Asher with no pacifier, Sarale with no bottle, a soaked-through Eliezer, and a late Moishy Ganz. This is going to be a lo-o-o-n-g day.

———◆———

I've always loved babies, and I've always known that I wanted to work with them. I earned degrees in early childhood education and psychology, and before my own children were born I worked in various preschool settings. After I became a mother, however, I didn't want to leave my babies, so I opened a babysitting group in my house.

In the beginning, I worked only mornings, but as my kids got older and our expenses grew, I extended my hours to the afternoons as well, eventually offering a full-day babysitting service, from 8:30 to 5:30, to accommodate mothers who work 9 to 5.

Unless someone has actually worked as a babysitter, I don't think she can understand what it's like to be responsible for a bunch of helpless infants. Most parents find it challenging to take care of one or two babies — how often do you hear mothers complain, "I can't get anything done with her around"? — and it doesn't get easier when the numbers multiply. I've always limited my group to five babies, because I don't see how it's humanly possible to take care of more, but I know of babysitters who will accept even 10 babies at a time. I shudder to think of what goes on there while the mothers are blissfully at work.

Even with "just" five babies, from the minute the first child arrives in my house until the last one leaves, I can hardly put a morsel of food in my mouth, and certainly can't take any sort of break. There's always someone who needs attention, and usually a few at the same time. I can't change more than one diaper or hold more than one baby at once, so I have no choice but to tend to the babies in sequence, leaving the others to cry while I feed, change, or soothe the one I'm currently dealing with.

Parents who have watched me handle a bunch of babies simultaneously have marveled at how calm and efficient I am, but no matter how efficiently I work, I can't be there for everyone at once, and I'm pained anew each time a baby has to wait to have his basic needs met.

I try to be organized, preparing each kid's food or bottle ahead of time and putting all the babies in for naps at the same time so that the house stays quiet and no baby's sleep is interrupted by another one's crying. But the parents make it very hard for me to stick to my schedule.

I've asked Mrs. Ganz several times to bring boisterous little Moishy at the same time every day, but she says it's impossible. Half the time she brings him while the other babies are napping, and he promptly wakes them up. The other half of the time, she brings him after the other kids are already awake, when *he* needs a nap. Of course, he doesn't sleep for very long with all the noise of the kids playing, and he's cranky and irritable the rest of the day.

And no matter how organized I am, there are always little things that throw me for a loop. A pacifier, a bottle, a stretchie — these things may sound petty, but they mean a world of difference to a baby who depends on them for his physical or emotional comfort. And when you're taking care of a bunch of babies, it's not so simple to compensate for these items. I can't run out to the grocery to pick up a new pacifier, and I can't prepare formula against the mother's express wishes that her daughter be weaned off the bottle.

Right now, Asher is screaming, and all the other kids have to wait while I comb my house for an old pacifier that he'll be willing to take. He only uses the old-fashioned rubber kind with the big bulb, while I only have the silicon kind in the house... Wait! I think there's an old rubber one in the toy dishes box! I quickly rummage through the dishes, and, miracle of miracles, there's an

Asher-style pacifier. Now I have to sterilize it — *Eliezer, I'm coming, I know you're still soaked* — and then hopefully Asher will stop howling.

Phew! That's one down. Now a stretchie for Eliezer. He had a spare outfit here, but I sent it home with him the last time he arrived wet — that was just a couple of days ago, I think. I should have washed it myself instead of sending it home for Mrs. Barnett to wash. I climb up on a chair and pull down a box of my son's old clothing. Ah, here. Size 18 months. It might be a little big, but it'll do. I just hope Mrs. Barnett doesn't complain that her kid is dressed in someone else's hand-me-downs. She wasn't happy the last time Eliezer came home in one of my children's old outfits.

Next is Sarale. She's the real challenge here today, since she's not used to eating food and I have no bottle for her. I coax her into gulping down some rice cereal, and then I rock her to sleep, which is no mean feat, since she's clearly thirsty for her bottle.

And then Moishy Ganz shows up, all bright and preppy, just as I've finally gotten all four of the others to settle for a nap.

It's not that I mind going the extra mile to accommodate Mrs. Ganz, or any other busy mother. I don't. And I'm happy that the mothers place so much confidence in me and trust me implicitly with the care of their precious little bundles. I just wonder if they realize what they are doing to their babies, and to the other babies in the group, when they bring them to me in less than tip-top shape, or at a time that disrupts my carefully planned schedule.

Who am I fooling? Of course they don't realize. Mrs. Yaroslawski doesn't call to find out how Sarale's managing without her bottle, and Mrs. Kepler doesn't ask how Asher managed without his pacifier when she comes to pick him up. It's as though they've outsourced their motherhood to me by dropping their kids off at my doorstep: *Rina will figure it out. She's the best.*

I don't blame these mothers. Mrs. Kepler has six other kids besides Asher, and if Mrs. Yaroslawski has decided to wean Sarale cold turkey, there must be a good reason. They, and all of the other mothers who entrust me with their babies, are working hard to support their families, in whole or in part. If they could afford it, they'd probably hire a private babysitter to come to the house instead of sending their kids to me — although I *have* had some mothers who delude themselves into thinking that it's better for a baby to be with other kids.

How many times have mothers told me that they want their infants to have some "social stimulation"? I never know whether to inform them that from a developmental standpoint a young baby is much better off playing the starring role, without a host of other babies competing for attention. There's a reason why *HaKadosh Baruch Hu* designed this world in such a way that human babies are usually born one at a time, and not in a litter, like most animal species. A baby needs a mother, and he needs that mother to be the primary figure in his life, not just the one who dumps him in his crib at night and whisks him out of the house in the morning.

Let's face it. If a kid spends most of his waking hours with a babysitter and sees his mother for a few minutes in the morning, when she's in a huge rush, and for a couple of hours in the evening, when she's worn out and trying to get supper together and throw in a load of laundry, when does he have a mother? On weekends? And if there are a few siblings in the mix, how much mother can possibly be left for him?

I'm the one who sits on the floor and plays peekaboo with the babies. I'm the one who notices when they cut a new tooth, and I'm the one who kisses them when they bump their heads. Poor mothers, they don't even know what they're missing.

I like to think of myself as a competent babysitter who truly loves the kids in her care. But at the end of the day, I'm just a babysitter. The babies are not my own, and at the end of this year or maybe next year, they'll leave me and continue with someone else. Whatever bonding we do in the time they are with me will quickly disappear.

But I don't have much time for such morbid musings; I need to get back to caring for my babies. I have to make a *parnassah*, too, just like the other mothers.

I also have to get ready for my next client. The Ganzes are moving to a different neighborhood very shortly — dare I admit that I'm looking forward? — and a brand-new baby, Chaim

Lieberman, is going to take his place. He's a *bechor* — he actually had his *pidyon haben* exactly a month ago, as his mother told me wistfully when she came to introduce him to me a few days ago.

"I begged my boss to give me more time off work," she said, "but she told me that eight weeks is the absolute limit. So now I have to give him over to you."

I felt like crying, both for Chaim and for his mother. I thought of Yocheved placing her newborn son in the Nile River, and I couldn't help but think that the two situations were not all that different — except that Yocheved was able to care for Moshe for two whole years, until he was ready to be weaned, while the sweet, young Mrs. Lieberman had only two months to be Chaim's mother before rushing back into the grind of her work as a computer programmer.

I know that for the first few days it's going to be torture for Mrs. Lieberman to go back to work and leave little Chaim in the hands of a stranger. Maybe I'll reassure her that in my experience mothers get used to leaving their babies after a short while — a shockingly short while — and that in a mere few days or weeks, she won't even be thinking about her baby when she's at the office. Or maybe I'll tell her that she can feel free to call or even drop by at any time to visit little Chaim. That'll happen once, twice, three times, and then Chaim will be all mine — missing pacifier, bottle, and all.

Postscript:

Many working mothers felt unfairly attacked and condemned by this story, and they used words such as "preposterous," "outrageous," and "deeply insulting" to describe the way "Rina," the protagonist, expressed herself.

But the reactions of the babysitters were no less visceral. A number of babysitters left messages on the LifeLines voice mail, and when I called them back, they voiced their disappointment over the mild tone of the article. "It was so pareve," one babysitter complained.

Each of these babysitters reported similarly shocking experiences: mothers who neglect their babies' medical care; mothers who send their children sick; mothers who dilute their babies' bottles; mothers who deprive their children of basic nutrition ("Hold him off for a couple of hours until I come pick him up"); mothers who can't tolerate being home with their babies.

The "Outsourced" story wasn't about cases of objective neglect, however. It was about the regular, everyday reality of mothers leaving their children all day in the care of hired babysitters. And the purpose of the story was not, chas v'shalom, to condemn these hardworking mothers, who struggle valiantly to balance motherhood and parnassah.

So what was the purpose of the story? I'll let this excerpt from a reader's letter about "Outsourced" answer that question:

> *I finished reading the gripping account as my train neared my station on my way home from work. As I bolted down the subway stairs, racing home to finally be reunited with my tot after the daily 10-hour workday separation, I was awash with pity for both sitter and charges. The article was a great motivator to keep searching for the elusive well-paying job with reduced hours.*

Sometimes a less-than-ideal situation becomes such an ingrained societal norm that we forget that this isn't the way things are supposed to be. As the stay-at-home mommy becomes an increasingly endangered species, we would do well to remind ourselves on occasion that babies weren't meant to be outsourced.

Bending the Laws of Nature

Have you ever gone through a time in your life when you felt that absolutely everything was going wrong? I experienced such a time, and now that I've safely reached the other side, *baruch Hashem*, I feel compelled to share my story.

My husband, Tzvi, was in *kollel* for the first two years of our marriage. I worked as a bookkeeper, while Tzvi gave bar mitzvah lessons in the evenings, and we managed to make ends meet respectably.

The birth of our second baby turned our lives topsy-turvy. Yanky was an adorable baby, but he had terrible feeding issues. Each time I would feed him, his body would swell up, he would screech frightfully, and eventually he would start to vomit.

The doctor told me it was reflux, and we put Yanky on medication. When that didn't help, the doctor changed his medication, but that didn't help either. Our baby wasn't eating, gaining weight, or sleeping — and I was sick with worry, not to mention lack of sleep.

I was busy with Yanky around the clock. Not only was there no way I could go back to work, I also needed Tzvi to help me in the evenings with Yanky and his older brother Bentzion, who was still a baby himself. Tzvi couldn't leave the house at night to give his bar mitzvah lessons, and there was not a penny of income entering our home at that point. We used up what remained of our *chasunah* money, and we literally had nothing left. Realizing that it was unlikely that I'd be able to return to work anytime soon, Tzvi began looking for a job.

In the midst of all this, we stopped receiving food stamps. Due to a technicality, the city was missing some of our financial information, and they cut us off this program just at the time when our income was reduced to zero.

Mendel, the owner of our corner grocery, was extremely kind to us. "Don't worry about paying me," he told us. "You can buy everything you need on credit, and when you have the money, you'll pay."

I didn't want to buy groceries on credit. I had never before had an account in the grocery; I always paid either with cash or with food stamps. But now, there *was* no cash, and our food stamps hadn't yet been reinstated, so what choice did we have?

Thinking that we would receive our food stamp benefit retroactively, we reluctantly took Mendel up on his offer.

Our landlord was not as understanding as Mendel the grocer. When we explained our situation and asked if he could give us some more time to pay our rent, he threatened to evict us. In the meantime, we also began receiving notices from the electric, gas, water, and phone companies that they were going to cut off our service if we didn't pay our bills.

My parents and Tzvi's parents helped with some of our expenses. They would have loved to help us more, but they're both in *chinuch*, and have children to marry off, so they weren't in a position to give us much money.

Tzvi and I considered debt a loathsome thing, and we were reluctant to borrow or put our bills on the credit card, even though our situation was desperate. "Borrowing money that you can't pay back is like stealing," Tzvi often told me. "Even if a person is hungry, he can't steal."

Tzvi calculated that we would soon be receiving several thousand dollars from the government in the form of a tax refund. The parents of two of the bar mitzvah boys he had taught also owed him money, and when he approached them, they both assured him that they would pay him within a week. With those assurances in hand, Tzvi asked a friend of his for a loan of a few thousand dollars.

The money we borrowed kept us afloat for several months. During that time, Tzvi tried his hand at a few different jobs. He worked as substitute rebbi in a *cheder*, he worked as a salesman in an appliance store, he worked in the office of a *tzedakah* organization. But none of those jobs lasted more than a couple of weeks. Tzvi is a bright, talented person, but his quiet, reserved nature was not suited to the positions that were open to him. It didn't help that he was under tremendous pressure to earn a living, or that he came home every night to a screaming baby, a neglected toddler, and a wreck of a wife.

By the time the money we borrowed was used up, we found ourselves right back where we had been several months earlier: destitute, in danger of eviction, still waiting for money to come in so we could repay our debt — and dealing with an undernourished, miserable baby. I found myself in a constant state of anxiety. Either I was worried about my baby, who couldn't eat and wasn't growing, or I was agonizing over the disastrous state of our finances.

I'm not the kind of person who likes to talk about my problems, and I didn't confide in anyone how much I was suffering. To the outside world, including my parents and siblings, I put on a big smile and pretended that everything was wonderful.

Months of bottling up my stress took a severe toll on me. One day, I just collapsed. I lay in bed for three days and cried and cried. I couldn't do anything; I couldn't even daven. The only thing I could do was open my *Tehillim* and say the words of *kapitel* 22 over and over again: "*Keili Keili lamah azavtani*" — where are you,

Ribbono shel Olam? As I continued through the *kapitel*, my *Tehillim* became soaked with tears, but I found a measure of comfort as I repeated the words of David HaMelech and Esther HaMalkah: "In You our forefathers trusted; they trusted and You rescued them."

Even in the midst of my suffering, I knew that I wasn't alone. Hashem was with me, and I knew He would help.

But I also knew that I needed to help myself, so I called a *rebbetzin* who has a great deal of experience counseling people. "I'm cracking up!" I cried to her. "What's wrong with me?"

"There's nothing wrong with you," she comforted me. "You're not depressed, and you're not having a nervous breakdown. It's just all the pent-up frustration coming out. Let it come out, it's healthy. Cry it out, daven, and Hashem will take care of you."

It was precisely then that a small glimmer of hope appeared. A woman named Mrs. Zaks who ran the public-relations department of an organization for special-needs children called to ask me if I could help her write some thank-you poems for their donors. I had volunteered for that organization when I was single, spending two afternoons a week in their after-school clubs for special kids. At some point, the people in the organization had discovered that I had a flair for poetry, and Mrs. Zaks had recruited me to write some poems for her PR materials. Now she was calling to ask if I could write more of these poems — for pay.

I made $300 that week writing poems, and that small paycheck made me feel like a human being once again.

After that, we had another big breakthrough. I tried feeding Yanky a special type of infant formula, and his symptoms disappeared! When I stopped nursing and switched him to the special formula completely, he was a new child, and I was a new mother.

My bookkeeping job had already been snapped up by someone else, so I asked Mrs. Zaks if I could write more poems or do other types of writing for her.

"Would you like to help us prepare the materials for our upcoming dinner and journal?" she offered.

Shortly after the dinner, I got a call from a woman from another organization who had seen the journal and wanted me to do some PR writing for her organization as well.

For the first time in months, I was earning some money. Our food stamps were reinstated, too, but we were still far from covering our monthly budget. Tzvi was having no success in his job search, and he was becoming extremely discouraged. On top of that, our actual tax refund was much less than Tzvi had anticipated, and the parents who owed him money never did pay him. Tzvi reluctantly borrowed more money, hoping that he would find work quickly and be able to start paying off some of the mountain of debt we had accrued.

It was around this time that a friend of mine mentioned to me that when she had been going through a difficult time, she had consulted with a great *tzaddik* in Eretz Yisrael, who had told her, "*Az a frau tosht zich in tznius, vet di Eibeshter toshen far ir di teva* — If a woman improves her *tznius*, Hashem will bend the laws of nature for her."

Hearing this made me confused. I didn't believe in making deals with Hashem; I believed that a person has to do what's right, period. But if a big *tzaddik* said otherwise — based on the statement of the *Zohar* (III:126a) that says that if a woman is modest, she merits distinguished children, and her husband is blessed with riches and more — who was I to disagree?

I knew that *al pi teva* our situation was hopeless. I was underemployed, Tzvi was unemployed, our job prospects were bleak, and we were falling further and further into debt. What did I have to lose by taking on something as a *zechus* for a *yeshuah*?

Now the question was what my *kabbalah* in the area of *tznius* should be. I wanted to do something meaningful, something that would truly make me deserving of *berachah*.

One afternoon, as I was standing in line at the grocery, I heard a woman talking on her cell phone behind me.

"Take the meat out of the freezer and put it on the counter. No, not the roast — the ground beef. And you can start peeling some potatoes, too."

It was quiet in the store, and I realized that every single person in line — male and female — was turned in her direction, unconsciously listening to her conversation.

When I went home to my apartment building, I saw my neighbor sitting on her first-floor porch and talking on the phone, and I noticed that people's heads swiveled in her direction as they walked down the sidewalk near her porch.

Right then and there I decided what my *kabbalah* would be: I would not talk on the phone outdoors. I didn't have a cell phone, but I often talked on my cordless phone outside on my porch or in the hall of my apartment building.

That same week, the phone company cut off our home phone line. It was a mistake: the company claimed that we hadn't paid an old bill, when in fact we had paid all of our bills up to that point. When I informed the phone company of the error, they apologized profusely for the misunderstanding and promised to have our line working again by the end of the day.

The next day, our phone was still not working. When I called the company, they said they had restored our service, and they couldn't understand why I had no dial tone on the line. They promised to send a technician, but when the technician finally arrived two days later, he was stymied. "There's no problem at all with your phone wires, but I can't seem to get the dial tone back," he said.

I borrowed a cell phone until my phone would be fixed, but I quickly learned that my apartment had poor cellular reception. I couldn't make any calls unless I stood right beside the window, and even then, my calls got disconnected every few seconds.

I experienced two conflicting emotions at that point. On one hand, I felt tempted to abandon my *kabbalah*, at least temporarily, because it seemed completely unfeasible to stick to it under these conditions.

On the other hand, the sudden malfunction of our phone line came at such an uncanny time that it was clear to me that this was a *nisayon* from Heaven to see whether I would abide by my *kabbalah* and refrain from talking on the phone in public. The knowledge that I was being tested made it much easier for me to endure the considerable inconvenience of being without a phone.

At the end of that month, when Tzvi went to pay our landlord — with borrowed money, yet again — the landlord handed half the money back to him. "You have a mysterious benefactor," he told Tzvi. "Someone just called and told me that he wants to pay half your rent for the next year, on condition that he remain anonymous."

We were flabbergasted. Neither of us had any rich relatives, and very few people outside our immediate families knew of our plight. Who could this secret benefactor be?

That same week Tzvi found a job working as a *mashgiach* in a local restaurant. The pay was decent, and his supervisor at the *kashrus* agency hinted that there was room for upward mobility within the agency if he proved himself out in the field.

My new career as a writer for nonprofit organizations was also starting to pick up, and by this time I had steady work writing fund-raising materials for three different organizations.

Now that Tzvi and I were both working again, we were managing to cover all of our monthly payments. But our accumulated debt of $30,000 dollars was weighing heavily on us, and the people Tzvi had borrowed from were demanding that he pay up immediately.

"What we need," Tzvi said, "is one large loan to consolidate all the debts, a loan that we can repay slowly over the next few years. But who's going to give me such a loan?

We found out a short while later. Tzvi was at a wedding in a different neighborhood, and he found himself seated beside a wealthy man from our community, Mr. Gordon. Tzvi and Mr. Gordon decided to take a taxi home together, and during the ride, Tzvi told him a little about our situation and asked him if he could possibly lend us the money we needed in order to pay off our debt.

"I want to tell you something," Mr. Gordon said. "I wasn't planning to come to this wedding at all. It was a shlep for me, I'm not familiar with the neighborhood, and I don't even know the *ba'al simchah* that well. I would never have agreed to give a loan to a stranger, but it's obvious to me that the reason I had to be at this wedding was so that I could sit next to you and take a taxi home with you and hear your story. So I'll take this as a sign *min haShamayim* that I should say yes to you."

With that, Mr. Gordon pulled out his checkbook and wrote out a check for $30,000. "You can pay me $500 a month for the next five years," he said. "Can you manage that?"

"I...I think so," Tzvi said quickly as he handed Mr. Gordon a signed IOU.

With that, all of our financial issues were settled. We both had work, our income was adequate to live off of and slowly repay our debts, and we had a loan that enabled us to get our creditors off our backs and even pay off our account in the grocery.

When the few people who knew about our desperate situation heard about the unlikely series of events that had led to our financial recovery, they each commented independently about the extraordinary *siyatta d'Shmaya* that we had merited. "What did you do to merit this?" they asked us. "What's your secret?"

Tzvi and I just smiled when we heard this question. The ways of Hashem are mysterious, and who were we to say why things happened the way they did? Yet in our own heads and hearts, the words of the *tzaddik* continued to reverberate: *Az a frau tosht zich in tznius, vet di Eibeshter toshen far ir di teva.*

Postscript:

Many readers have sent me stories of how they took on a particular kabbalah or segulah and saw a miraculous salvation. For the most part, I have studiously avoided those stories, because LifeLines isn't the venue for stories of the "I promised and I was saved" genre; I prefer to focus on internal growth rather than external deliverance.

Another reason I'm wary of stories like these is that they contain the implied promise that anyone who follows the same prescription will see the same results, and I'm not qualified to make such promises.

Why did this story make the cut? Well, for one thing, because the promise it contains was made by no less an authority than the Zohar. The narrator did not know the exact words of the Zohar, nor did she know where in the Zohar they are found, so I did quite a bit of research to locate the precise source, and I made sure to include it.

Another thing that was different about this story was that the narrator searched within herself for something to work on rather than reaching for the nearest magic 40-day formula or all-purpose spiritual potion. The change she made was innovative yet appropriate, small yet difficult, personal yet concrete. That's a genuine kabbalah.

Finally, what made this story different from the classic tale of "I did x and saw miracles" was the way it reframed the subject of tznius. Too often, discussions of tznius revolve around inches and centimeters and miss the heart of what tznius is. True modesty is about being inconspicuous, about switching the focus from the external to the internal, about finding fulfillment in concealment rather than exposure. The narrator of this story understood that.

To me, the real story here wasn't the miracle of her financial rescue. It was the miracle of how she was able to look inside herself and grow in a highly unusual way.

Wedding Spirit

The first thing I told Yitzy, my *chassan*, after we got engaged was, "We're not getting involved in planning the wedding. Let our parents work it out between themselves."

I knew that my parents had very definite ideas about what a wedding should look like, and I suspected — or more than suspected — that Yitzy's parents would disagree.

Yitzy's parents and mine belonged to the same income stratum, what you would call upper middle class. But while his parents viewed a wedding as a necessary stepping-stone to a marriage, mine viewed it as the culmination of 20-odd years of raising a child.

In my community, a wedding was a big deal. It was the night of a lifetime, and as such had to be accorded its due honor — and expense. It didn't matter if you had to mortgage your house, take on an additional job, or rob a bank; a wedding had to be an unforgettable event, by hook or by crook.

My older brother and sister had married within the community, and their weddings were respectable affairs. Respectable meant a lavish smorgasbord, followed by a meal that included six types of fish and 15 salads for the first course and seven types of meat for the main course. "Guests should not be given a choice of menu," my mother would say emphatically. "At my *simchah*, there's no such thing as 'Do you want prime rib or lamb chops?' You put everything on the table so that the guests can take as much as they want. Sea bass, tilapia, salmon, tuna steak — let them have everything!"

For my sister Shuli's wedding, my father had decided that a regular bar wasn't enough, so he went out and bought XO cognac — at over $100 a bottle — to put on each table. The guys in his shul talked about that for weeks afterward, and my father was so pleased he promised me that he'd do the same for my wedding.

"For me, you can skip the cognac, Abba," I told him.

"Yeah, save it for my wedding," my younger brother Benny piped up.

My siblings' weddings — just the wedding night alone — cost approximately $120,000, which was completely normal in our community. A wedding that cost less was "cheap," which, in the eyes of my parents and their friends, was about the most heinous crime imaginable, with mass murder perhaps a close second.

Generally, wedding guests gave monetary gifts, and if the hosts were not wealthy, those gifts went to cover the wedding costs. That was how my parents had made their two previous weddings, and that was how they planned to make mine.

Except that I strayed from the *derech* to some extent. In high school, I got a bug in my head — as my father described it — that I wanted to marry someone who would learn in *kollel* for a few years. That bug in my head only grew as I got older, and although my parents insisted that I date boys who would be able to support me, after a while they realized that I was serious about the *kollel* thing and I was not going to marry a medical student or an MBA. Throwing up their hands in despair, they agreed to let me go out with boys who were learning.

"But we're not supporting you," my father informed me. "That's your husband's job. This *kollel* business is ridiculous, and you're not cut out for it anyway. Don't say we didn't warn you."

I was duly warned, but undeterred. When I met Yitzy, a serious boy who had dropped out of college in order to pursue Torah study, I knew that we were meant for each other.

That didn't mean that our parents were meant for each other, though.

When Yitzy's father told my father that he thought $25 a person was a reasonable tab for a wedding, my father hit the roof. "We don't even make a *bris* for $25 a plate!" he exclaimed.

And when my mother saw the diamond that Yitzy's parents bought me, she practically cried. "What kind of business is that, to buy *kallah* a 60-point stone?" she fumed. "And the *chassan* didn't even send flowers for the *vort*! That's how they treat a *kallah*?"

When Yitzy had presented me with the diamond, I had actually liked it. Yes, it was small, but the setting was pretty and it was *mine*. Nor had it occurred to me that Yitzy should have sent me flowers. But now that my mother pointed it out, it did start to bother me that my diamond was a fraction of the size of those of the other women in my family. Come to think of it, it really wasn't nice that Yitzy and his parents hadn't thought of sending flowers to the *vort*. Didn't I mean enough to them to warrant even a simple bouquet?

Hearing Yitzy talk about his parents while we were dating, I knew right away that the wedding would be a major issue. His parents lived in a low-key out-of-town community, where a fancy wedding was one that featured grilled chicken instead of chicken on the bone.

Right after our engagement, the two sets of parents agreed that each side would pay for their own guests. But the type of wedding my parents envisioned was going to cost $200 a person, a lot more than my in-laws were willing to cough up. Gracious, generous people that they were, my parents didn't want to get into a confrontation with their new *mechutanim*. Instead, they put me to the task.

"Tell Yitzy that his parents should fly in to meet with the caterer," my father instructed. "They need to understand how things are done around here."

"And they can sit with the florist at the same time," my mother chimed in. "We need to plan a color scheme, you know."

I felt my jaw tighten. "Yitzy's parents aren't flying in for those things," I said. "They have jobs."

"So let Yitzy come in," my father countered. "He doesn't have a job."

"Yitzy's *learning*!" I protested. "His time is valuable, too! Besides, he wouldn't know a daffodil from a dandelion."

"That's the problem," my mother muttered.

"Abba, Ima," I begged, "who is this wedding for? Me and Yitzy, or the guests? What difference does it make if the color is lilac or plum? My mother-in-law couldn't care less, and neither do I!"

"Your wedding day is the happiest day of your life," my mother said, a touch of wistfulness in her voice. "Everything has to be just right."

"But Ima, if a wedding is supposed to be a happy day, then why should there be all this stress between you and my in-laws?"

My father's eyes narrowed. "Aliza," he said, "this might be your wedding, but it's our *simchah*. And if your in-laws can't understand that there's a way to make a *simchah*, they have a problem. How dare you take their side?"

This isn't my problem! I wanted to shout. *How did I get involved anyway? Didn't I tell Yitzy the minute after we drank l'chaim that we were not going to have anything to do with planning this wedding?*

My parents kept insisting that I intervene, that I speak to Yitzy, that I get him to make his parents understand "how things are done around here." Yitzy didn't understand, though, and no matter how delicately I broached the subject, it invariably resulted in friction between us.

"I don't get why we need a full orchestra, plus a professional singer," Yitzy said. "What's wrong with a one-man band?"

"Nothing's wrong with a one-man band," I said desperately, "but that's not the way it's done! My parents would never be able to lift their heads in public again if they did that."

"Why not?"

My temples started to throb.

Before my engagement, I had always been thin, but now I found myself eating out of nervousness, and I started to gain weight. Twice I brought my wedding gown to the seamstress to let out, and she said nothing. The third time, she waved her thimble-topped finger at me threateningly and said, "I not fix zees dress vun more time! You close mouth and stop to eat now!"

Then came the next hurdle.

"So how many friends are you and Yitzy planning on having at the wedding?" my father asked.

"Oh, probably about 50 each," I said.

My father blanched. "Fifty friends *each*? Do you know how much that's going to cost me?"

"It doesn't have to cost so much," I said. "My friends don't care whether you serve steak or salami sandwiches, and neither do Yitzy's."

"Don't be silly," my father scolded. "At a wedding you serve steak. Shuli had 20 friends at her wedding, and that's more than enough. You can tell that to Yitzy, too."

"But Abba," I complained, "having my friends at my wedding is more important to me than the food!"

"You can invite as many friends as you want to the *chuppah*," he said with finality. "If you want more at the dinner, the money for that will have to come off what we're paying for your furniture."

A few weeks into our engagement, Yitzy came to spend Shabbos with us. When he arrived, he presented me with a bouquet of carnations.

"Carnations for a *kallah*?" my mother moaned when he was out of earshot. "Not a rose in sight! Did you ever?"

Her horror notwithstanding, she decided to use the opportunity to take care of the wedding invitations, and she drove us to the printer Friday afternoon to choose samples and look at monograms.

While in the car, she turned to Yitzy and asked, "So who in your family is going to be walking down to the *chuppah*?"

"Me," Yitzy said. "And my parents, of course."

My mother chuckled. "Yes, yes," she said. "But what about your younger siblings, and your cousins? We need some flower girls, you know. And we usually rent tuxedos for the little boys. The whole thing is just adorable."

I already knew Yitzy's opinion on flower girls, and it wasn't a favorable one.

"Ima," I said carefully, "I think Yitzy and I would prefer not to have any flower girls."

"What?" my mother shrilled. "What's a *chuppah* without flower girls? That's the cutest part of the whole wedding!"

That was when I lost it. "A wedding is not about cute!" I exploded. "Can't we get past the flowers and the tuxedos already?"

Yitzy didn't say anything, but I could tell that he was appalled by my outburst. For the rest of the drive, and during our meeting at the printer, he was quiet and withdrawn. During the Shabbos *seudah* that night, he barely spoke to me, and when I suggested that we take a walk, he said he was too tired.

Alarm bells started ringing in my head. *He's going to break the engagement*, I thought.

The next morning, when Yitzy came home from shul with my father, I motioned to him to come with me to a quiet corner of the house.

"You're upset that I spoke to my mother that way, right?" I asked.

His eyebrows arched in surprise. "How did you know?"

"Look," I said, "I'm upset at myself, too. I don't usually speak that way to anyone, and certainly not to my parents. But if you would know how much stress I'm under because of this silly wedding — I mean, it's not silly, but all these *details* — you'd understand why I blew up. I'm hearing about this stuff all day, every day, and I feel hopelessly caught between my parents and you and your parents. Do you know how many Advils I've taken since we got engaged? I'm trying to keep the peace between everyone, but at some point, it just becomes too much for me! Honestly, I'd rather elope and forget about this whole wedding!"

"Thanks for explaining this," Yitzy said. He seemed calmer, but from then on there was this tension in the background that didn't go away for the duration of our engagement.

With time, and after lots of bickering, my parents and in-laws each made concessions. Neither side was happy with the compromises, though. My in-laws thought the wedding was going to be over the top, and my parents were so embarrassed at how simple it was going to be that they didn't invite some of their friends, who they knew would be aghast.

At the wedding itself, my mother overheard some relatives talking about how surprised they were that there hadn't been sushi at the smorgasbord, or even meat carving. One relative mentioned that he was disappointed that there was no XO cognac. My mother was deeply insulted, and she tearfully relayed these remarks to me just before the start of the second dance.

"Ima," I said, "this is such a beautiful wedding! Everyone I danced with was so happy. It's the spirit that counts!"

She didn't look convinced. It didn't help that my brother Benny moped the whole week of *sheva berachos* that there hadn't been a professional singer at the wedding. "My friends were so disappointed," he lamented. "Why couldn't you get a *real* singer?"

That Shabbos, the *rav* of our shul got up and began to praise my parents for the tasteful wedding they had made. "Everyone in this community should do the same," he declared. "I especially liked the fact that the *chuppah* was serious, with no children walking down the aisle."

My parents didn't know whether to be proud or mortified.

Everyone says that *shanah rishonah* is challenging, but for me, it was a cinch compared to my engagement. Yitzy didn't care if I served plain chicken for supper, and I didn't care if he bought me carnations for Shabbos. He mopped the floors every Friday and washed the cholent pot every *motza'ei Shabbos*, and that, to me, was worth more than roses.

With time, my parents have made peace with the fact that they made a "*nebbach*" wedding, and they've even come to respect my in-laws. They're especially impressed that Yitzy changes diapers; Shuli's husband doesn't do that, and neither does her two-carat diamond ring.

I feel bad for people whose wedding day is the "happiest day of their life." The wedding lasts just a few hours, and then what? Downhill all the way?

Of course a wedding should be a happy event. But what makes a wedding happy is not the flowers, the prime ribs, or even the cognac. It's the spirit that counts — not the spirits.

Postscript:

Here's a letter I received from a skeptical reader:

> *Dear C. Saphir,*
>
> *Your stories are always interesting, but please keep them plausible. I've attended many fancy weddings, at the Waldorf Astoria, Sheraton, etc. — yes, kosher ones. The mechutanim were not millionaires, they were billionaires. The weddings were extremely fancy and elaborate. However, I never heard of or saw six types of fish, 15 salads, or seven types of meat served at the meal. This would make a circus of any chasunah. Let's be real, keep it real.*

This was my response:

> *Thank you for your e-mail. There is a rule in writing: fiction has to be plausible, but truth doesn't. I do change details in my stories, but the outlandish details aren't the ones I would make up. In this story, the part about the menu options was the plain truth, told to me by the protagonist herself. The story happened in a particular community that you probably have no contact with; in this community, these are the norms, even if there are billionaires making weddings in the Waldorf who don't serve as many menu options.*

It's ironic that what this reader — and probably many others — consider implausible is considered completely normal in the community to which the protagonist of "Wedding Spirit" belongs.

It's frightening to think that we, too, might subscribe to social conventions that we consider completely normal — but that an outsider might consider a "circus."

Part 4

חַיִּים שֶׁל חִלּוּץ עֲצָמוֹת

A Life of Health

A Hole in the Heart

It was supposed to be a routine 20-week ultrasound scan. I was 22 years old, expecting my second child, and I had no reason to think that anything might be wrong, until the technician abruptly left the room. "I'm going to call a doctor," she said.

This is strange, I thought, left alone in the darkened examination room. I thought back to the 20-week ultrasound I had taken when I was expecting my first baby, Menachem. I didn't remember any doctor being present.

A minute later the technician returned, accompanied by a gray-haired man in a white lab coat. "I'm Dr. Stevens," he said. "Libby, our technician, asked me to take a quick look at your baby's heart."

The "quick look" seemed interminably long, at least from my vantage point.

"There appears to be a defect in your baby's AV canal," Dr. Stevens finally said.

"A-what?" I asked blankly.

"It's a congenital heart defect. Basically a hole in the heart," Dr. Stevens explained gravely. "It looks very serious."

This can't be happening, I thought to myself, feeling panicky and confused. *He's being an alarmist.*

I listened in a daze as Dr. Stevens gave me a list of instructions. "I'm referring you to a pediatric cardiologist at Columbia University Medical Center," he said. "You'll have to undergo further testing to verify the precise diagnosis and determine a treatment plan."

"Thank you," I said shakily.

I left the office clutching the pile of papers he had given me, wondering how all the other people in the office could be smiling and happy when my entire world had just caved in. I had walked through the doors of the office feeling light and joyous about the new baby I hoped to meet shortly. Now I was walking out, heavy, weighed down by the knowledge that I was carrying a baby who might not live long enough to take his first breath.

As I drove home, I thought of all the stories I had heard about ultrasound mistakes. My own cousin had been told that something was very wrong with her unborn baby, yet the baby had been born perfectly healthy, to the astonishment of all the doctors. *I'm sure there was a mistake here, too*, I comforted myself.

But when I went for another ultrasound, accompanied this time by my husband, Zev, I learned that the prognosis was even worse than Dr. Stevens had described.

"Your baby has a right dominant AV canal defect," the pediatric cardiologist at Columbia informed us. "He's going to need open-heart surgery immediately at birth or shortly thereafter."

My initial reaction of denial and hope gave way to shock and grief. I cried straight through the next week, even as I kept running to more doctors and undergoing more tests. For the rest of the pregnancy, I davened, I said *Tehillim*, I went to get *berachos* from *tzaddikim*, and I listened to inspirational speeches, bracing myself for what was to come.

About 10 days before my baby was born, my aunt Blimi succumbed to her battle with Hodgkin's. At the *shivah* my uncle was like a rock, repeating over and over again the words "Hashem knows what He's doing and we don't ask questions."

With these words ringing in my head, I checked into Columbia Medical Center to give birth. A special team of medical staff was on hand during the delivery, and the moment my son was born, they whisked him away to hook him up to a respirator. They did not give me my son to hold, nor did they even show him to me. But as they were wheeling him out of the room, I caught a glimpse of his face, and I knew.

Oh, Hashem! Help me! I thought, gulping very hard.

I realized then, just minutes after my son's birth, that there were two roads before me: the road of pain, bitterness, and complaints, or the road of "Hashem knows what He's doing and we don't ask questions." In that split second, I chose the latter.

"Zev," I said, taking a deep breath, "it looks like we were *zocheh* to a special *neshamah*."

"What do you mean?" Zev asked.

"I…I think our baby has Down syndrome," I said. "I caught a glimpse of his face, and I could tell."

"The doctor didn't say anything about it," Zev said doubtfully. "And besides, you didn't even get a good look at him! Let's hope for the best."

Five minutes later, my doctor walked back into the room, a dismal expression on his face. "I have bad news for you, Mr. and Mrs. Handelsman. Your baby has Down syndrome."

"That's not bad news!" I declared stubbornly. "He's our son, and we're going to love him however G-d made him."

Zev vigorously nodded his agreement.

Now we had to call our parents and relatives and share the news of our son's birth with them.

"Everything's going to depend on us," Zev said. "If we're proud of this baby, then the rest of the family will be proud of him. But if we're embarrassed and sad, they'll pick up on that and they'll also be sad and uncomfortable."

"Absolutely," I concurred. "This is a *simchah*, not a *tzarah!*"

I took a deep breath and dialed my mother's number. "Hi, Ma," I said excitedly. "I just had a beautiful baby boy."

"*Mazel tov*!" she said. "How is he?"

We had told my parents and Zev's parents that our baby had a heart defect, so my mother was understandably concerned.

"We don't know yet about his heart," I said, "but we do know something else about him — he has uppies!"

"Uppies? What's that?"

Zev threw me an encouraging glance, and I forged ahead. "Well, some people call it Down syndrome, but we're calling it uppies!"

That was the way we broke the news to all of our relatives and friends. They were all shocked at first, but as Zev had predicted, they followed our lead and congratulated us instead of walking on eggshells around us or trying to console us. Which was good, because I didn't want anyone's condolences; I wanted the freedom to enjoy the precious gift Hashem had given me, without the shadow of other people's grief clouding my ability to appreciate my child.

Zev and I decided that from then on, when we would wake up in the morning, we would immediately say, "*Hodu laShem ki tov*," before the horrible, sinking feeling of "Help, what's happening to us?" would have a chance to take hold.

The next morning, right after I said *Modeh Ani*, I said, "*Hodu laShem ki tov*." All of a sudden, I had the feeling that Hashem had zeroed in on me and Zev, choosing us for the special privilege of being this child's parents. I knew it wasn't going to be easy, but I felt utterly secure in Hashem's hands.

Thankfully, the doctors decided that our baby could wait three months before having his first surgery. He was allowed to go home after only a few days in the hospital, and remarkably, he was able to have his *bris* on time. We named him Shlomo.

Shlomo was a beautiful, cuddly baby, and because of his heart condition, he slept a lot. It was as though he wanted to make things easy for us.

At the age of 3 months, Shlomo underwent his first open-heart surgery, during which the doctors placed something called a PA band around his heart to slow down the blood flow and ease the pressure on his lungs. After the surgery, when he was recovering in the ICU, I jumped every time the machines started to beep.

"Don't worry about the beeping," the nurse assured me. "He's fine."

"But how will I know if something's wrong?" I persisted.

"Just look at my face," she said. "You'll know."

A few minutes later, the machines started to beep again, and the nurse hurried over.

"Is he O.K.?" I asked anxiously.

She ignored me. I saw her face, and I knew something was very wrong. Then she started doing CPR. I heard the words "cardiac arrest," and in seconds, Shlomo's incubator was surrounded by medical personnel.

As Shlomo fought desperately for his life, I davened to Hashem with an intensity I had never before experienced. "Save his life!" I begged.

And then, finally, a resident announced, "We got him back!"

Shlomo came home a few weeks later. For the next year and a half, he developed beautifully, with the help of wonderful therapists. He had sparkling blue eyes and an adorable, irresistibly charming personality. He loved everyone, and everyone loved him — especially his older brother Menachem, who would climb into his crib to play with him every time I turned around. Around his first birthday, Shlomo learned to say "ma-ma-ma" and "da-da-da," and he would blow kisses to anyone who passed him outside in the street.

When Shlomo was a year and a half old, he underwent another open-heart surgery, which was supposed to be the first of a series of three. This time, there were complications during the surgery, and the surgeon's assistant came out to the waiting room to tell us that Shlomo wasn't going to make it out alive. On the spot, Zev added the name Refael to Shlomo's name.

After six hours of surgery, Refael Shlomo came out of the OR, his blood pressure at a barely livable 60/45.

After the surgery, the doctors kept telling us that he might die any day. But Refael Shlomo proved them wrong time after time, prompting the pediatric cardiologist to shake his head in wonderment and say, "If there's ever a nuclear war, I want to be near this kid."

Refael Shlomo was alive, but he wasn't doing well. Just before his second birthday, he suffered a stroke that paralyzed one side of his little body. Had we allowed ourselves to succumb to misery and despair, we could easily have fallen apart. I mean, whose kid has a complicated heart defect, Down syndrome, multiple major surgeries, *and* a stroke — before the age of 2?

At one point, when I tried to daven, I felt very discouraged and disconnected. *What's the use of davening?* I thought to myself. *Whatever's meant to happen will happen anyway.*

Then I realized something. I wasn't davening for Hashem's sake — I was davening for my own sake! Refael Shlomo was in Hashem's hands with or without my davening, but if I were to stop davening, I would lose *my* connection to Hashem, the very connection that gave me strength to keep going. That thought was more frightening than anything.

From then on, my *tefillos* took on a new significance. Before, I had davened that things should turn out for the best: the way *I* thought was best. Now, I davened that things should turn out for the best: the way *Hashem* thought was best. Whatever happened, I knew I was guaranteed one thing: *kirvas Elokim*. And so I continued to daven for Refael Shlomo to recover completely, even as I let go of my need to be in control and allowed myself to accept whatever Hashem wanted to happen.

Refael Shlomo spent five months in the hospital, followed by six weeks in a rehab center. Finally, he was allowed to come home, much to the delight of 3-year-old Menachem, who had missed him terribly during his absence.

Refael Shlomo had to be on oxygen and needed full-time nursing care, but we were so excited to have him back home, we couldn't think of complaining about how busy he was keeping us.

"Hey," Menachem said to me one day, "why does Shlomo only have half a smile?"

"Well," I told him, "while he was in the hospital, he learned a new trick; he learned how to smile with only half of his mouth! Let's see if *you* can do that!"

I sat there and practiced it with him, until he, too, learned how to smile like his younger brother, whose face was paralyzed on one side.

Refael Shlomo's stay at home was short-lived. Within two months, he was back in the hospital with pneumonia, hanging on to life by a thread yet again.

He recovered, by a miracle.

A few weeks after his bout with pneumonia, while he was still in the hospital, Refael Shlomo was scheduled for a routine procedure, something to do with his feeding tube. Less than 24 hours after the procedure, his heart rate shot up to 200 — normal is about 120 or 130 — and his temperature climbed to 107 degrees.

"Sepsis," the doctors said grimly. They whisked him away to do a CT scan, hoping to pinpoint the source of the infection raging through his little body. "It might be a problem with his feeding tube," they told us.

I honestly thought my son would be fine. If he had survived open-heart surgeries, a stroke, and severe pneumonia, he could survive this, too. I davened for a while, and then went to his hospital room to rest. It was 1 a.m.

About an hour later, my husband called me on my cell phone. "You'd better come down here," he said quietly.

Once again, I knew.

The corridors of Columbia Medical Center, practically my second home, were dark and eerily quiet at that hour of the night. I could hear my own footsteps squeaking down the corridors, and I felt very alone, but at the same time enveloped by Hashem's presence. I had said so much *Tehillim* since that first ultrasound two and a half years earlier that the words of *Tehillim* echoed through my mind constantly. Now, the words that came to the tip of my tongue were *"Gam ki eileich b'gei tzalmaves lo ira ra ki atah imadi* — Even as I walk through the valley of death, I will not fear, for You are with me."

Then, suddenly, the words of *Havdalah* started echoing through my mind. *"Hinei Kel yeshuasi evtach v'lo efchad* — Behold, You are the G-d of my salvation; I will trust and I will not fear." I was saying *Havdalah* for my son.

When I came down to the radiology department, where Refael Shlomo had been taken for a CT scan, the doctors were furiously doing CPR on him. His pure, beautiful little body was covered with bruises from all the medications and blood thinners he had been taking, and he had marks in all the many places where needles and IVs had punctured his skin. He had suffered so much in his short life, yet he was a source of joy to everyone around him: always smiling, always happy.

After 45 minutes, the doctors gave up. "There's nothing more we can do for him," they said sadly.

For Zev and me, there *was* something more to do. We had to say the *berachah* of *Dayan ha'emes*, blessing Hashem for taking back the *neshamah* of our beloved little boy. I wanted to say it the way it was meant to be said: with love and acceptance, just as I would say a *berachah* upon hearing good news.

I couldn't do it right away. I had to wait a few minutes. Finally, I felt that I was able to say the *berachah* with love and acceptance. "*Baruch...Dayan ha'emes.*" My voice rang out loud, clear, and confident. And then, with tears flowing from our eyes, Zev and I whispered, "*Hodu laShem ki tov.*"

———————————

We've just marked Refael Shlomo's sixth *yahrtzeit*, on 20 Elul. The pain of losing him is still raw and deep, and there will always be a hole in my own heart that throbs with longing for his beautiful smile. Yet I feel fortunate that he was given to us when we were young, at the start of our parenting career, because thanks to him, I live with a heightened appreciation of the gifts Hashem has bestowed on me.

Refael Shlomo's entire existence was a struggle for life, the very same struggle that we all experience when we cry out "*Zachreinu l'chaim!*" on Rosh HaShanah. Many times, I've thought to myself how appropriate it is that he passed away just before Rosh HaShanah, because he taught me — and so many other people — just how precious life is.

Postscript:

Does the "hole in the heart" ever heal? Do the births of other children provide comfort? Refael Shlomo's mother has this to say:

Having another child after losing one is not a replacement for the child who was niftar, nor does it bring comfort; the loss is still there. On the other hand, when there are simchahs to celebrate, it helps boost the family's positive emotions.

As family members reach milestones, and as more children join the family, we want to know that we are still connected to the child we lost. The first time I gave birth after losing Refael Shlomo, I felt so connected to him because my non-Jewish roommate named her son Refael. The next time I gave birth, on the very last day of my hospital stay, the nurse who was assigned to me was the very same woman who was our home-care nurse for Refael Shlomo! (She said she never does mother-baby care, since she is usually in the NICU, but the mother-baby unit was short-staffed, so she was asked to fill in.)

The third baby after Refael Shlomo was born in the same month that, l'havdil bein chaim l'chaim, Refael Shlomo was. And the fourth baby was a daughter whom we named Batsheva. She was named after Rebbetzin Kanievsky, who had given us endless chizuk during Refael Shlomo's life and after his petirah.

Until today, the hardest question that I am asked is "So how many children do you have?" Such an innocent question, yet it still causes us pain... Do we leave out Refael Shlomo? Do we include him in the number? What if they start asking us who his rebbi is?

It gets complicated. Well, I have such hakaras hatov to Hashem that I now have a comforting answer. I can say with such confidence that I have seven, because my seventh child's name is Batsheva!

Our Refael Shlomo will always be a part of our family. He will never be forgotten, and the incredible spiritual benefit that we gained through our journey will be ours forever.

Before and After

If I had to divide my life into two phases, before and after, the dividing line would unquestionably be my visit to the neurologist.

Before the visit to the neurologist, life was tough. We had six young children, the third of whom was an 8-year-old autistic boy named Motti. *Parnassah* was a struggle, and *shalom bayis*...well, you know how things are when you have your hands full taking care of little kids and money's tight and the house is too small *and* you have a very demanding special-needs child.

Motti is nonverbal, and his behavior is best described as "out of control." Our house is constantly in disarray, because one of Motti's favorite activities is to empty shelves and cupboards. He's not 2 years old anymore, though, so his reach extends far beyond that of the typical toddler who likes to play in the kitchen. Mealtime, bedtime, outings — everything becomes a challenge with Motti.

On top of the physical difficulties of living with Motti, I experienced a great deal of heartache as well. This was not the way my life was supposed to turn out! I was meant to have a beautiful Shabbos table, set with china and glasses, just as I saw growing up. My home was meant to be filled with visitors; I dreamed of hosting *bachurim* every Shabbos and turning my house into a home away from home for guests. But my Shabbos table does not even get set!

Then there were the worries about the future. What will be with Motti once he is all grown up? How will we care for him? Can our other children grow up normally if Motti saps us of our energy and makes our home a chaotic place to live? Who will want to marry our other children? And once they are married, will their spouses want to come to us for Shabbos?

My husband, Daniel, would tell me to lighten up. "Chava, smile!" he'd say. "You don't have to be so stressed out all the time." I did try. But it was so hard.

At one point, when I was feeling particularly overwhelmed, Daniel decided to take me on a one-day vacation to a beautiful beachfront hotel. As we were walking along the beach, enjoying the sun and the magnificent view, I felt cramps in my arms. Then my fingers started to tingle. *That's weird*, I thought. *Must be from all the stress in my life.* But I was determined to enjoy my vacation, so I decided not to pay any attention to it.

The next morning I woke up feeling as though my fingers had been burned. I also continued feeling strange sensations in my arms and now, also, my legs. These symptoms worsened when I returned home.

I visited my doctor, who sent me for some blood tests, all of which came back normal. "Come back in a few weeks if things don't improve," she said. They didn't. She referred me to a neurologist in Manhattan.

"I'd like to send you for some tests," the neurologist said. "An MRI, an EMG — that's a muscle and nerve test — and some others."

I didn't like the tone of his voice. "Are you concerned about something in particular?" I asked.

He frowned. "I'd like to rule out motor neuron disease," he said. "Also known as Lou Gehrig's disease, or ALS."

Lou Gehrig's.

"It's a progressive disease that robs people of their voluntary muscle activity and slowly shuts down the body," he added.

I imagined myself slowly losing control over each muscle in my body. I'd stop being able to walk, speak, swallow, use the bathroom. My mind would function, as would my emotions, so I'd understand exactly what was going on. Eventually, I'd stop being able to breathe, and then…

No! It can't be! I'm so young! I have a family! I have a child with special needs! Who's going to care for them?

———— • ————

I staggered out of the neurologist's office, and the first thing I did was reach for a *Tehillim*. I had never really been much of a davener; in fact, I don't think I had ever completed *sefer Tehillim* in my adult life. But now I'd be completing *sefer Tehillim* every other day.

I didn't know how to deal with the diagnosis, or possible diagnosis. I stopped talking to my friends. How could I talk about silly things like what Shiffy should wear to her sister's wedding? Who cared what Bracha should make when she'd host her in-laws?

Don't you realize how unimportant this is? I wanted to scream. *The only important thing in life is your health and your family!*

I want to yell to the whole world, *Just hold on to your kids! Kiss them and tell them how much you love them. Get off that phone and tell them how special they are! Listen to them! But really listen to them! Stop worrying about when you'll get a raise, how you'll manage to clean the house for Pesach, how you'll lose those five pounds you put on over Yom Tov. Don't you realize that life is short? You never know what will be tomorrow! Grab hold of today, and don't waste your time and energy on frivolities.*

From the day of my visit to the neurologist, I spent every minute I could with my kids. I sat on the trampoline with them, and I sang to them while combing my fingers through their hair. I took them to the park every day and pushed them on the swings instead of sitting on the bench and chatting with the other mothers.

Suddenly I had endless patience for my children — even Motti. Bedtime, which had been the most dreaded and difficult part of the day, now became my favorite time. Once, I had thought that three bedrooms for the eight of us was impossibly tight. Now, I didn't care if we'd have to live in a one-bedroom apartment, as long as I could hug my children and we could all be together and healthy.

Sometimes I would picture myself in a wheelchair, paralyzed, watching my children. They would be running around the house, doing all the things kids do: playing, doing homework, bickering. They would talk to each other, but not to me, because I couldn't talk back. It's hard to have a conversation with someone who can't respond, so eventually they would learn to ignore me, their own mother. I'd be there, in the living room — there, but not there. No one would come and tell me about his day, or cry to me that his brother tore his paper, or ask for my opinion on anything.

Suddenly, it dawned on me: Hashem is here, right here with me, yet how often do I talk to Him? He is my Father, my dear Father Who has cared for me from the day I was born. He is here, yet He is ignored. Suddenly, I felt His pain.

Hashem, I am so sorry for not talking to you about my day! When I needed help or advice, I asked my husband, I called my mother, my sisters, my friends, but I forgot that You are here!

I began talking to Hashem. A lot.

Hashem, please let me be healthy! Hashem, thank you for giving me the ability to wash my hands. Thank you for allowing me to drive a car and pick up my daughter from playgroup. How I love to see her smiling face when she sees me at the door. Please, Hashem, let her always be smiling!

My appointments for the tests the neurologist had ordered were a few months away. "I feel that I need to go to Eretz Yisrael to daven at *kivrei tzaddikim*," I told Daniel. "My *yom hadin* is approaching, and I need to know that I have done everything possible to receive a favorable judgment."

Even though money was scarce, Daniel joined me, as he saw I really needed the support.

In Eretz Yisrael, we went to Kever Rachel, to the Kosel, and to Meron. I davened as never before, begging Hashem to grant me life and health and make the tests come back clear. At one point, I opened my ArtScroll *Tehillim* to *perek* 107 and my gaze fell on the brief introduction: "This psalm calls upon those who experience G-d's deliverance — whether national or individual — to publicly proclaim their gratitude. They must proclaim that His kindness endures forever!"

I will do that, Hashem, I pledged. *If You keep me healthy, I will let the world know of Your kindness! I will sing Your praises forever and ever!*

Daniel ran from Rebbe to Rebbe, accumulating *berachah* after *berachah* for me. One Rebbe gave Daniel his assurance that everything would be fine, and I left Eretz Yisrael with a sense of optimism. I had done all I could do. Now I had to leave the rest up to my loving Father.

The first test was the MRI. I had to lie in a tunnel, motionless, for 30 minutes. Half an hour without moving. Imagine months or years of not moving! That was what was going through my mind as I lay there. It was such a relief to be able to get up after 30 minutes and drive home to my beautiful family.

Next came the electromyogram (EMG). As needles were inserted through my skin and electrical currents shot through my limbs, I closed my eyes and repeated the words "*Hashem Hu haElokim… Ein od milvado…*"

On my way to the neurologist a second time to receive the test results, I thought about how my life had changed over the past few months. I was davening every day, saying *Tehillim* every day, and giving *tzedakah* every day. I was learning from Rav Ezriel Tauber's book on *emunah* and *bitachon* every night. I had taken the Internet out of my house. I had volunteered for the local Bikur Cholim and was driving people to and from hospitals once or twice a week. I was more careful with *shemiras halashon*.

As we drove, I looked at the cars driving on the other side of the road. "Soon we'll be driving on that side, going home," I remarked to Daniel. "Who knows how life will change in the next half-hour? How will we be feeling when we drive down the opposite side of the road?"

We drove in silence the rest of the way.

When we entered the neurologist's office, I was shaking. As he peered into the computer, viewing my results, I scanned his face, desperate for a sign. I couldn't read his face, though.

Finally, after what seemed like an eternity, he turned to us and said, "All the tests came back clear. You do not have Lou Gehrig's or any other form of motor neuron disease. I can't explain your symptoms, but they'll probably go away on their own. I don't need to see you again."

I staggered out of his office, and the first thing I did was reach for a *Tehillim*. Again. I opened my *Tehillim* and cried, but these were different tears: tears of joy.

———•———

If I had to divide my life into two phases, before and after, the dividing line would unquestionably be my visit to the neurologist. But not the second visit. The first.

After the second visit, I went from fear to relief, from despair to rejoicing, from darkness to light. But after the first visit, I went from a dreary, arduous existence to an existence in which every small gift was cause for celebration and thanks to Hashem. And that was by far the greater transformation.

Do I think that I'll be able to carry this feeling of intense appreciation with me forever? I'd love to say yes, but I know that as time goes on, the euphoria of being spared from a dreaded illness will fade, and I will likely revert to focusing on the daily struggle of caring for Motti and my other children while living in cramped quarters on a tight budget. The real challenge will be to hold on to my new perspective on life even without the prospect of a dreaded disease hovering over me. I am publicizing my story here as a tangible reminder to keep on singing Hashem's praises, forever.

Postscript:

Imagine being incapacitated, utterly dependent on others for your every need. You're at their mercy: if you're hungry, you need them to feed you; if you don't like the food they bring you, tough luck. You need them to dress you, wash you, lift you, and move you around. Sometimes they are rough with you; sometimes they are gentle.

You try to communicate with the people around you, but they're busy with other, more important things, and your message isn't heard or understood. You cry out softly, hoping that someone will notice your discomfort. No one pays attention. Do I matter? you wonder. Does anyone care? Now the discomfort is compounded by loneliness, even desperation.

Help me! I need you! you want to cry out, but you aren't able to. Finally, someone comes to take care of you. But the person is tired and grumpy and overwhelmed, and you know that you are a burden.

Imagine what it's like to be a baby…

———◆———

We all hope to remain in full possession of our physical and mental faculties. We daven never to become dependent on others. Yet it's good, every once in a while, to imagine what being incapacitated feels like. Not only because it helps us to appreciate the gifts we have, as illustrated in this story, but also because it helps us to be more compassionate and understanding toward the people who are dependent on us, demanding and challenging as they may be.

From Head to Toe

It was Shavuos night 5771, and I was sitting with my 10-year-old son Mordechai studying the review sheet his rebbi had given him to learn over Yom Tov.

Mordechai was reading the questions to me, and when he reached the third or fourth question, he asked, "What's the phone number for Hatzlacha?"

We both laughed, as Hatzlacha is a grocery store in Monsey, where we live. "Did your rebbi actually put that question on the sheet, or are you making that up?" I asked.

He laughed again. "No, Daddy, that's the question."

Then he looked back at the question and realized he had made a mistake. "Oh, it says Hatzolah, not Hatzlacha. What's the phone number for Hatzolah?"

I didn't know the number, and I told Mordechai to skip to the next question, thinking that the Hatzolah question must have been the rebbi's way of jolting us awake. But Mordechai insisted on answering the question. "The number is 425-1600, Daddy. The rebbi gave it to us in class."

We reviewed the sheet three times, and each time we got to that question, Mordechai made me repeat the number.

The Sunday after Shavuos, I went out to cut the grass with my John Deere lawn tractor. The grass was quite long, so I lifted the discharge chute up and out of the way in order that the cut grass could flow more freely. I was nearly finished mowing the lawn when a hose got caught in the blades, shutting down the mower. I had to push the mower to the garage to untangle the hose from the blades.

When I jacked up the tractor, I was shocked to see just how close the mower blades were to the discharge chute. *This is really dangerous*, I thought, making a mental note never to mow with the discharge chute up again.

I restarted the mower and drove it back to the spot where the hose had become entangled in the blades. But before I could lower the grass chute and continue mowing, my son Dovid came out of the house. "Can I have a ride?" he asked.

"Sure," I said. I often took the kids with me in the tractor when I mowed the lawn.

As Dovid walked toward me, I noticed two balls in the tall grass, and I forgot all about the discharge chute.

"Dovid, can you pick up the balls and throw it them out of the way?" I asked.

He picked up one ball and threw it to his right, and then picked up the other ball and began to throw toward the tractor. "No, Dovid!" I shouted. "Throw it away!"

But he didn't hear what I said, because the engine noise was too loud. So I said, "Bring the ball to Daddy!" and he walked toward me with the red ball. As my little, innocent 4-year-old extended his gentle hand to give me the ball, he stepped close to the tractor. At that point, I heard the most horrible sound I have ever heard, and an unimaginable, life-altering nightmare began.

Dovid had stepped right into the tractor's discharge chute and was thrown backward to the ground. As he fell backward, his confused, frightened eyes locked with mine. I will never forget that look on his face.

Everything went into slow motion. I jumped off the tractor and lifted Dovid from the ground. The front of his little sneaker was in shreds, and as I picked him up in my arms, I looked up to Heaven and yelled louder than ever before in my life. *Hashem*, I screamed silently, *how could You have allowed this to happen?*

I raced up the stairs of our backyard deck and into the house. The slow-motion haze continued as I reached for the phone and tried to retrieve Hatzolah's number from my memory. But my mind drew a total blank. Knowing that there was not a second to waste, I decided to call 911 instead, even though I knew the response time would be longer and the level of care would not be comparable.

As my finger moved toward the 9 on the keypad, everything slowed down even further. All of a sudden a vision blew into my mind, and I saw myself sitting with Mordechai on Shavuos night. "Daddy, what's the phone number for Hatzolah?" he was asking. In the vision, I responded, "425-1600." As that number entered my consciousness, I simultaneously dialed it into the phone.

The Hatzolah *tzaddikim* arrived within minutes and expertly assessed the situation. Dovid had lost several toes. They immediately contacted nearby hospitals to determine which one had the best doctors available to handle his condition. They decided to take us to the leading trauma center in the area, after learning that a top pediatric foot surgeon was on call at the hospital.

When my wife, Faigy, and I arrived at the emergency room with Dovid, the surgeon on call informed us that although Hatzolah had recovered the severed toes, she would not be able to reattach them due to the small size of the nerves and capillaries. At that point I wanted to dig myself a hole in the ground and never return.

Mustering all my strength, I asked the surgeon, "Will my son ever be able to walk again?"

"We haven't gotten the X-rays back," she said, "so I can't answer that."

A wave of despair and howling guilt washed over me.

Within minutes of our arrival at the emergency room, a coworker of Faigy's who had heard what happened called to tell us that her son-in-law, a doctor, had worked with one of the top pediatric foot surgeons in the world. I called this surgeon right away, and he told me that as long as Dovid's metatarsal bones were in place, he should be able to walk almost perfectly. "At this young age, he'll simply adjust to walking without the missing toes," the surgeon assured me.

When Dovid came out of his initial surgery, he was assigned a plastic surgeon, who was scheduled to operate on him again on Tuesday. For some reason, I didn't feel comfortable with him, and I began calling medical referral organizations to find out whether he was competent. But none of the people I spoke to at ECHO, the medical referral organization, or Bikur Cholim had ever heard of him.

My boss, whose grandson had been run over by an SUV some years earlier and almost lost his arm, urged me to request a surgeon named Dr. Kent, who had operated successfully on his grandson at the same hospital Dovid was in. The ECHO representative I spoke with held Dr. Kent in high regard, but she told me it was unlikely that he would agree to work with Dovid once another surgeon had been assigned to the case.

"If you do meet with Dr. Kent," she advised, "tell him that you want his hands on your son's foot."

I put in a request with the head of the Pediatric Emergency Unit to meet with Dr. Kent.

In the midst of this turmoil, a memory hit me like a lightning bolt. Exactly two years earlier, my mother had sent me an e-mail containing the story of a man named Lee Spivak in Cincinnati whose fingertip had been cut off during a model airplane demonstration in the toy store where he worked. Mr. Spivak's brother Alan, a Harvard research scientist, had been conducting experiments with a medication named MicroMatrix that was used to regenerate ligaments in horses. Alan instructed his brother Lee not to graft the finger, but rather to apply the MicroMatrix "pixie-dust" powder to the finger every day.

Miraculously, within 10 days Lee's fingertip regrew, with fresh skin, a completely new nail, and Lee's original fingerprint. I had found the story fascinating, and I had sent it to countless people.

Remembering this story, I began searching for information regarding this pixie-dust medication. I learned that the name of the manufacturer was ACell, and that although the medication had been used successfully in other patients and had earned FDA approval, it had not yet gained traction with doctors and hospitals. When I contacted the company, they informed me that if we wanted the medication it would have to be prescribed by the doctor or hospital.

I asked many medical people if they had heard of Lee Spivak's story and the MicroMatrix medication, but no one seemed to know what I was talking about.

In the meantime, the doctors put Dovid into a hyperbaric chamber, a metal and glass tube filled with pure oxygen that is supposed to accelerate the healing process. Not all doctors believe that it is at all beneficial, though. In addition, an ENT informed us that because the chamber puts extreme pressure on the eardrums, if we wanted Dovid to continue using the hyperbaric chamber, we would need to put tubes in his ears to relieve the pressure. More decisions...

Dovid had been through so much Did we want to put him back in the OR for another procedure? And did we want to put him through the additional trauma of spending two hours at a time in a hyperbaric chamber?

As we agonized over this decision, a friend who works for a medical organization came to visit us in the hospital. Seeing how torn we were over whether to put Dovid in the hyperbaric chamber, he put me in touch with a Mr. Goodman, a Florida resident whose daughter had been underwater in a swimming pool for 20 minutes without breathing.

"I have a hyperbaric chamber in my house," Mr. Goodman told me. "I put my daughter in it every day. It's a great thing."

In the course of our conversation, Mr. Goodman mentioned that there was a fellow in Cincinnati who had lost a fingertip. "You should get the medication he used to grow his fingertip back," he urged me.

"How do you know this story?" I asked. "I've been trying so hard to get this medication, but no one seems to know anything about it!"

"I don't just know the story," Mr. Goodman said quietly. "Lee Spivak is a friend of mine."

After this conversation, my wife and I consented to have tubes inserted in Dovid's ears to relieve the pressure and allow him to continue the hyperbaric treatments.

The next day we had a meeting with Dr. Kent. I told him that Dovid was due back in surgery in 48 hours, and I requested that he perform the procedure. "I'll be there at the surgery," he assured me.

"Great!" I said. "So you'll operate on Dovid?"

"I'll be in the OR while his doctor is operating," he clarified.

Realizing that Dr. Kent had no intention of doing the surgery, I started to feel panicky. Just then, I remembered what the woman from ECHO had told me to say. I didn't think it would help, but it was a last-ditch effort.

"Dr. Kent," I pleaded, "I am a guilt-ridden, scared father. Please! I want your hands on my son's foot."

Dr. Kent looked down at the floor, cocked his head gently, and said, "Let me clear it with the other doctor, and I'll take over the case."

But getting Dr. Kent to do the surgery was only the first step. Now I had to convince him to order a medication that no one had ever heard of before and use it on my son in a procedure that was to take place in 48 hours.

Sheepishly, I explained to Dr. Kent that there was one more thing I needed from him. I told him the story of Lee Spivak, and asked that he used the ACell medication.

"I have my own way of doing things," Dr. Kent replied. "I'm not using some mumbo-jumbo pixie dust I know nothing about."

I begged and persisted, though, until Dr. Kent finally agreed to check out the product. "Don't count on it, though," he warned.

We and our wonderful community davened fervently for Dovid. I prayed that Hashem would open Dr. Kent's heart and mind to the possibility of using this unfamiliar medication, in the hope of sparing Dovid the painful grafting surgery that would traditionally be used to heal this type of wound.

When I spoke to Dr. Kent the next day and inquired tentatively about the medication, he said, "Oh, didn't my assistant call you? The hospital approved the medication, and I spoke with the company. They're sending a representative to assist me in the procedure."

This, from the man who, just 24 hours earlier, was calling it mumbo-jumbo pixie dust!

The next morning, the ACell representative arrived. He assured us that although the medication couldn't regrow Dovid's toes, it would heal the wound completely without the need for grafting.

During surgery, Dovid's wound was cleaned and the pixie dust was sprinkled on his foot. After the procedure, the representative left a supply of medication with Dr. Kent, with the instructions that it be applied every other day.

Dovid was discharged from the hospital, but he had to return every other day to have his bandage changed and the medication reapplied and to spend two hours in the hyperbaric chamber.

The medication was doing a wonderful job of healing the wound, but it was prohibitively expensive — $100 per application — and once the hospital's initial supply ran out, the expense was not covered by our insurance. As we were wondering how to cover the cost, we received an unexpected call from Jonathan, the ACell representative.

"I have some good news for you," he said. "Our company would like to donate as much medication as Dovid needs until the wound is completely healed."

During one of our last appointments with Dr. Kent, I was greeted by another ACell representative, who wanted to see the progress of Dovid's foot. By that time, the hospital had begun using the pixie-dust medication on other patients, with dramatic success.

"Why hasn't anyone heard of the medication before?" I asked the representative.

"We were involved in a patent infringement lawsuit with another company," she explained, "and it was not until the middle of May that the suit was settled in ACell's favor. At that time, we moved the medication into the market."

Dovid's accident happened two weeks after the lawsuit was settled.

The summer after the accident we had our *mezuzos* checked. All of the *mezuzos* were fine, except the one on the front door, which was *pasul* because three words were smudged. Those three words were *"bneichem al ha'adamah,"* which literally mean, "your children on the ground." That was eerily reminiscent of the sight of Dovid falling backward onto the ground after his foot met the lawn-mower blade.

After several months of treatment, Dovid's foot healed completely. Thanks to the medication, he has no scar; he just looks as though he was born without a few toes. And he's totally uninhibited about it. Sometimes he'll hear people whispering to me, "How's his foot?" and he'll announce, "You wanna see my foot?" Then he'll pull off his sock and show off his foot.

Sometimes we even tease him. "Dovid, which foot do you like better? The one with toes or the one without?"

And without a moment's hesitation, he'll say, "The one without!"

Banter aside, it took me a long time to be able to look at his injured foot, the foot that I myself had mutilated. By now, two years after the accident, I am able to kiss his foot and massage it, but I am pained afresh every time I see it.

Faigy was incredible throughout the ordeal. Dovid is her son, too, and his pain is her pain, but not once did she say a negative or accusing word to me about my role in the accident. "This had to happen," she's told me many times.

My respect and gratitude to Faigy have grown tremendously because of the compassion and understanding she displayed to me. This is what makes a marriage: not beauty, not money, not superficialities, but the ability to show caring even in moments of weakness.

For me, the main *nisayon* has been coping with the guilt. My *rav* and my close friends reassured me over and over again that this was a *gezeirah* from Heaven, something that had to happen.

It has required tremendous effort on my part not to walk around carrying the guilt on my shoulders and instead to turn to Hashem and recognize that it was ultimately for our good, not merely a whack. I tell myself over and over and that Hashem loves me, as He loves all His children. And I know it's true, because He held our hands every step of the way.

He made me review the number of Hatzolah with my son Shavuos night, and He made me remember the number just when I needed it. He made me read Lee Spivak's story, and He ignited my memory to recall the story amid total chaos. He put me in touch with a friend of Lee's who urged me to get hold of the pixie-dust medication, and He made sure the patent-infringement lawsuit was settled just before the accident happened. He made Dr. Kent agree to take over Dovid's case and to use a medication he'd never heard of instead of the more conventional treatment of grafting. And finally, He made Dovid's toes heal in a way that allowed him to walk, run, and play soccer, his favorite sport.

Why the accident had to happen, I don't know. I see it as a call to *teshuvah*, a shake-up to get me to introspect and improve myself, and I certainly have a lot to work on. But I have to walk the fine line between using this experience as a springboard for growth and viewing it as a punishment for my own inadequacies. Because if I'd allow myself to believe that this was all my fault, I'd sink into depression and despair.

At the moment of the accident, when I turned to Hashem and wondered how He could let this happen, it seemed to me that what had happened was out of the realm of possibility. I have since learned that *nothing* is out of the realm of possibility. We humans are utterly fragile and dependent on Hashem's mercy for absolutely everything, from head to toe.

Postscript:

One of the more challenging aspects of writing a LifeLines story is sifting through a huge amount of information and distilling the story into compact form, with one main idea running through it. To do that, I have to go through every detail and ask: Is this critical to the story line? Or will the story's message be clear enough without it?

If I determine that the story can stand without a particular piece of information, then I label that piece an outlier and delete it. Often, I have to eliminate material that is interesting or colorful or informative, and the work of cutting and discarding can feel painful, even merciless. That was the case with this particular story, which started out at over 6,000 words and had to be chopped to about half of that.

But, as the story itself so poignantly conveys, it's sometimes necessary to destroy in order to create.

One Good Heart

I was born with a hole in my heart. Lots of people are, actually. Some holes in the heart go away on their own, while others require medical intervention. Mine didn't need any special treatment, because it wasn't medically dangerous. It did, however, lead the doctors to discover a more serious cardiac issue: severe aortic regurgitation, a condition in which blood leaks back from the aorta into the left ventricle of the heart.

When I was growing up, this condition didn't affect me at all. I was a very active, athletic kid, and I played all kinds of sports, including soccer, softball, tennis, and team swimming. (No, I didn't grow up *frum*.) The only thing I couldn't do was join a competitive sports league for elite players, because that would have posed too much of an endurance challenge to my heart.

Another thing that didn't affect me at all growing up was my Jewish background. I was your typical public school kid who didn't fast on Yom Kippur, didn't eat matzah on Pesach, and never spun a dreidel on Chanukah. I barely even knew I was Jewish.

At the beginning of my freshman year at college, a rabbi approached me and asked, "Are you Jewish?"

"My mom is," I answered.

"Then you are, too," he said.

"Cool."

"Would you be interested in coming to a Friday-night dinner?" he asked.

"Double cool."

The first time I attended a Shabbos meal, I looked down at my seat in confusion when the rabbi said that we were going to "*bentch.*" From there, however, I took the fast track to becoming a *ba'alas teshuvah*, much to my parents' consternation. The summer of my freshman year I was already doing a two-week summer program at Neve Yerushalayim, and by the time I was in my junior year of college, I was basically *frum*.

That year, I spent a full semester at Neve. When I came back to the United States, I started *shidduchim*, with the blessing and approval of my mentors, who knew that my commitment to *Yiddishkeit* was authentic and healthy.

Having learned a thing or two about *frum* society by that point, I figured that I should probably tell any prospective husband about my congenital heart condition. I spoke to a *rav* about this, and his *psak* for my specific circumstance was to tell "after three dates, or when things get serious."

The first *shidduch* set up for me was with a *ba'al teshuvah* named Aharon who was learning in a yeshivah in New York. Aharon flew out to meet me, and we hit it off right away.

Our first date was so great that I decided that if things went well on our second, I would disclose my condition. The *shadchan*, an FFB, agreed that it was a good idea, especially since Aharon was going to be flying back to New York two days later.

Aharon took my disclosure remarkably well. In fact, he told me, he himself had been diagnosed with a slight cardiac issue in his childhood.

"Between the two of us, we have one good heart," he joked.

We went on a third date, which also went well, and then Aharon flew back to New York. *A few more dates, and we'll be engaged*, I thought happily.

Then disaster struck. In the course of telling his parents about me, Aharon mentioned my heart issue, and his mother went ballistic. She's a nurse, and she works in a geriatric ward where people die of heart failure all the time. "The last thing you need is to marry a girl with a heart condition," she told Aharon. "I won't hear of it! Don't even think of meeting this Debra again."

Aharon was torn. On the one hand, he really liked me. On the other hand, his mother was forbidding him to see me. He decided to ask his *rebbeim* in yeshivah what to do.

The *ba'al teshuvah* yeshivah he learned in encouraged its students to stay — or become — emotionally healthy and to maintain good ties with their parents and family. Ever since Aharon had embarked on his path to *Yiddishkeit*, he had tried very hard to follow this approach. He had been close with his parents before becoming *frum*, and despite the inevitable glitches that cropped up due to his religious observance, he had succeeded in keeping up a good relationship with them.

Knowing that Aharon's parents were normal, loving people, the *rebbeim* in the yeshivah advised Aharon not to pursue the *shidduch*. "We wouldn't want you to get married without your parents' support and blessing," they told him. "This isn't a battle you should be fighting."

When the *shadchan* called to tell me that Aharon wouldn't be seeing me again, I was devastated. Never before had I been "punished" because of my minor heart condition: a condition I hadn't chosen and one that had no bearing on who I was as a human being.

I didn't only feel rejected by Aharon. I felt rejected by Hashem, too. "Look what I did for You, Hashem!" I felt like yelling Heavenward. "I threw everything I knew out the door, stood up to my parents, took on a life of modesty, moved off campus and into the *frum* neighborhood 20 minutes away, and this is how I get repaid? I get rejected by a guy's *mom* because of a condition I have no control over?"

This could easily have turned into a crisis for me, either in terms of my *frumkeit* or in terms of my mental health. Luckily for me, however, I had a huge support network cheering me on.

The *shadchan* and his wife, Mr. and Mrs. Sherman, were my number one cheerleaders. As I sobbed at their kitchen table, they did their best to console me. Mr. Sherman also tried to get Aharon to reconsider. "I married my wife despite my parents' reservations," he told him, "and we've been happily married for 20 years."

When Aharon apologetically repeated that his *rebbeim* had advised him not to risk alienating his parents over this *shidduch*, Mr. Sherman urged me not to take the rejection personally. "This isn't about you," he said. "You're still an excellent candidate for *shidduchim*."

I also had a community *askan* and a *rebbetzin* on my team, both of whom felt that Aharon's mother was dead wrong. They called Aharon's *rebbeim* repeatedly to plead my case, but to no avail. His mother wouldn't budge, and the *rebbeim* felt that it was unwise to pit a fresh *ba'al teshuvah* against his parents.

People told me the same thing, but I was unconvinced. Aharon and I were ideally suited on so many levels: we shared the same *hashkafos*, our personalities meshed, we had numerous common interests, and we really enjoyed each other's company. After meeting Aharon, I couldn't imagine ever finding anyone else like him.

A few weeks after Aharon called off the *shidduch*, I visited New York for a wedding, and while I was there, I worked up the courage to call Rabbi Erlanger, Aharon's closest rebbi.

"Is there any chance he might change his mind?" I asked anxiously. "Maybe now his mother can be convinced?"

"I'll try to talk him again," Rabbi Erlanger said doubtfully.

Rabbi Erlanger called me back to say that he had spoken to Aharon and that nothing had changed. "This isn't going to happen," he told me. "You should try to look into other *shidduchim*."

My team of advocates and cheerleaders assured me over and over again that *shidduchim* were *bashert*. "Aharon's reason for calling off the *shidduch* does seem harebrained," they told me, "but it might just be Hashem's way of protecting you from a marriage that wouldn't have been good for you."

At first, I found that hard to swallow. If Aharon wasn't right for me, then why did I have to meet him in the first place?

"We don't always understand why things are right for us," my *rebbetzin* told me. "Sometimes we discover the reason later, and sometimes we never do."

Right for me or not, it hurt. And I didn't exactly have parents or siblings who could understand what I was going through. But having other people around me who cared, who were willing to listen and let me cry, allowed me to slowly heal.

Eventually I decided to put Aharon behind me and start dating other people. By that point, however, I was already in the damaged-goods category. So many people had been involved in trying to salvage the *shidduch* with Aharon that my heart condition was practically public knowledge. To a host of would-be *shadchanim*, a *ba'alas teshuvah* with a heart condition was just the thing for any boy out there with a problem.

The first boy I went out with after Aharon was an FFB with a severe limp. He was a nice guy, and I admired his tenacity, but we had zero common ground in terms of *hashkafah*. He wanted to have a television in his house; I hadn't looked at a TV in at least three years.

I can't describe how insulting it is to be set up with someone who is completely unsuited to you and whose only qualification as a potential marriage partner is the fact that he has a physical defect. But once *shadchanim* who deal with "special issues" got wind of me, I was inundated with *shidduchim* of this sort: "He's so wonderful, he'll make a great husband even though he's in a wheelchair. And he's only 15 years older than you, don't you worry."

I did go out with some "regular" boys, *ba'alei teshuvah* who hadn't grown up with *shidduch* hysteria and didn't think a minor medical issue was a nonstarter in a marriage. I tried to push Aharon out of my mind, but none of the other boys I met came up to Aharon's toenails, at least in my estimation.

Then came the next blow. I visited my cardiologist for a routine checkup, and he informed me that I needed heart surgery. "We've been monitoring this leak in your aorta for a long time," he said, "and until now, your heart function has been okay. But now it's time to intervene."

So the shadchanim were right, I thought sadly as I stumbled out of the doctor's office. *I really am damaged goods. I guess it was Aharon who was saved from me, not the other way around.*

This was where belonging to a *frum* community paid off. Knowing how amazing the people in the community were, I asked around for names of cardiologists, and people connected me with two *frum* cardiologists who were considered tops in the field. These doctors were kind enough to review my records on their own time, and each of them independently concluded that I didn't need surgery.

My parents, who were still highly skeptical about the whole "*frum*" thing, were astonished at the way people in the community had networked on my behalf to direct me to these specialists.

I felt vindicated, both for becoming *frum* and for thinking of myself as a healthy person who didn't have "special issues." *So Aharon and his mom were wrong*, I thought. *I'm not sick, and I never have been sick.*

I still didn't know why Hashem had deemed it necessary for me to meet Aharon, but after mourning him for a long time, I was finally able to banish his ghost from my mind. I had cried enough, I had hated his mother enough, and now I was ready to move on with my life. *It's their loss*, I told myself.

By that point, I really meant it.

With the benefit of time and healing, I was able to see that losing Aharon had turned me into a stronger person and had actually reinforced my commitment to *Yiddishkeit*. I wasn't *frum* only because I thought that a religious lifestyle was beautiful and appealing; I was *frum* because it was right, even if it involved difficulty. Having emerged from this painful experience intact, emotionally and spiritually, I saw that I could cope with adversity in my life and not fall apart. I felt at peace with myself, and ready to face the future without being haunted by the past.

I remember exactly when I reached that feeling of peace. It was just after Lag BaOmer, and just under a year after I had first met Aharon.

The very next week, I got a phone call from Rabbi Erlanger while I was in the college computer lab. I ran outside, wondering why he would be calling me. "Have you been davening?" he asked. "Because Aharon wants to fly out to see you."

My hands were trembling so badly, I could barely hold on to the phone. "I have to think about it," I said. "I'll get back to you tomorrow, O.K.?"

After I hung up, I needed to sit down. I had thought the roller coaster was over, but it seemed that Hashem had other ideas.

A few months earlier, I would have jumped at the opportunity to see Aharon again. At this point, however, I had closed the door that said "Aharon," and I wasn't sure I wanted to open it again.

At the time, I was boarding with a *frum* family, and I asked the parents what they thought. "Go for it," they urged me. So I did. *At the very least, I'll get a free dinner out of this*, I told myself.

Aharon took me out to dinner and apologized sincerely for putting me through so much heartache. Then he explained why he had decided to give the *shidduch* another go.

Turned out, the *kiruv* rabbi who had first met me on campus and invited me for a Shabbos meal had recently sent a bunch of college kids to the *ba'al teshuvah* yeshivah in New York where Aharon was learning. Some of these boys knew me from college, and the rabbi sent them off with instructions to "find a good guy for Debra."

One of the boys spotted Aharon and decided that he'd be a good match for me. Not knowing that Aharon had already met me, he walked up to him and started to describe this great girl from his hometown, without giving my name.

"I knew right away that he was talking about you," Aharon said, "and I couldn't ignore the handwriting on the wall anymore. After dating so many 'wrong' girls, I realized that there was something special about you, and I saw that I wasn't going to have that same connection with anyone else. I asked Rabbi Erlanger to call my mom and explain the concept of *bashert* to her. He told her that when two souls are connected, you shouldn't stop them from coming together, and he added that it would be a crime for me to lose my *bashert* because of her. When she heard this, and she saw that I was still thinking about you a year later, she reluctantly agreed to the *shidduch*."

To put Aharon's mom at ease, I arranged for my medical records to be sent to a cardiologist in New York who was a friend of Aharon's parents. "You have nothing to worry about," the cardiologist friend told them, and he proceeded to explain exactly what my condition was and how it might affect me in the future.

The next step was to meet Aharon's parents. Oddly, by the time I met my future mother-in-law, I no longer felt angry or spiteful toward her. I guess I had processed all the hateful emotions in the months before.

My mother-in-law was far more nervous than I was during our first meeting. She didn't stop talking, and she was clearly uncomfortable and embarrassed.

Shortly after our engagement, my mother-in-law invited me out to lunch in a fancy restaurant. "I'm really sorry for trying to keep you and Aharon apart," she stammered over her poached salmon. "All I wanted was to protect my son. I didn't know you, and of course I didn't mean to hurt you."

I laid my hand gently on her arm. "It's O.K.," I said. "I understand that it wasn't personal; you care about Aharon, and you want what's best for him. No hard feelings."

This is where I'm supposed to say, "And they lived happily ever after." We really did, except that in the real-life version, it took me a while to feel secure in my marriage and stop feeling threatened by Aharon's relationship with his mother.

If we're doing full disclosure here, I'd have to admit that things haven't been smooth sailing between me and my mother-in-law. I can honestly say, however, that I don't bear her any grudge over her initial opposition to our *shidduch*. Whatever issues we've had over the years have been normal relationship issues, many of which were caused or compounded by the fact that Aharon and I are *frum* and she isn't. Thankfully, Rabbi Erlanger stepped up during our engagement and during the first few years of our marriage to mediate between us and Aharon's parents, and to this day he continues to advise us on how to maintain our principles without offending our parents.

We've been blessed with a few children, and my medical issue continues to have very little bearing on my life — except that sometimes, when I'm tired or cranky, I tell Aharon, "You've got to cut me some slack. I have a heart condition."

Postscript:

In this story, a ba'al teshuvah's rebbeim advised him to break off a promising shidduch because his mother was opposed to it. Although at the end the shidduch did go through, the message of the story most certainly was not that ba'alei teshuvah — or anyone else — should get married in defiance of their parents.

In another LifeLines story, entitled "Winning Choice," a ba'al teshuvah's parents took an immediate dislike to the woman he wanted to marry, but his mentors encouraged him to proceed despite his parents' misgivings. The marriage turned out to be a disaster and ended in divorce. The narrator of that story learned, the hard way, that "Mom and Dad are still my parents, and they still understand me better and love me more than anyone else." ("Winning Choice" was not included in this book; space constraints made the selection process quite grueling, and this was one of the stories that didn't make it in.)

So who's right — the fellow in "Winning Choice" who discovered that it's not a good idea to disregard your parents' opinion of a prospective spouse, or the fellow in "One Good Heart," who ultimately married the woman his mother had spurned initially?

The answer, of course, is that the two situations are completely different. The lessons of these two stories may seem to conflict, but the truth is that both are correct — in different situations.

I like to write stories that are on opposite bookends to each other, because together, they convey a more universal message than either of the two on its own. ("Building My Rabbi Akiva" and "Crowning the Queen," which appear in the last section of this book, are another two such stories.)

The point of these stories is to provide food for thought, not to offer instructions for how to navigate similar situations. Because when it comes to matters of the heart, no one else's experience counts.

Silencing the Voice

I'm sitting in my 10th-grade classroom, listening to our biology teacher drone on about symbiotic and parasitic relationships in the animal kingdom. Suddenly, the word "cancer" drifts across my mind like a little neon light. "Say 'cancer'!" A Voice in my head commands. "Say it loud, and say it four times. Otherwise someone in your family is going to get cancer!"

The little neon light becomes a blinding floodlight, and I hear the word "cancer" screaming in my head. I clamp down on my lips to keep silent, but the Voice is overpowering. "Say 'cancer' right now! NOW!"

Looking around furtively, I quickly whisper the dreaded word, as if to purge myself of its tentacles. But the Voice is not satisfied. "Say it again! Four times! And say it louder!"

I feel the blood rushing to my head as I try desperately to control myself and ignore the Voice. What will my friends think? Finally, when I can bear it no longer, I bury my head in my elbow and say *"cancer" aloud four times. Then I look around to see if anyone noticed. To my relief, my friends seem too absorbed in their own daydreams to have noticed my rapid blinking. I struggle to focus my attention back on the biology lesson, but all I can think of is the neon word "cancer" dancing around my head and daring me to shout it out.*

From the time I was about 12 years old, I was a slave to the Voice in my head that forecasted disaster. At times, the Voice commanded me to perform a specific action, such as blinking rapidly, shaking my head a certain way, or saying certain words. More often, however, the Voice simply predicted catastrophe, conjuring all sorts of horrific scenes and frightening me to the core.

On the outside, I was Tova Bergman, a typical teenager — perhaps a bit insecure, but not exceptional in any way. I earned good grades in school, went to the right camps and seminary, and surrounded myself with friends and fun. On the inside, though, I was living in the torture chamber of my mind, dying a thousand gruesome deaths, while suffering the torments of spinsterhood, infertility, trauma, illness, and bereavement — all before the age of 18.

Painfully real as these agonizing thoughts were, I knew that I could never share them with anyone. At best, people would dismiss my fears as foolish; at worst, they would consider me "touched." I was normal enough to know that my thoughts were crazy, even as I wholeheartedly believed every one of the Voice's dire predictions.

The fact that the Voice's predictions rarely materialized did not weaken the Voice's authority in the least. If I didn't drown in the camp lake, it must have been because I obeyed the Voice's instruction to fold my arms a certain way. If I was accepted into seminary despite the Voice's warning that no one would take me, it must have been because I didn't glance at a mirror for a full month. If I became engaged several months after graduating seminary, it must have been because I verbalized the offensive words the Voice plastered in my head.

I knew about obsessive-compulsive disorder (OCD), but I assumed that people with OCD do things like wash their hands continually or check a million times whether they locked the door. I didn't engage in any bizarre behaviors, nor did anyone seem to think there was something wrong with me, so it never occurred to me that I was suffering from OCD. I knew exactly what my problem was: I was an evil person, and I deserved to have bad things happen to me because I sometimes spoke disrespectfully to my parents, I sometimes didn't have *kavanah* when I davened, and I sometimes read things I shouldn't have read.

I tried desperately to placate the Voice while at the same time maintaining the happy-go-lucky veneer of a normal young woman. I would dance spiritedly at my friends' weddings while picturing myself lying in a coffin at my own funeral. I would offer the *kallah* a drink, imagining myself choking on the glass of water I was holding. No matter how happy or enjoyable the occasion, my mind was always conjuring nightmare scenarios, any or all of which were certain to be my fate.

I felt condemned to a lifetime of misery, even though to all appearances I was living a fairy-tale existence. I landed a plum job right after seminary, and I was one of the first girls in my class to marry. I went through the motions of being a great wife, and on the outside my husband Gavriel and I looked like a perfect pair.

Between us, however, things weren't all that rosy. Although I had a great deal of experience in pasting an artificial smile on my face, it didn't take long for my husband to uncover the negativity and noxious thought patterns hiding behind the smile. He mistook my constant state of apprehension for lack of trust in him and was perturbed by my inability to "loosen up and relax."

Gavriel was the first person I ever confided in about my intrusive thoughts, and what I told him was only the tip of the iceberg; I didn't dare reveal the extent of my craziness. To my surprise, he reacted with incredible equanimity when I told him about the Voice and its doomsday predictions. He managed to be understanding and sympathetic while at the same time insisting that I get help.

I wish I could say that things improved after that, but they actually got worse before they got better. I went to see a psychiatrist, who diagnosed me with OCD and prescribed a regimen of pills for me.

"OCD is caused by a chemical balance in the brain," he explained, "and medication is the best way to correct that imbalance." He also recommended that I go for cognitive behavioral therapy (CBT) in conjunction with the medication.

Because psychiatric medication precluded having children, Gavriel and I opted to try CBT alone, before trying the medication.

In the meantime, one of my longtime fears began to materialize. I experienced several miscarriages in succession, and these were attributed to an underlying fertility issue that my doctor said would make it difficult for me to bear children. This diagnosis gave the Voice its best ammunition ever; one of its favorite predictions — "You're so evil, you'll never have kids" — had finally earned credence. For the first time in my life, I actually had a *real* problem to deal with, in contrast to the imaginary worries I had suffered with for almost a decade. Now, most of my intrusive thoughts began to center around fertility, and I started obsessing about the childless future that no doubt awaited me.

Gavriel, on the other hand, was unruffled by the diagnosis. "Hashem holds the key to childbirth," he said calmly. "The doctors didn't say it's impossible for us to have kids and, *b'ezras Hashem*, we will."

His attitude astounded and annoyed me at the same time. Where did he get such *bitachon* from? Was he human?

I was overcome with guilt at making Gavriel's life so difficult, and I apologized to him incessantly for burdening him with my problems. Once, I even offered to let him divorce me. "What do you need me and my crazy problems for?" I asked despondently. "You can get rid of me and marry someone normal."

For the first time, I saw Gavriel become really angry. "Don't ever speak that way again, Tova," he admonished me. "A marriage doesn't happen by accident. If Hashem brought us together, it means that he wanted me to go through these *nisyonos* along with you. I won't have any talk of divorce in my house, *ever*."

The insecure child in me didn't want to believe that Gavriel really wanted to stay married to me, and I often had an urge to goad Gavriel into reiterating his devotion to me. I controlled myself after this incident, however, and refrained from mentioning the *D* word from then on. But the thought that Gavriel would one day decide to get rid of me persisted relentlessly in my mind.

I was at my lowest point ever when I started going for CBT. I was struggling to build a stable marriage while dragging a huge weight of emotional baggage with me: years of obsessive-compulsive behavior coupled with grief and anxiety generated by my recent miscarriages and medical diagnosis.

CBT was liberating and agonizing at the same time. It forced me to take a step back, evaluate my thought patterns objectively, and differentiate between unhealthy, obsessive-compulsive thoughts ("the Voice") and healthy thoughts. Once I knew to identify unhealthy thoughts ("Oh, hi, you're an obsession"), I learned to use specific CBT techniques to combat them.

One technique I learned was postponing, or stalling. When the Voice would issue a proclamation, I would mentally respond, "Sorry, I can't deal with this thought right now. Can you please come back in two hours to discuss this?" I discovered that if I could push off the Voice for even a short amount of time, it lost much of its urgency and authoritativeness.

Another technique I learned was exposure, which involved exposing myself to the consequences of ignoring the Voice. Rather than believing the Voice's threats and following its commands, I learned to stand up to it and do exactly the opposite of what it instructed me. If the Voice said, "Tova, blink!" I deliberately refrained from blinking. If the Voice said, "Don't blink!" I deliberately blinked.

I also forced myself to analyze the Voice's terrifying predictions and determine whether they had any logical basis. If I determined that they were illogical, I would announce to the Voice that I was paying it no heed.

On paper, these strategies sound simple and logical, but in practice, they were pure torture. I was terrified of the Voice, and obeying it provided me with a certain comfort and security, while defying it left me feeling vulnerable and panicky. My CBT counselor explained to me that OCD is a vicious cycle: the more you capitulate to the disorder, the more you exacerbate it. In contrast, the more you force yourself to ignore or disobey the Voice of OCD, the more you weaken its grip on you.

"You have to constantly tell yourself that the comfort of giving in to OCD is fleeting and deceptive," she told me, "while the discomfort of transcending OCD is what will ultimately allow you to live a happier life."

While I was struggling to implement the CBT strategies I had learned, Gavriel suggested that we begin learning *Sha'ar HaBitachon* in *Chovos HaLevavos* together. "If you work on relying on Hashem while doing CBT, you might have an easier time letting go of your obsessions," he said.

Armed with *Chovos HaLevavos*, CBT, and my husband's unremitting support, eventually I learned to take control of my thoughts and not allow the Voice to dominate my life. When it was difficult for me to withstand the Voice's demands, I would visualize myself gift-wrapping the obsessive thought and throwing it Heavenward. "I'm in Hashem's hands," I would say to the Voice.

Freeing myself from the Voice's shackles finally allowed me to enjoy the many blessings that Hashem had bestowed upon me, most notably the blessing of a husband who loved and accepted me unconditionally. With all the progress I made, however, the pain of infertility was still very real. The difference was that now I was able to distinguish between pain that was normal (yes, it's hard to see all the neighbors pushing baby strollers while I walk unencumbered) and pain that was unhealthy (no, I'm not a failure just because I struggle with intrusive thoughts and infertility).

After six years of waiting, I finally gave birth to our first child. He was followed by three siblings, each of whom arrived miraculously after several years of waiting.

I've had plenty of ups and downs over the years, and the Voice is still a prominent player in my life. I've come to accept the fact that the Voice will remain my constant companion; the only question is whether I will rule him, or he will rule me. He makes inroads occasionally, but for the most part he's been rendered impotent by now.

Prior to the birth of my last child, when I was recovering from yet another failed pregnancy, I decided to train as a CBT counselor and begin helping people who suffer from OCD and other mental illnesses such as schizophrenia, depression, panic attacks, and anxiety disorders. Becoming a therapist was a catharsis for me, representing the culmination of a two-decades-long battle against OCD. Although the battle isn't yet over, I've arrived at a point where I can reach out to others and use my own personal experience to help them.

Today, I feel that my own OCD is my greatest asset as a therapist, since it allows me to truly empathize with my patients and enter their tortured minds. The recommendations I make to clients are based on firsthand knowledge that CBT really does work, and the confidence I have in the techniques I impart goes a long way in convincing clients to implement my recommendations despite the difficulty or discomfort involved.

I feel a tremendous sense of gratitude to Hashem (and to His messenger, the angel Gavriel) for lifting me from the abyss of mental illness, and I view my work as a therapist as a small way of expressing this *hakaras hatov*.

Postscript:

Tova has now been working as a CBT counselor for several years. This is how she describes her work:

> *My office is specially designed to dispel the needless distress my patients are experiencing. The office is nicknamed the "White Room," since the whole room is covered in white; there are even white mattresses lining the floor! When patients enter, they are invited to recline on an ultrasoft cushion, which resembles a puffy white cloud. Bright, delightful props and fixtures are artfully arranged along the wall, intended to put patients at ease. I start treatment with slow breathing exercises, with calm, relaxing melodies wafting in the background. It is a private, wonderful world where people can feel loved and secure, a safe haven where they can bare their souls, unleash their emotions, and peel off the painful layers of pointless suffering.*
>
> *My patients vary in age and condition — OCD, fears, phobias, anxiety — although the majority are children aged 9 to 12 who suffer from OCD. I adore working with these*

tender, innocent charges and helping them overcome their inner battles.

When a young, vulnerable patient takes timid, tentative steps into this white island of serenity and empathy, he senses that he is trusted. His words will be taken seriously, with a listening ear and great sympathy. He then allows himself to unload his personal and emotional cargo and is gently introduced to a new and fascinating therapy named CBT in an easy and exciting manner geared to his level of understanding. Together, we form a plan of treatment according to his abilities. Throughout the sessions, the strong ropes that bind him to his OCD loosen and unravel before his eyes as he gradually becomes master of his own feelings. With the conclusion of each session, he leaves with a spring in his step, determined to succeed.

Baruch Hashem, I have seen awesome results and high success rates. Before I begin my work, I beg Hashem for guidance and ask Him to send me His children who are afflicted with OCD, so that I can help relieve them of their suffering with the magnificent tool called CBT. After all, it is only my duty to thank Hashem for overcoming my own OCD by aiding those who are calling for help.

Part 5

חַיִּים שֶׁיֵּשׁ בָּהֶם
יִרְאַת שָׁמַיִם וְיִרְאַת חֵטְא

A Life in Which There Is Fear
of Heaven and Fear of Sin

And the Angel Says, "Amen"

Let me introduce myself. I'm the guy who sits behind you in shul. Or maybe in front of you, or at your side. It doesn't really matter.

I'm not the *rav*, or the *gabbai*, or even a *talmid chacham*. I'm just a regular *baalebos*, like you. I work hard to support my family and pay my children's tuition. During the week, I wear blue shirts, striped shirts, gray pants — anything but black and white, unless I'm going out to a *simchah*. I get up at 5:30 a.m. every day to go to my *daf yomi shiur*, daven, and then rush off to Manhattan. In the afternoon, I drag myself away from my desk and join the nearest Minchah *minyan*, doing my best to clear my mind of the deals that have been buzzing around the office, but usually unable to muster any real *kavanah*. By the time I get to Ma'ariv, I'm wiped.

I spend my week on a continuous treadmill, juggling the demands of my job and my family. The treadmill speeds up on Friday afternoon, when I dash out of the office, run some last-minute errands for my wife, fly into the house, help get the kids ready, jump into the shower, set up the Shabbos candles, and then burst into shul in time for Minchah. But then, as *Kabbalas Shabbos* begins, I feel myself winding down. The business deals, the e-mails, and the deadlines start to fade into the background, and the switch on my motor clicks into Shabbos mode.

I'd never come out and say this openly, for fear that I'd be branded as odd, eccentric, or *farchenyukt*, but here, in the comfort and privacy of these pages, I'll admit that I actually look forward to the Shabbos davening. For one thing, I enjoy the *chazzanus* and the singing. Mainly, however, I appreciate the opportunity to reconnect with my Creator. (How politically incorrect is that?)

But what usually happens in shul Friday night is this: as the *chazzan's Lechah Dodi* starts to lull me into the Shabbos spirit, I start to hear snatches of...something else.

"The Yanks really blew it last night," a fellow behind me tells his friend. "They had it in the bag! On home turf! Why didn't they call in their closer?"

"Yeah," the other guy says. "And the infield was asleep! Did you see the ground ball they let through in the eighth inning? And the two stolen bases?"

I'm turning around to the back of the shul, bowing as I say *"bo'i kallah,"* and my mind is one big jumble. Out pile the Yankees from the dugout to meet the Shabbos Queen on the hills of Tzefas...or is it Yankee Stadium?

The conversation continues unabated through Ma'ariv, dropping to a whisper during *Shema* and *Shemoneh Esrei*.

"The trade was a disaster..."

"Player to be named later, my foot..."

"I'd fire that general manager. . ."

When I leave shul that night, I have a sneaking suspicion that one of the *malachim* accompanying me is wearing a baseball uniform — an Anaheim Angels uniform, maybe? — and is quite pleased to give a resounding *berachah* that I be equally befuddled next week upon my return home from shul.

In the morning, I get up at the leisurely hour of 8 o'clock, refreshed and ready to daven, and I head off to shul with Yudi, my 6-year-old son. The shul is quiet, mostly empty, as I start to say *Pesukei D'Zimrah*. "*Hodu laShem kiru bishmo... Hashamayim mesaprim kevod Kel... Kol haneshamah tehallel Kah... Kol atzmosai tomarnah...*"

It's there, around *Nishmas*, when the humming begins. This time, it's from the front of the shul, right near the sign that says, "If you talk in shul, where do you go to daven?"

"So I agreed to be on the dinner committee," a middle-aged member of the shul is saying, "but I didn't realize how hard it was going to be to put together the journal. We're practically giving away the ads just to fill up pages! I committed to bringing in at least five platinum donors, and so far I only found two. I'm thinking that your friend, what's his name, the one whose face was all over that splashy brochure — Kahan, that's the one — you could work him a little bit, no? Tell him a little about what our organization does, tell him you know me, tell him it'll look good for his corporation. He can take it right off his advertising budget, *nisht Shabbos geredt*."

The *rav*'s face is turning purple. He looks in the direction of the dinner committee member, who's too engrossed in his sales pitch to even notice. Finally, the *rav* claps his hands together, and the conversation stops abruptly.

But as the *tzibbur* wends its way through *Shemoneh Esrei*, the two pick up right where they left off.

"I can't approach Kahan now," the other guy says. "I just hit him for another organization, and I'm also working on closing on a property with his company. But I have another idea for you. You know that young guy, Sternberg, who davens in the *shtiebel* down the block? His business just went public, so he has some cash to throw around, and he's the type of guy who'll stand on his head if you give him a little attention. Make up some new honor for him, and you'll have him eating out of your hand."

The *rav* can't save me this time, since he's also in the middle of *Shemoneh Esrei*. I wonder whether he's going to give another *derashah* about talking in shul when he speaks after *Krias HaTorah*.

He just spoke about this topic a few weeks ago. "People come to shul to daven for *parnassah*, for health, for *shiduchim*," he said, "and by talking in shul we close the gates to Heaven and rob our friends, and ourselves, of the chance to receive the *yeshuos* we desperately need. If we drive Hashem away, how do we expect Him to answer our *tefillos*? This is what the *Shulchan Aruch* means when he says that the sin of talking in shul is too great to bear!"

The congregation listened soberly, and Mussaf that week was a silent affair, for a change. But the next week, it was business as usual, with at least four different conversations going on during *Krias HaTorah*.

Fed up for my own sake, and indignant for the *rav*'s sake and Hashem's sake, I went over to one of the offenders during a break between *aliyah*s. "It's really disturbing when there's talking during davening," I said in a low voice.

"Oh, and since when are you Mr. Frum?" he replied. "I know a shul that's looking for a new *rav*, in case you're interested in the position."

His rejoinder reminded me of the last time I attempted to stop a conversation in shul. That time, Hershy Klein, who sits on my bench, was earnestly explaining to Bentzion Muller, one of the shul's wealthier members, that his brother-in-law would make a great addition to Muller's accounting firm. The *chazzan* was about to start *Kaddish*, so I gave a loud, "Ssssh!"

"Sruli, what's the matter with you?" Hershy hissed. "I'm trying to get my brother-in-law a job! This is a *devar mitzvah*, the highest form of *tzedakah*! You're allowed to talk in shul for a *devar mitzvah*."

If I'd allowed myself to talk in shul, I would have answered that my *Shulchan Aruch* doesn't say anything about an exemption for a *devar mitzvah*. But since I don't allow myself to talk in shul, even for a *devar mitzvah*, I couldn't answer him then. I saw no point in raising the issue again after davening — unless I wanted to make another enemy.

After that incident, I gave up. If people want to talk, I can't stop them.

I've thought about switching to a different shul, but I know that it won't make any difference. Talking is endemic in the shuls in my neighborhood; it's just a fact of life.

I think back to the shul where I davened with my father as a boy. It was in a basement, with only 15 or 20 *mispallelim*, and despite the lousy acoustics, you could hear a pin drop from *Mah Tovu* until after the last Kaddish. My parents used to invite many nonreligious people to join our Shabbos meals, and these guests would often accompany us to shul. Most of them couldn't read from a siddur and were unfamiliar with the shul proceedings, but they donned yarmulkes and sat quietly and respectfully for the duration of the services.

In the yeshivos I attended, talking during davening was similarly unheard of. If you couldn't hold yourself back, you went out into the lobby, got what you had to say off your chest, and then slipped back into the *beis midrash* and rejoined the *tzibbur*.

I'd be happy to daven in a yeshivah *minyan* today, even though now I feel more comfortable in a shul of *baalebatim*, but there are no such *minyanim* in reasonable walking distance.

But where was I? Oh, still in middle of *Shemoneh Esrei*. I quickly finish up, my concentration shattered.

"I hear that Sternberg is going to be receiving the newly minted Amud HaKehillah award. Maybe someone should tip him off, *nisht Shabbos geredt*."

Behind me, the two Yankee fans are back to their play-by-play armchair analysis. My son Yudi's head is turned in their direction, and he's hanging on to every word.

That's it. I've had enough. I close my *siddur*, motion to Yudi to leave, and the two of us walk out of shul right then and there, Yudi not quite understanding what's going on.

We walk into the house an hour earlier than usual, and my wife looks like she's going to fall off her feet in shock. "Is everything okay? Are you sick?"

"Yeah," I mumble. "I *am* sick. Sick and tired."

Yudi scampers off to play with his younger brother and sister, and I go into my study and finish davening, alone. I sing the songs the *chazzan* usually sings, humming some harmonies in between, and I have my heart-to-heart with Hashem without any side conversations to distract me. Of course, I feel good and guilty for not hearing *Krias HaTorah* and not finishing davening with a *minyan*. I also feel bad that I missed the *rav*'s speech. But mostly, I just enjoy the serene *tefillah* in my own little private shul.

I'm thinking about davening in this little shul next week, too. It's a nice place to daven, actually. Okay, the acoustics aren't great, but it's quiet and peaceful: no sports commentary, no dinner campaigns, no *devar mitzvahs*. So I don't get to daven with a *tzibbur*, but hey, the whole point of davening with a *tzibbur* is that Hashem is with you. I think Hashem would rather be with me, in my shul, than with you and the Yankees in yours.

Do I hear the angel saying, "Amen"?

Postscript:

The narrator of this story originally wrote a letter to Mishpacha's inbox decrying the talking in shul that was endemic in his community. I contacted him, heard the details of his story, and wrote it up as a LifeLines piece.

In his letter, the narrator described himself this way:

> *If you'd meet me in the street, you would never have guessed it was me who wrote this letter. . . I don't dress in black and white and am very chilled and easygoing overall, but I am a religious person who strives for basic yiras Shamayim, which for starters means not talking carelessly while the King is in the room.*

After I wrote up the story and sent it to the narrator for approval, he wrote back:

> *I feel like the article really needs more "shtarkness" to show the frustration of the writer and how much the careless talk in shul truly irks him deep inside. . . You need a few powerful lines that hit the reader, allowing the message to sink into his realization that talking in shul is really bad — like, evil. Not a frum thing.*

In the end, we decided to leave the story as is. "The power of the message is in its subtlety," I wrote to him, "and it's better to err on the side of less mussar and more story."

Do you agree?

Life and Death

The first thing that struck me about Nosson was how *large* he was. He was only in the seventh grade, but he seemed to stretch six feet in every direction. He was a gentle boy, though, the type who would walk around an ant rather than step on it.

Nosson wasn't learning much in school, nor had he learned much at any stage of his educational career, because he was extremely dyslexic, and couldn't tell an *alef* from a percent sign. His parents were desperate to finally get him to read and had hired me, a *kriah* specialist, to work with Nosson in school several times a week.

Nosson's lumbering frame didn't lend itself to athletics, which meant that he was as much of a failure in the school yard as he was in the classroom. The only thing Nosson did have going for him was his last name. His great-grandfather had founded the yeshivah he was learning in — which went from pre-kindergarten all the way up to *beis midrash* — and within the yeshivah's walls, his family was considered royalty. By virtue of his pedigree,

Nosson had friends, he was respected by his classmates, and he actually had a decent self-image.

Nosson was quiet and well behaved in class, and no rebbe had ever complained about his behavior. Until he entered the seventh grade, the yeshivah had tolerated his presence, both because of his *yichus* and because he didn't make any trouble.

I worked with him for most of that year, and with much *siyatta d'Shmaya*, I was able to teach him basic reading, enough to enable him to finally daven from a siddur. That didn't mean that he was able to learn *Mishnayos*, though, or even make out a *pasuk* of *Chumash*. But he was delighted with his progress, and so was I.

I thought the yeshivah would be pleased, too, but then, toward the end of the school year, I received a desperate phone call from Nosson's mother.

"Miriam," she cried, "you'll never believe what happened! They asked me to find a different yeshivah for Nosson!"

"A different school?" I asked. "Why?"

"The *hanhalah* says that he's accomplishing very little, and he could be learning a lot more if he were in a special remedial class."

"But this is your family's yeshivah!" I exclaimed. "How can they kick you out?"

"That's exactly what I told them," she said. "But they said that if he's not learning, he doesn't belong there, even if he's named after the old *rosh yeshivah*."

So much for protektzia, I thought. "I don't know how much my opinion is worth," I replied, "but I think moving Nosson out of the yeshivah would be terrible for his self-esteem. It probably wouldn't help him much academically either. His problems are very individual, not the type you can address in a group setting."

"I know," she said, sighing. "But it's not as though they're giving me a choice. None of the three eighth-grade *rebbeim* are interested in having Nosson in their class next year. They claim he'll gain much more in a different environment."

"Gain much more." Where had I heard those words before?

I remembered. And I shuddered.

A number of years earlier, I had been working in the resource room of a Bais Yaakov elementary school. Three of my students — Rivka, Yehudis, and Atara — were in the same class, and all three were extremely weak academically. I had been working with these girls since the third grade, and I knew them to be wonderful, hardworking kids who just had not been blessed with the greatest minds.

When these girls were in the third and fourth grade, I worked with their teachers to modify tests for them, and I shepherded the girls through the material the class was learning so they could succeed to the best of their ability. "Call on Atara for *pasuk yud beis*," I would advise their teacher before *Chumash* class, "and on Yehudis for *pasuk chaf*. I drilled them on those *pesukim*, so they should be fine reading and translating them. Don't call on Rivka today at all. She was tired yesterday and didn't catch what I was teaching."

The third- and fourth-grade teachers had been understanding and compassionate, and all three girls had done well — relatively — with them. The fourth-grade teacher noticed that Yehudis was artistic, and she actually placed her in charge of all the bulletin boards, which did wonders for Yehudis's self-esteem.

Then came the fifth grade — and Mrs. Klein. Mrs. Klein was the type of teacher who crammed her students with information, covering twice as much ground as any of the parallel fifth-grade teachers. What's more, she insisted on speaking only Hebrew in class, even though all of the other teachers in the school conducted their classes in English, and the girls started fifth grade barely understanding a word she said.

"A child's mind is like a sponge," Mrs. Klein often remarked in the teachers' room. "The more material you throw at them, the more they'll learn."

Mrs. Klein's tests were notoriously difficult, but she refused to allow me to modify them for her three weakest students. "You can't mollycoddle kids," she maintained. "They have to learn how to cope in life, even if they're not bright."

A couple of weeks into the year, Atara's mother realized that her daughter was suffering, and she prevailed upon the principal to switch her daughter to a different class. She had to put up quite a fuss, but in the end Atara was switched.

Rivka was having trouble in Mrs. Klein's class, too, but she came from a troubled home, and her parents were barely aware of her academic woes, so she remained in the class. She was stronger scholastically than the other two, however, so despite her difficulty keeping up with Mrs. Klein's rapid-fire teaching style, she made it through the year relatively unscathed.

That left Yehudis, whose mother was deeply concerned about her inability to keep up in class, but was too timid to go head-to-head with the school. "I spoke to Mrs. Klein, and to the principal, and I didn't get anywhere," she told me. "They keep saying it's fine, Yehudis will adjust, I just need to give it time. I see that she's not adjusting, but I don't have it in me to fight. I hope they know what they're doing."

Yehudis flunked every single test that year, handing in most of her test papers completely blank. By the end of the year, Mrs. Klein had decided that Yehudis was "slow," and she persuaded the principal that Yehudis belonged in a remedial class, together with other weak and learning-disabled students. "She can't stay in this school," Mrs. Klein declared one day in the teachers' room. "She hasn't learned a thing all year."

"But Yehudis is happy," I protested. "She's well behaved, she has friends, and she's not bothering anyone. Why rock the boat by uprooting her from her milieu?"

"Everybody's busy today with kids being happy," Mrs. Klein retorted. "Bottom line, a kid is in school to learn, and if Yehudis is not learning here, that means this is the wrong place for her. I think she stands to gain much more by being in a school for kids with learning disabilities."

When I met Yehudis's mother a few months later, she told me that Yehudis was miserable in her new school. "Every single kid in that special class of hers has serious emotional and behavioral issues," she said. "The first day of school Yehudis came home crying, and she asked me, 'Mommy, why did you put me into a crazy class?' She hates going to school, and I can't get her out of bed most mornings. I wish I could put her back into Bais Yaakov, but they won't take her."

The following year, Yehudis was switched to a third school, and by the end of that year, she was on her way off the *derech*.

Here and there, I'd meet Yehudis's mother, and she would tearfully update me on Yehudis's latest deterioration. In the eighth grade, she stopped wearing socks. In the ninth grade, she stopped wearing skirts. In the tenth grade, she stopped keeping Shabbos.

"You can't imagine what this is doing to our family," Yehudis's mother confided to me once, her voice breaking. "I feel like our entire home fell apart the day Yehudis was asked to leave Bais Yaakov."

Several years later, when I was no longer working in that school, I bumped into Mrs. Klein at a *simchah*.

"By the way," she asked casually, "whatever did happen with Yehudis?"

"Oh," I said, shifting uncomfortably, "you didn't hear? She's completely off the *derech*. The remedial class was a disaster for her. From the time she left your class, she went into a downward spiral, and now she's a mess."

I hoped Mrs. Klein wouldn't feel attacked by my words, since I was basically implying that she had been the catalyst for Yehudis's downfall. I needn't have worried, though, because Mrs. Klein chuckled and said, "I could have sworn it would happen. I could have predicted it!"

I couldn't believe what I was hearing. She could have sworn it would happen? She *made* it happen!

That conversation left me shaking.

———◆———

Hearing that Nosson could "gain much more" by being switched from a mainstream environment into a remedial class brought back memories of Yehudis and set off alarm bells in my head. *There is nothing to gain!* I wanted to scream. But what was the use? Nosson's parents were just about the most influential parents in the school, and if all three eighth-grade *rebbeim* were refusing to teach their son, what chance did I have of convincing the school to keep him? Besides, if the *hanhalah* was advocating that he leave the yeshivah, what business was it of mine? I was just Nosson's *kriah* teacher, after all.

But I thought of Mrs. Klein, and how her actions had led directly to the implosion of Yehudis and her entire family. *There's more than one way to destroy a kid*, I reflected. *You can destroy him by labeling him a problem child and placing him in the wrong environment, or you can destroy him by standing on the sidelines and watching passively as he withers away.*

I tossed and turned that entire night, the words *"Lo sa'amod al dam rei'echa"* echoing through my mind. *No one will ever blame me if Nosson goes off the derech*, I told myself. *But after seeing what happened to Yehudis, I'll never be able to live with myself if I don't speak up.*

The next morning, before leaving for work, I called Nosson's mother. "Tell me something," I said. "You know all of the eighth-grade *rebbeim*. Which of them do you think would be the best for Nosson?"

"Hmm," she responded. "Rabbi Levine and Rabbi Kranzler are excellent *rebbeim*, but probably too demanding for Nosson. Rabbi Hertzfeld is more laid back. I'd say he's the best bet. He already told the principal that Nosson wouldn't do well in his class, though."

"Do you mind if I call him?" I asked.

"Go right ahead," she said. "But it's probably a waste of your time."

My heart pounding, I dialed Rabbi Hertzfeld's number.

"My name is Mrs. Levenstein," I said, getting straight to the point. "I'm calling you about Nosson. You *must* take him into your class. It's a matter of life and death."

Rabbi Hertzfeld was a bit shocked. "This is not a student I can teach," he said. "Why shouldn't he go into a classroom where he can actually learn something?"

"I want to tell you something, Rabbi Hertzfeld," I said. "With all the progress we've made in special ed in recent years, we've forgotten something crucial, which is that children come a certain way, and we can't always 'fix' them. For some kids, a remedial class is a godsend, but for Nosson, it will do nothing besides kill his self-esteem. Even if he's not learning a thing, this yeshivah is his home, and his last name gives him something to be proud of and live up to."

"But isn't it worth a try?" he persisted.

"Let me ask you something," I answered. "We know that a fish needs to swim in water. But maybe there are some fish that can swim better in other liquids — say, apple juice. For Nosson, this yeshivah is water. A remedial class in a different school would be apple juice — and I'm telling you, Rabbi Hertzfeld, this kid is going to drown in the apple juice! Is that worth a try?"

As I spoke, I pictured Yehudis pleading with her mother not to leave Bais Yaakov. Yehudis in pants. Yehudis on the street.

"Let's say Nosson sits in your class next year and doesn't learn a single *pasuk*, a single *mishnah*, or a single *blatt* Gemara," I said. "Let's say all you do is keep him *frum*, off the streets, and out of trouble. Will it have been worth having him in your class?"

Rabbi Hertzfeld cleared his throat. "That's a heavy question, Mrs. Levenstein," he said. "I guess if you put it in those terms, the answer would be yes. I'll try my best to help this boy."

The next year I wasn't working with Nosson anymore, but I followed his progress through the grapevine. To everyone's surprise, he flourished in Rabbi Hertzfeld's class. Apparently, Rabbi Hertzfeld's smiles and total acceptance of Nosson despite his scholastic limitations had given him the impetus to learn and impress his rebbi. He wasn't getting hundreds on his Gemara tests, but he *was* getting 70's, which for him was a major achievement. When I met his mother, she happily informed me that his confidence was soaring.

That summer, when I went up to visit my own boys in camp on visiting day, I met Nosson. He was standing behind the canteen counter, wearing a walkie-talkie and a huge ring of keys on his belt, and a bunch of younger kids were gathered around him.

"Nosson, can I help you unload the boxes?" one kid begged.

"Nosson, can you give me the key to the soda machine?" a counselor called out.

In the meantime, Nosson was calmly serving dozens of customers while supervising some boys who were stocking the canteen shelves. His was clearly in his element.

Several years later, my *mechutan* made a *vort*, and while I was there, a woman tapped me on the shoulder and told me that her husband wanted to speak to me. I didn't recognize the man, but he introduced himself as Rabbi Hertzfeld.

"I want to thank you for that conversation we had a couple of years ago," he told me. "Not only did Nosson do well in my class, but he actually moved on to a regular yeshivah high school. He may never become a great *talmid chacham*, but I've watched him grow and blossom into an *ehrliche ben Torah*. And it's all to your credit."

"No," I answered, "it's to *your* credit. You're the one who had to deal with Nosson in the classroom every single day, and you're the one who built him up all year."

He flushed slightly. "Thank you," he said. "I can't say it was easy, but in hindsight, I don't think Nosson would have gained much by being in a remedial class."

"Rabbi Hertzfeld," I said, "this wasn't about what Nosson had to gain. It was about what he had to lose! You saved him from dying a spiritual death!"

I could tell he thought I was being overly dramatic. But having seen what happened to Yehudis, I knew that a *mechanech* holds the key to life or death for a child. Literally.

Postscript:

Here's what one reader had to say after this story:

> *Saphir, you just hit the nail this week. Were you thinking of me? This is exactly what I've been struggling with for the last ten years with my son. My hands were shaking when I finished reading this article. Yes, it's truly a matter of life and death. I have a meeting with our school district this week. This is what I will be distributing to each person at the meeting.*

Not every reader agreed with the premise of the story, though. Take this parent, for instance:

> *As the parent of a child who has learning disabilities, I was very disturbed with the LifeLines story titled "Life and Death." It implied that a child who has a learning disability is better off*

staying in his mainstream school and just "floating through" rather than attending a special program because doing so may send him off the derech.

While I understand that this is a story about only one child, a parent who may be faced with this difficult dilemma of how to properly deal with a child who is struggling in school (as I myself was) may be impacted into making the wrong decision out of fear of this story's strong connotations. It's important for a parent to know that although at times it is appropriate to keep the child in a mainstream school, at other times allowing the child to remain can result in a dire outcome.

Having a child sit in a regular class day after day, week after week, where the language and pace of learning is way over his head, is unfair and does a great disservice to the child. This feeling of failure is what eventually may lead a child to engage in negative behaviors and look for fulfillment and happiness in all the wrong places. I, too, struggled with the decision because of what people might think or say, but looking back now, and seeing the true successes that my son has experienced in a special program, not sending my child to a special program would have been the real "Life and Death."

Another reader offered a model for how issues like the one described in "Life and Death" should be handled:

Your article "Life and Death" stabbed me right though my heart! I hereby invite all principals to visit my alma mater to learn the ABCs of chinuch from our wonderful menaheles, Rebbetzin K.

Never did a teacher independently dictate the rules of acceptance regarding a student; every neshamah counted! Rebbetzin K. cared about each student like a bas yechidah, and such an incident could never have happened under her jurisdiction. She would never have allowed a teacher to destroy a child like that. Her nachas was to see each girl's success. She wanted to build each girl's confidence somehow and have each girl shine, either via the classroom or through extracurricular activities such as the chagigah, Shabbaton, or production. She wanted to see each girl happy, have friends, be as successful scholastically as she could be, and grow in ruchniyus. Each girl had the security that Rebbetzin K. was there no matter what — always worried about each girl in high school and after, including shidduchim, jobs, and beyond.

In response to all these letters, the narrator of "Life and Death" wrote the following:

It seems from the letters to the editor that the only one who really got it was that student who wrote, "Never did a teacher independently dictate the rules of acceptance regarding a student." This was the problem to begin with. The teacher (not the principal) was in charge of deciding whether it was okay to modify a test for this child. As a special educator for many years, I have seen many children flourish in special remedial classes, and there is much to be said about those success stories. However, I have worked with too many children who were dumped — yes, dumped — into self-contained classes because the teacher decided that "you can't mollycoddle kids." As mechanchim, it is our chiyuv to go out of our way to mollycoddle every single Jewish child! As principals, it is our chiyuv to oversee teachers who refuse to do so.

Teachers are humans. Teachers are sometimes young kids just returning from high-pressure seminaries in Israel and convinced that their fourth graders are their peers. Teachers are sometimes tired mothers just returning from postpartum breaks. True, we have problems with learning-disabled children, but guess what? Many innocent kinderlach suffer from TD teachers (as in teaching disabled). It is the responsibility of every one of our principals to be in charge of those teachers. They should be the ones to make those decisions. They should be the ones dictating to the teachers, not the other way around! This article was not about knocking the validity of self-contained education. It was about caring enough to save those neshamos who didn't require it!

Sometimes I feel that the dialogue generated by a story is more valuable than the story itself. The story highlights one facet of a *particular issue, while the subsequent dialogue illuminates other critical facets and completes the picture. This story was a case in point.*

Computer Trouble

It was a long and frustrating *motza'ei Shabbos*. My wife, Shiffy, was out at some *melaveh malkah* fund-raiser, and I was baby-sitting. I've never enjoyed getting five kids to bed, but on this particular night my 4-year-old daughter, Miri, gave me a really hard time, coming out of bed every two minutes and then crying her head off for an hour after I warned her that she'd better not come out of bed again.

I had been planning to learn the next day's *daf* so I'd be prepared for my *shiur* the next evening, but after finally settling everyone down, I didn't have the head to open my Gemara. Instead, I decided to check my e-mail.

I own a landscaping and snow-removal business, and although I do maintain a small website, most of my work comes through the old-fashioned way: through word-of-mouth recommendations and advertisements in the Yellow Pages and local circulars. Some of my customers communicate with me by e-mail, but it's rare that an urgent e-mail will come in over Shabbos. If there's an emergency — "Mr. Balter! The squirrels dug up my tulip bulbs!" — I'll usually get a call on my cell phone.

The only client e-mail that *motza'ei Shabbos* was from Mrs. Milner, an old customer who wanted to know how often to water her new hydrangeas. There was one other e-mail, from Phil Schwartz, a shul buddy of mine. The subject line said "Hilarious!!!! Must See!!!!!!!" and the mail contained a link to some YouTube video. I clicked on the link, just so I could respond to Phil with an LOL (or maybe LOL!!!!!!!!!!!!!).

I don't know how it happened, but after I viewed the short slapstick clip, I must have accidentally clicked on a nearby link to a different video. The moment I clicked on the link, I knew that this was not something I wanted to see. But my curiosity was uncontrollable. Just one quick peek…

One quick peek, and I spent the next hour in front of some of the worst images the *yetzer hara* has to offer. My heart was pounding with horror and revulsion, but as much as I willed myself to click on the *X* in the corner of the screen, I couldn't do it. Only when I heard Shiffy's key turning in the door did I quickly hit "Close all tabs" on the Internet browser and then frantically delete the browser's history.

I was terrified that Shiffy would notice that my hands were shaking badly or spot the guilt written all over my face. But she came in all happy and excited, telling me that she had won a new coffeemaker at the Chinese auction and going on and on about how little space on the counter the new machine takes up.

I felt sick. Sick that I had allowed myself to sink so low, sick that I had gone behind Shiffy's back and done something that would hurt her terribly, if she only knew.

I walked around the next day, and the rest of the week, with a heavy burden of shame and disgrace hanging over me. Shiffy — who's a pretty astute person — remained blissfully oblivious to the awful secret I was carrying, and the more she carried on with life as usual, the worse I felt about myself.

When Shabbos came, I could no longer bear it. After Shiffy lit candles and wished me a *gut Shabbos*, I blurted out to her what I had done.

Her eyes widened. "Danny, how could you?" she whispered. "I can't believe it." And then she started to cry.

I found her tears strangely comforting. All week I had been living in dread of this reaction, and now that it was over, I felt weak with relief.

Still, it was one of the saddest Shabbosos of our married life. The lowest point was when Shiffy reminded me of what I myself had said when she had asked that we install a filter on our home computer.

At the time, I had scoffed at the idea. "A Jew needs a filter on his *neshamah*, not on his computer," I had declared. "A guy who needs a filter to stop him from looking at bad stuff is going to find ways around the filter anyway, and a person who has *yiras Shamayim* doesn't need K9 or NetNanny to babysit him."

When Shiffy replayed that conversation accusingly, my whole body burned with shame. I swore to Shiffy that I would never do it again, but the look of betrayal in her eyes lingered, making me feel rotten and worthless.

Immediately after I made *Havdalah*, Shiffy stalked over to the computer and installed a filter on it. I was humiliated, but I couldn't say a word.

I helped her get the kids to bed, and then I told her that I was going out to Rabbi Weissman's *daf yomi shiur*. Instead, I went to my office, settled myself in the empty chair where my assistant, Steve, usually sits, and logged on to the Internet. I really wasn't planning to hit those bad sites again; I just wanted to check my e-mail without Shiffy hovering over me, and without running afoul of the new filter any time I clicked a link.

To my chagrin, not a single e-mail had come in for me since Friday. No official from Namibia informing me that I had won $13 million, no friends writing to tell me that they were stranded in Madrid with no cash, not even a virus notification.

I clicked the refresh button a few times, hoping that somehow an e-mail would materialize that would make it worth having lied about the *shiur*. But there was none, so I found myself typing, as if possessed by an invisible demonic force, the words that would bring me to the online netherworld I had stumbled upon the previous week.

It was close to midnight when Shiffy called to find out when I was coming home. A flood of guilt washed over me when I heard her voice, and I hurriedly shut down the computer and left the office, feeling like a cesspool.

When I came home, I told Shiffy that I had a headache and went straight to bed. Thankfully, she was on the phone, and she didn't ask any questions.

I made up my mind that I wasn't going to go to those ruinous sites ever again, and for a few weeks I managed to keep myself away. But then, one afternoon when Steve was gone and I had to take care of something at the office, it happened again.

I came home feeling like a clod of dirt, and when Shiffy greeted me, I told her in a low voice that I had stumbled again.

Shiffy was flabbergasted, and furious.

"You promised! You told me you were never going to do this again! How could you?"

The more she carried on, the more oddly detached I felt about the whole thing.

When she demanded that I go for therapy, I didn't put up any fuss. She booked me an appointment with Dr. Randolph, a psychotherapist.

I obediently explained to Dr. Randolph that my wife had a problem with my Internet use. "How do *you* feel about your Internet use?" he asked.

"It's not such a big deal," I averred, hoping that the session would end quickly.

We talked a bit about behavior modification strategies, and then Dr. Randolph ended the session, saying that he was confident that I'd be able to make a positive change in my life.

The moment I returned home, Shiffy started cross-examining me. "What did you tell him? What did he say? How long do you have to go for therapy?"

"It went really well," I assured her. "We're working wonderfully together."

I met with Dr. Randolph a few more times, and each time I reported to him that things were going "just great." I didn't bother telling him that I hadn't implemented any of his strategies, but I managed to hem and haw my way around his questions so that he'd be satisfied with my answers.

After every meeting with Dr. Randolph, I'd stop at the office on my way home instead of going to my *shiur*. I felt horribly guilty about it, but I just couldn't control myself. Besides, the lascivious images that were flashing in my head made it impossible for me to concentrate in the *shiur*.

Davening also became very difficult for me. I felt that Hashem couldn't possibly love me, and I started to put off davening until the latest possible time; there were days when I put *tefillin* only minutes before sunset. In other areas, though, I became even more scrupulous than before. I insisted on a particularly stringent type of *shechitah*, and I stopped relying on the local *eiruv*. I guess I wanted to feel holy somehow.

Shiffy discovered the truth about my Internet habit when Bracha Schwartz, Phil's wife, met her one day and innocently mentioned something about my dropping out of the *shiur*. That day Shiffy had another fit, and I didn't really care.

But the next day, when she told me that she had spoken to Rebbetzin Weissman, I did care.

"How could you do that?" I whispered, shocked to the core that Shiffy would go behind my back and speak to the *rav*'s wife about this.

"I have to take care of myself," she said softly. "Rebbetzin Weissman told me that this has nothing to do with me, it's between you and Hashem. I know that this is hard for you, and I am davening that Hashem will help you."

From then on, Shiffy completely dissociated herself from my problem, no longer questioning me about my Internet use or about my therapy with Dr. Randolph. She behaved kindly and politely to me, and we'd go through the motions of normal family living, with Shiffy dutifully serving Shabbos meals and me singing *zemiros* and reading the kids' *parashah* sheets at the table. But the feeling of closeness and trust in our relationship was missing, and that pained me greatly.

To my surprise, I realized that I *wanted* Shiffy to ask whether I was misusing the Internet, I *wanted* her to tell me that what I was doing wasn't okay, I *wanted* her to cry and carry on. I couldn't stop myself, and being left to my own devices was extremely scary.

One evening, when I came home, I announced to her that I had just been surfing the Net.

"I'm so sorry," she said calmly. "This must be very hard for you. I am davening for you."

There was no trace of anger in her voice, only pity.

We went through similar exchanges a few times, until eventually I felt that I was going to explode with guilt and shame. Shiffy and I were like strangers, like ships passing in the night, and although I wanted desperately to regain the warmth that had previously characterized our marriage, I couldn't break through the invisible wooden barrier that had sprung up between us. Finally, when I saw that Shiffy was dead serious about not listening to any confessions from me, I realized that in order to escape from the clutches of the *yetzer hara*, I was going to have to reach out for help.

I hadn't seen Dr. Randolph since Shiffy had stopped booking my appointments, but I knew that he wasn't going to be able to help me. I decided to unburden myself to Rabbi Weissman.

Rabbi Weissman listened empathetically, looking more saddened than shocked. "This is unfortunately very common," he said. Then he gave me the name of a therapist, Benjy Sanders, who specialized in Internet addictions. "A regular therapist isn't going to be able to help you," Rabbi Weissman explained. "You need someone who is trained to deal with this specific problem."

It was shocking to think of myself as an addict, but I subsequently learned that the designation is critical, since addictions don't respond to standard forms of behavioral therapy; they're in a class of their own. Benjy Sanders was a recovered addict himself, and, unlike Dr. Randolph, he knew exactly how to deal with a client like me.

"In order to heal," Benjy told me, "an addict has to decide of his own accord to pull himself out of the mud. If you've reached that point, I can help you."

He explained that in the past, when I had admitted to Shiffy that I was viewing inappropriate images, the very act of unloading the burden of secrecy had given me an emotional release, which in turn encouraged the cycle of my addiction.

"Confession alone is a dangerous thing," Benjy informed me. "If it's not followed by immediate action to prevent further slipups, it positions you to fall back into the same behavior, since you've cleared your slate of some of the guilt."

With Benjy's encouragement, I swore off the Internet, rejoined Rabbi Weissman's *shiur*, and instructed Steve to put a filter on my office computer, making sure I didn't know the password. Benjy also advised me to join GuardYourEyes.com, a website that provides resources and support for *frum* people who struggle with viewing inappropriate material.

I asked Shiffy to white-list Guard Your Eyes on the maximum-strength Internet filter on our home computer, and through that site I discovered that there were other *frum* people who were suffering — or recovering — from the same problem I had. Knowing that I was not alone with my problem gave me tremendous *chizuk*, and hearing again and again from my anonymous Guard Your Eyes friends that Hashem still loved me no matter what spurred me to work on rebuilding my relationship with Him.

I began davening to Hashem to remove the *yetzer hara* to surf the Net and to help me regain Shiffy's trust and respect, and through Guard Your Eyes, I joined a phone-in twelve-step addiction recovery group.

In the meantime, Shiffy learned from the Guard Your Eyes website that there is a support group for wives of *frum* men with Internet addictions. Being part of this group helped her reinforce the belief that she was not to blame for my problem and view my problem as a difficult *nisayon* for me rather than a betrayal of her. We also went for marriage counseling to restore the shattered trust in our relationship.

Shiffy and I have gone through Gehinnom as a result of my addiction, even if on the outside we managed to maintain a semblance of normalcy in our lives. I'm grateful to her for giving me the space to work out this issue on my own, and I'm grateful to her for working on herself to accept and respect me despite my problem. In the beginning, it was extremely difficult for her not to take my issue personally, but she's grown to recognize that it's not about her; it's about a trap of the *yetzer hara* to which even the most filtered *neshamah* can succumb in the absence of safeguards.

It took close to five years for Shiffy and me to rebuild the trust in our marriage, but *baruch Hashem* today our relationship is stronger than ever. I wish I could say that I'm cured of my Internet addiction, but part of moving past an addiction is recognizing that recovery is a lifelong process, and that the word "cure" doesn't exist in an addict's lexicon. Unless you're constantly on guard, you're fair game for the *yetzer hara*.

Postscript:

What does Shiffy have to say about this experience?

While we were going through this test, it was the most difficult thing; it seemed so black. But looking back, I can say, "Thank You, Hashem, for the opportunity to grow and help others through our pain, and thank you for letting us come out stronger people on the other end." It made both of us more humble, accepting, understanding, and less judgmental. It was something we had to go through together in order to gain wisdom and understanding and a broader vision of Hashem's plan.

Seeing a Different Picture

About 15 years ago, my parents moved from a sleepy town in the Midwest to a new Anglo community in Israel. My parents had always dreamed of making *aliyah*, and when my father was offered the option of working for his software engineering company remotely, they jumped at the opportunity. They never imagined the price that realizing their dream would exact.

I was 12 years old at the time, possibly at the worst stage in my life to be uprooted from my natural habitat and transplanted to a foreign country, language, and culture. Plucked from a small, cozy community school with lots of room for individuality, I fell smack into a massive, factory-style Bais Yaakov where I was expected to exchange my bobby socks for beige bulletproof stockings, my Baby-Sitters Club library for unintelligible Hebrew novels, and my broad Midwestern grin for a prim, tight-lipped Middle Eastern smile.

Rather than trying to break into the ranks of the sabras, I gravitated to the other kids of fresh-faced, idealistic American *olim*, and we became a fringe group that earned the suspicion of the school and the neighborhood. In America, I had been a popular, academically successful, but otherwise run-of-the-mill student from a typical middle-class family. To my Israeli peers and their parents, I was a rich, modern, brazen American upstart whose hairstyle was wrong and whose attempts at pronouncing a *r-r-reish* evoked smirks and giggles.

Prior to our move, my parents had an O.K. marriage, but the process of acclimating to a new environment and a scaled-down lifestyle — living in a small apartment instead of a ranch-style house; taking buses instead of owning two cars; buying made-in-China overpriced junk instead of quality, affordable clothing and housewares — took a toll on their *shalom bayis*, and I was witness to a lot of friction between my parents.

Do the math and you get a very disgruntled, disenfranchised, disillusioned teen.

Since our community was so new, my posse pretty much represented the first wave of American at-risk youth in town, rivaling the Israeli dropouts. We were the trailblazers, and the local teens-at-risk have been faithfully following in our footsteps ever since.

When I started the ninth grade, my reputation preceded me, and the staff was determined to quash my rebellious nature. I was put under a microscope, my every action subject to intense scrutiny. If I bought a new skirt, the principal knew about it the next day. If I came a minute late to class, the teachers had instructions to pounce on me and not afford me the slightest leeway ("Give this kid a finger, she'll take an arm"). If I was spotted in conversation with a "good" girl, her parents would get a phone call advising them to tell their daughter to keep her distance.

There was only one person in the school who I felt genuinely cared about me, and that was my homeroom teacher, Morah Elisheva. She was under tremendous pressure from the principal to keep me in line, so she had to admonish me constantly about my earrings, my boots, and my skirt length, but behind the *mussar* she was paid to deliver was a gentle, compassionate soul whose love came through even as she handed me a ponytail holder or tugged at my rolled-up sleeves.

At the end of the ninth grade, when my parents were told that I was not welcome in the school the next year, Morah Elisheva showed up at my house to present me with a gift: a *Tehillim* with a beautiful inscription.

I was too angry at the school and at the world to even come to the door to greet Morah Elisheva, and the last thing I wanted was a *Tehillim* from her, or from anyone. Yet nestled somewhere beneath the layers of wrath was the warm feeling of knowing that there was someone in the school who didn't think I was garbage.

On the outside, I may have seemed tough and defiant, but on the inside I was just a little girl crying out for unconditional acceptance and social belonging. Other than Morah Elisheva, though, there were pitifully few people who looked past my veneer. On the whole, the adults in my life did a lot of hand-wringing, writing me off as an at-risk menace.

"What's going to be with that kid?" was written all over the faces of my teachers, principals, neighbors, and relatives. My parents were worried sick about me, and everyone else seemed certain that I was headed for serious trouble.

Were they wrong? That's a good question. The girls I was hanging out with were definitely up to no good — boys, smoking, alcohol, drugs — but I myself was not doing anything really dangerous, even if I dressed like the others and adopted their swagger. What could have pushed me over the edge, and almost did, was the expectation that I was going to mess up my life big time.

A 14-year-old is still a kid, and her self-definition is primarily a reflection of the way the authority figures in her life view her. Had people believed in me, seen the still-pure *neshamah* that was lurking beneath the shaggy hairdo and droopy earrings, I probably would have had a much easier time extricating myself from the youth-on-the-fringe quicksand. The confidence of the adults around me could have constituted the strong arm that I could have grabbed hold of in order to pull myself up from the mud.

Instead they fretted, they warned, they punished, they shook their heads and clucked their tongues. My self-image came to mirror their lack of faith in me: I started seeing myself as a "bad girl," the type who could — and would — do really "bad things."

People don't seem to realize that worry is not harmless; it can be extremely damaging, a self-fulfilling prophecy. It happened to many of my at-risk friends, and it almost happened to me.

What saved me was my chutzpah. I was so defiant, I had to defy *everything*, including people's gloomy predictions for my future. If they said that I was going to be a street bum, that I was going to go off the *derech* completely, that I was never going to raise a normal family, then I had to prove them wrong. (I should point out that my experience was highly unusual, and reverse psychology of this sort should *not* be employed as a strategy for dealing with defiant kids.)

Because I was determined not to mess up my life the way everyone thought I was going to, I drew certain red lines for myself. I'd wear really short, tight skirts, but I wouldn't wear pants. I'd stay out late at night with friends who were smoking, but I wouldn't smoke. I'd talk to boys, but I'd keep total physical distance.

Looking back, I realize that these distinctions were laughable, and that I could easily have landed in big trouble despite my self-imposed red lines. It was only by the *chesed* of Hashem, and the confidence of certain key individuals in my life, that I never crossed into the world of substance abuse and promiscuity. Unfortunately, many of my friends did, and today a large percentage of those kids are depressed, divorced, or dead.

In desperation, my parents decided to send me back to America, to a tiny Bais Yaakov–type school in a Midwest hick town. I said no way, José.

There was an American *rebbetzin* in Yerushalayim — I'll call her Rebbetzin Feder — who had taught in that Midwest school before making *aliyah*, and my mother dragged me to her for an interview. During our meeting, I tried to convince the *rebbetzin* that I didn't belong in a Bais Yaakov, and that I'd be a horrible influence on the other students there.

She looked me up and down, and then, peering over her glasses, she smiled at me. "You'll do just fine," she assured me.

"But I don't wear socks!" I protested. "I talk to boys!"

"You'll do fine," she repeated. "You're fine." Clearly, she saw a different picture of me than the one other people saw.

In case I thought Rebbetzin Feder's words were lip service, she then went and put herself on the line by convincing the school to accept me and arranging for me to board at a local family, the Brandweins. After that show of confidence in me, there was no way I could let her down.

I could, however, give my mother a hard time, by refusing to get on the plane, which is what I did. But my mother convinced me to come with her to America to visit some relatives and also to check out the school in the Midwest, "just to see what it's like." We visited the school together, and then my mother took me to meet the Brandweins. At both the school and the Brandwein home, I was deliberately rude, scowling the whole time and sticking out my chin defiantly, just to make sure they wouldn't want me to stay.

Mrs. Brandwein was gentle and easygoing, and she started shmoozing with me in the kitchen while my mother spoke to Mr. Brandwein in a different room. At some point, I realized that I was no longer hearing my mother's voice, and I turned around to see where she was.

She was gone. She had hopped into a taxi, sped off to the airport, and boarded a plane, taking my passport with her.

To this day, I'm not sure if my mother did the right thing. On the one hand, switching to that school saved my life; on the other hand, that breach of trust ruined my relationship with my mother. I still can't fully forgive her for dumping me 6,000 miles away from my family and friends, in a town where I knew not a soul, and forcing me to stay there against my will. I understand that she did it because she cared about me, but I wish she could have found a less painful way to go about it.

In the beginning, I was terribly homesick and absolutely miserable. But the school was perfect for me, and I hit it off well with the Brandweins. My at-risk behavior didn't seem to scare anyone in this slow-paced, do-your-own-thing school, and with no crowd of juvenile delinquents to hang out with, I eventually just fell into line.

In Israel, I had been viewed as a problem kid, which turned me into one. Here, I wasn't seen as a threat, so I stopped seeing myself that way. Also, living with a stable, happy family rather than in the tense environment of my parents' post-*aliyah* home gave me a feeling of security and calm.

While I was still in high school, I decided that I wanted to work with at-risk kids one day.

I came back to Israel for seminary, and then attended a *frum* college while working as a dorm counselor in a residence for off-the-*derech* girls. Before I completed my degree in adolescent psychology, I met my husband, Uri, also a former at-risk youth who had decided to turn his life around. Uri's parents were divorced, and when he dropped out of yeshivah in the tenth grade, the message he picked up from the hand-wringing adults around him was "Well, his parents are divorced, what do you expect?" It was almost as if being a child of divorce gives you the license to do any type of delinquent behavior. Uri, fortunately, defied those expectations.

Our *vort* was the event of the century. Everyone who knew me or Uri from our previous lives *had* to be there, and it seemed to me that the entire community came to share the *nachas* of one of its first at-risk success stories. I got the feeling that for many of the parents, it was a relief to see me and realize that their own shaky kids might also turn out *frum* at the end. If I had a hand in helping them envision a different future for their children, I consider that a tremendous *zechus*.

The day after our *vort* I bumped into the person who deserved much of the credit for helping me survive my rocky adolescence. I was visiting a friend in a Yerushalayim seminary, and there, walking down the hall, was Rebbetzin Feder! I introduced myself and told her that I had just gotten engaged. Once again, she peered over her glasses and smiled. "Exactly the way I thought you'd turn out," she said.

Looking at me today, with my *sheitel* and double stroller, the troubled teens who come to me for therapy find it hard to believe that a mere 12 years ago I looked exactly the way they do now. Of all the forms of therapy I can offer them, I think the best therapy I provide is holding up a picture of themselves a few years down the line — *frum*, settled, and happy — and showing them that this is the picture I see for them, too.

Postscript:

One reaction to this story stands out in my mind. "Are teachers in Israel really called by their first names?" a certain mechanech wanted to know. I guess he was surprised that I referred to the high school teacher in this story as "Morah Elisheva."

The answer is that, yes, teachers in Israel are called by their first names. (In chareidi schools, the title "Morah" is typically used, along with the teacher's first name.)

This may seem like a minor detail, but it speaks volumes about cultural norms and nuances, such as the informality that characterizes Israeli society. Cultural differences like these aren't the typical factors people consider when contemplating aliyah, but it might be worthwhile to take them into account, especially when there are teenagers involved.

Anybody know how to say "Mister" in Hebrew?

Upstairs, Downstairs

The most frequent question I asked growing up was "Where's Dad?" and the most frequent answer was "Upstairs." That's where he worked. In fact, that's pretty much where he lived. Except when he was reading the newspaper during dinner or sleeping in front of the television.

I grew up in a typical Jewish home in the American Northeast. Not religious, we were the Rosh HaShanah/Yom Kippur/Chanukah/ Passover type of family with a smattering of *kiddush*es and bar mitzvahs, and a few hora dances thrown in at family weddings for good measure.

Dad was a diamond setter, Mom a librarian. Both sides of the family trace their lineage back to strong chassidic dynasties, but that heritage was jettisoned upon the approach to Ellis Island.

Dad typically brought work home from the diamond district in Manhattan and then went upstairs to his work bench to begin the eye-straining, back-wrenching job of setting hundreds of diamonds into myriad settings while listening to the radio or the hum of the TV in the background. He was almost always around, but rarely available physically or emotionally. Work was his religion.

Except when he found out about a good yard sale. And he always knew where there was a good yard sale. He would cut out that part of the classified ads early on Saturday morning and often spend the day hunting for bargains, showing up hours later, his car packed with loads of other people's stuff. My mom would sigh as he unloaded it all into the basement week after week, only to reach the breaking point herself and make her own yard sale just so she could find her way through the basement to the washing machine.

As a child, I quickly learned that any relationship I wanted to have with my father would have to be on his terms, either having something to do with his revered work or with his beloved yard sales. Some days I'd come home from school and go upstairs to spend some time with him. "Hi, Dad," I'd say. "What can I do here?"

He'd hand me a huge box that contained hundreds, maybe thousands, of specialized drill bits and say, "Here, organize these. I'll give you a dollar."

On Sundays, he'd drag me to one yard sale after another, exulting over the opportunity to sift through other people's junk. I hated every minute of it.

Once, Dad spotted a huge safe at a yard sale and decided he just had to have it. "Gimme a hand, Michael," he ordered as he began lifting the safe, which must have weighed a few hundred pounds.

"Dad," I begged, "Mom's going to hit the roof! Why on earth do we need this monstrosity?"

Dad ignored my protestations. "Grab that side, will you?"

I wouldn't. I was 12 years old, and I'd had enough.

When Dad saw that I wasn't budging, his face turned red with anger. He then lifted the safe into the car himself, giving himself a hernia in the process. He had to undergo surgery, but the surgery was botched, and he suffered from the hernia for the rest of his life. It was all my fault, of course, and I never stopped hearing about it. But that was the last time Dad ever took me to a yard sale.

By the time I hit adolescence, I wanted nothing to do with Dad. I was going to be my own man.

The trouble was that I didn't know how to be a man. I knew I didn't want to be like Dad, but, having no other frame of reference for what a man is supposed to be, I naturally mimicked his behavior, even as I swore that I'd never make the mistakes he did.

Dad had always vacillated between explosive anger and brooding, disconnected silence, with no range in between. Those, in turn, became my two behavioral bookends. Like Dad, I had trouble making and keeping friends, and although I desperately craved closeness in relationships, I didn't have the skills to create that closeness.

What's more, I still needed a father. Outwardly, I was grown-up and macho, needing approval from no one, but inside, I was a hungry little boy eager for his father's attention and love. To cover up my emotional neediness, I could never admit to being wrong or apologize for hurting someone.

That my first marriage ended in disaster is no surprise, viewed in the context of my lack of a male role model and my inability to connect with people on a deep, meaningful level. But the fact that the divorce was partly my fault didn't make it any less painful.

When my wife and I broke up, I drove over to the house of my friend Clark, the only person I considered a true friend. He wasn't Jewish, but he was a deeply spiritual person, and he was the first man I ever met whose personality I considered worth emulating.

"Mike," he said after I cried on his shoulder for hours, "rather than focus on what you don't have anymore, maybe sit and write down what it is you really want."

So instead of stewing in my grief, I took Clark's advice and wrote a dissertation that described every quality I was looking for in a wife. Less than two weeks later, Nicki walked into my life. After seeing Nicki a few times, I could see that she possessed every one of the qualities on my list.

This time I knew better than to jump into a new relationship without first taking steps to ensure that I'd be a better husband

and father than my dad was. During our courtship, Nicki and I both enrolled in a year-long family and child counseling seminar offered through the University of Santa Monica. The program provided intensive training in how to build and maintain healthy relationships, and I augmented that training by reading numerous books on the subject.

When I was confident that I had expanded my bookends to include a broader, healthier range of emotional tools and relationship skills than I had learned from Dad, I married Nicki. We were both committed to making our marriage work, and we managed to forge a relationship based on trust, respect, and open communication.

But there was something missing. As wonderful as our marriage was, as happy we were to be in a stable, healthy relationship, we felt a gnawing sense of emptiness. There had to be more to life than just living, even if living was good.

Along with shedding Dad and his yard sales, I had long since dispensed with the bagels-and-lox, HaTikvah brand of Judaism I grew up with. In the Conservative Hebrew school of my youth, I never once heard G-d mentioned. In fact, G-d was mentioned far more often in chiropractic school than in any religious venue I attended.

Unfortunately, the experiences Nicki and I had had with Orthodox Judaism up until that point were highly unfavorable. But we were forced to rethink our attitude toward Orthodoxy when we heard a popular radio talk-show personality emphasize that the only way to raise happy, healthy, holy children was to have religion in the home — and that religion, she insisted, had to be the religion we were born into. Our children meant everything to us, so we gave up and gave in.

I called an observant patient of mine and asked the question that would change my life forever.

"Is there an Orthodox rabbi in town who welcomes people who don't own any black and white clothing?"

When my patient recovered from her laughter, she gave me the name and number of a Rabbi Geller. "He works with people like you," she assured me.

I immediately dialed the number she had given me, expecting an accented, affected, white-shirted, black-panted stereotype to answer. Not the case. Instead, a pleasant-sounding fellow answered, responding to my questions in clear, unblemished English. The sounds of young children were distantly heard in the background as we agreed upon a day and time to meet.

I hung up, nonplussed. "I don't think my patient gave us the number of someone who can really help us," I said to my wife.

When we arrived at the address Rabbi Geller had given us, we saw the rabbi emerge from a Honda Civic. Now I was certain that we had been misled. After all, these guys were supposed to drive beat-up station wagons!

But as I sized up Rabbi Geller in his round black hat, long black frock, starched white shirt, and long reddish-white beard, I concluded that he definitely looked like one of "them," his car notwithstanding.

"We have to get out here!" I cried. "She got us in with a zealot!"

"We're not going anywhere except inside to talk with him," my wife rejoined. "I didn't spend $200 on a hat and dress just to have you chicken out!"

So we went inside, and we sat down and talked. And talked. Rabbi Geller listened to us for well over an hour. Our dysfunctional childhoods, the loss of faith, the search for a path, the trials and tribulations, heartbreaks and breakthroughs. And finally this: the return.

What impressed me the most about Rabbi Geller was his equanimity and inner balance. Here was a guy who, on the surface, looked like the stereotypical black-and-white Orthodox Jew that I never wanted to have any contact with, and yet his personality was so reassuring, so pleasant. For the first time in my life, I felt myself drawn to an adult Jewish male role model.

With time, Rabbi Geller became not only my rabbi, but my father figure as well. I began davening in his shul every Shabbos, and I latched onto him as both a spiritual mentor and an emotional anchor. I learned to forge a relationship with G-d and with my fellow congregants by observing and emulating Rabbi Geller, who to me represented a fusion of G-dliness and normalcy.

Upstairs, Downstairs / 261

Rabbi Geller was steeped in Torah, Chassidus, and Jewish tradition, and he seamlessly combined that with a down-to-earth, caring, comfortable manner of relating to people. I saw the way he treated his wife and children, I saw how he spoke to his congregants, and I knew with certainty that this was my spiritual father — although he wasn't more than a year or two older than I was.

About six months after we joined the shul — which was several miles from our home — we took the bold step of buying a new house closer to Rabbi Geller's shul and community. The Shabbos after we moved in, however, Rabbi Geller announced in shul that he was taking a year's sabbatical.

I was so stunned and hurt that I stood up and walked out of shul. When Rabbi Geller approached me, I refused to talk to him. He called me and asked me to meet him, and I begrudgingly agreed.

"I know you're upset with me," he said. "I just want —"

"You'd better believe I'm upset!" I interrupted. "What exactly were you thinking to go on sabbatical right after I picked up and moved into your neighborhood to be part of *your* shul?"

"I'm not leaving you," he said. "I will be available to you, just not as available as before. And it will only be for a year."

I was livid. Here I was, trying my hardest to cram myself into Rabbi Geller's vision of what a Jew should be, and he was pulling the rug out from under me. How could he leave me alone just when I had made the full commitment to the lifestyle he championed? He was supposed to be my island of stability, my rock of Gibraltar, my lighthouse, my guru!

Without Rabbi Geller, I had no place in the community, no place in the world of G-d. Instead of guiding me to truth and inner peace, Rabbi Geller had led me down yet another path that led to disappointment and pain. The adult Mike felt angry and betrayed; the little boy Michael felt orphaned and bereft.

"Michael," Rabbi Geller said gently, "I'm not going to leave you. I'll give you my phone number, and you can call me any time of the day or night. I might not be here in shul every day, but I'll be thinking of you when I'm gone, and I'll make sure that you have all the help you need in adjusting to the neighborhood. You'll see, my absence will be a blessing for you."

I didn't believe him then. But after he left, I slowly realized that I *could* function in the community without him. When I needed his advice, I called him, and he answered the phone and gave me all the time I wanted. From afar, I sensed his compassion and understanding as he patiently answered my queries and gave me the spiritual advice and practical guidance I sought.

As it turned out, Rabbi Geller's sabbatical was one of the best things that ever happened to me, because it taught me that a person can be there emotionally even if he isn't there physically. Dad had always been physically present but emotionally absent; Rabbi Geller, on the other hand, remained a reassuring presence in the background even during the year he was away from the shul.

With Rabbi Geller away, I learned that I could be connected to someone without being attached to him at the hip 24/7. This was a process of differentiation and individuation I had never experienced with **my** own father, since I had never been close enough to him to go through any such process.

In halachah, a person's *dalet amos* are his domain, his boundaries, his defined area. Due to his personal limitations, Dad had never been able to create any emotional or behavioral boundaries for me, which left me feeling insecure and untethered. Forging a relationship with Rabbi Geller and becoming a member of his community created an *eiruv* of sorts around me, setting boundaries on my conduct and giving me a sense of belonging. And just when I reached emotional terra firma, Rabbi Geller pushed my boundaries to a new level, by showing me that you can leave without leaving and be close even if you're distant. I could be part of his expanded domain while still maintaining my own *reshus hayachid*, being my own unique self and building my own relationship with Hashem.

Fifteen years after that initial meeting with Rabbi Geller, my wife and I have seven beautiful boys, and I am the president and chief bottle washer at our shul. My clothing are black and white (mostly), and I could easily be mistaken for a zealot. A happy zealot.

Just over a year ago, my Dad passed away at the age of 87, three weeks short of my parents' 65th wedding anniversary. A few days after completing Kaddish for Dad, I had a dream. In the dream, I was calling my mom on my cell phone while on my way to work Sunday morning, as I usually do, and when I called her, Dad answered the phone.

"Hello!" he boomed. His voice was clear as day, just like in old times, and he was sitting and working at his diamond-setting bench on the second floor of our home, drills whirring, radio in the background. I said, "Oh, hi, Dad," and he responded, "Yeah, I'm back upstairs now."

I woke up, comforted by the thought that Dad's stormy soul had finally found peace upstairs in *Gan Eden*. Then I thought about my own life, my own journey, and the island of stability I had carved out with Rabbi Geller's help, and I silently thanked Hashem for helping me find peace, serenity, and truth downstairs in this world.

Postscript:

Finding peace, truth, and serenity in this world is everyone's dream, but the fact is that this is a world of work, struggle, and challenge. As was the case with our forefather Yaakov, just when we think we've arrived and can look forward to a bit of a respite, we discover yet another hurdle ahead of us in our journey.

When "Michael" — a chiropractor by profession — first told me his story, it had a happily-ever-after ending. But when I asked him for a postscript a couple of years after the story was published, he told me that he had recently suffered a career-ending injury. Sidelined by multiple herniated discs in his back, he could no longer help the many patients who came to him for help with their herniated discs. A chiropractor friend of his helped restore his ability to function, but not his ability to do the physically strenuous work he had performed and loved for 30 years.

In his words:

> *I had to confront the biggest fear of my life. How could I possibly survive if I couldn't work as a chiropractor? Without my job, I wondered, how would I pay the bills? And even more to the point, who am I?*

So I hired a life coach — which is possibly the least understood profession out there — to guide me through my maze of confusion and fear, and he helped me set new goals and develop strategies for actualizing them.

I benefited so greatly from his approach that I decided to become a life coach myself, and in the process, I dramatically increased my skill set and brought to the fore personal strengths that had previously existed only in potential.

My injury brought me to an all-time low, but in the end it was a huge gift, because it enabled me to make significant strides. I can say today, with confidence, that my life is happier and more meaningful than ever before.

The hurdles in our lives may seem huge, even insurmountable, when they loom ahead of us. But when we look back at them, we can often see how they were positioned precisely to help us leap higher.

Part 6

חַיִּים שֶׁאֵין בָּהֶם בּוּשָׁה וּכְלִמָּה

A Life in Which There Is No Shame or Humiliation

Quitting the Teacher

As far as I can remember, my class was generally well behaved up until the seventh grade. Other than the occasional *chutzpadik* remark, I don't recall much in the way of anti-authority behavior.

Our sixth-grade general studies teacher was Mr. Krauss, a veteran whose style of teaching was engaging and interesting. He also knew all the tricks that boys like to play — he never sat down on his chair without first examining the seat — and we knew better than to start up with him.

Our general-studies teacher in the seventh grade was supposed to have been Mr. Dadusc, an old-school disciplinarian whom the entire student body feared greatly. When he had yard duty, there were never any fights. One icy stare from "Ol' Daddy" was enough to instill terror in the heart of even the most enterprising troublemaker.

Ol' Daddy was notorious for working his students to the bone, giving them assignment after assignment, and his classroom resembled a military school. Woe to the student who slouched in his seat for even a moment when Ol' Daddy was at the front of the class.

The seventh graders finished learning *limudei kodesh* at 4 o'clock, and by then who had patience for things like geography and spelling? General studies was supposed to be a time to let your hair down and chill a little, not to stand at attention for Ol' Daddy's math drills.

At the end of my sixth-grade year, Mr. Dadusc announced his retirement. My class rejoiced. "No boot camp for us!" we crowed to each other. "We're gonna have a normal teacher next year!"

On the first day of the seventh grade, a slight, youngish-looking fellow with beige slacks and a comb-over hairdo entered our classroom.

"Good afternoon, gentlemen," he said brightly. "My name is Geoffrey Miller. That's Geoffrey, spelled G-E-O-F-F-R-E-Y."

There were a few titters in the room. Mr. Miller's eyes darted around, trying to see where the titters were coming from. "That's the British spelling," he explained. "My father is from England. I've been working in information technology until now," Mr. Miller continued. "Unfortunately, with the economy as it is, I was laid off recently, and I decided to make a career shift and come teach you guys instead."

He paused, looking expectantly at us for a reaction.

For a few seconds, there was silence. I shifted in my seat uncomfortably. Then, Gershon Lieber, who sat behind me, began to clap politely. I followed his example, and before long the entire class was applauding. Shimmy Fishman let out a low whoop.

Mr. Miller looked rather pleased. "Thank you, gentlemen. Now, I'll ask you to please take out your composition notebooks. I'd like you to write a two-page paper entitled 'My Summer Experience.'"

"I don't have a composition notebook," Yisrael Newhouse whined.

"Me neither," a few others piped up.

"Oh, dear," said Mr. Miller. "I guess you can use foolscap, then.'"

"What's a foolscap?" Aharon Ribnitz inquired.

A paper airplane whizzed across the room. Made of foolscap presumably.

"Gentlemen." Mr. Miller's face was turning red. "I expect better decorum from a class of yeshivah boys. We'll leave the 'My Summer Experience' assignment for tomorrow. Please make sure to have your composition notebooks by then. In the meantime, we'll begin our arithmetic lesson."

By the time the bell rang at 6 o'clock to announce dismissal, Mr. Miller was mopping his brow and breathing heavily. He seemed even more relieved than we were to leave the classroom.

"Don't forget the composition notebooks!" he called as we stampeded out the door.

I, for one, was certain that there would not be a single kid in the class with a composition notebook the next day.

I walked home with Gershon Lieber and Yisrael Newhouse. "Good thing we didn't get Ol' Daddy," Yisrael remarked.

"Yeah," Gershon said. "This guy's a piece of cake."

"'G-E-O-F-F-R-E-Y,'" I mimicked. "Do you think that's going to be on our first spelling test?"

Gershon and Yisrael guffawed.

It took a full two weeks before we all had our composition notebooks and Mr. Miller could finally assign his "My Summer Experience" paper. By then, Mr. Miller was talking more about chutzpah and *derech eretz* (he pronounced it "*dare cheiretz*," much to our amusement) than about science or English literature. "Gentlemen!" he would plead. "I can't shout over you. Please, some *dare cheiretz*."

One day, when Mr. Miller was giving us a spelling test and the class was quiet for a change, Yisrael Newhouse raised his hand frantically. Raised hands were something of a rarity in Mr. Miller's class, so Mr. Miller immediately called on him.

"How do you spell your first name again?" Yisrael asked. "I wanted to write it on my paper, but I forgot how to spell it. J-E-F… then what?"

"No, no," Mr. Miller corrected him. "It's G-E-O-F-F —"

He was drowned out by raucous laughter.

"Chutzpah!" he yelled.

"But why?" Yisrael asked, wide-eyed. "I needed to know how to spell your name!"

Mr. Miller's Adam's apple bobbed up and down furiously. "Okay," he said. "Let's move on to the next word. The next word is 'intention.' That's the last word on our spelling test. Now, here's the bonus word. The word is 'discombobulate.' One bonus point for spelling it correctly, and one bonus point for using it correctly in a sentence."

I saw a wicked gleam in Gershon Lieber's eyes, and I peeked at his paper to see what he was writing. He wrote, "Mr. Miller was discombobulated when his student forgot how to spell Geoffrey."

I tried to control myself from laughing, but instead a funny noise came out of my throat, sounding like a gulp. Shmuli Zimmerman, who was sitting next to me, turned in my direction, and I pointed to the sentence that Gershon had written. Shmuli dissolved into helpless laughter.

Mr. Miller marched over to Gershon's desk and snatched his paper. His eyes widened when he saw Gershon's bonus sentence. "Is it good, Teacher?" Gershon asked innocently.

"No bonus points for you!" Mr. Miller bawled.

Gershon's face wrinkled up. "I thought I knew how to spell discombobulate," he said. "Oh, well."

Mr. Miller dismissed us early that day. I felt a surge of satisfaction, mixed with a bit of... Was it guilt?

— · —

Our rebbi that year was Rabbi Feldman. He was a little on the dry side, but no one misbehaved in his class. We saved all our shtick and pent-up energy for Mr. Miller.

Practically every day one kid would shut the lights in our windowless classroom, another kid would quickly tack a large piece of cardboard over the window in the door, and the entire class would breathe, "Oooooohhhhh." As Mr. Miller would fumble toward the light, we'd start chanting, "Teacher's getting angry, Teacher's getting angry."

One day, Yisrael Newhouse slipped out of the classroom and knocked on the door. When Mr. Miller opened the door, there was no one there. Yisrael knocked again a couple of minutes later, and again he ran away before Mr. Miller opened the door. By the time Yisrael knocked a third time, Mr. Miller was good and mad. He raced to the door and yanked it open, hoping to apprehend the culprit before he could make his escape. This time, however, Yisrael had leaned a wooden bench against the outside of the door. When Mr. Miller pulled the door inward, the bench fell forward, smacking Mr. Miller on the forehead. His arms windmilled crazily, and he fell backward. Luckily for him, his fall was broken by Shimmy Fishman's desk.

In the ensuing pandemonium, Yisrael slipped back into the classroom safely.

A couple of weeks later, Shmuli Zimmerman made an astounding discovery. In the next classroom, where the sixth graders learned, there was a piece missing from the drop ceiling. "If we can get hold of a ladder," he said excitedly, "we can climb into the ceiling and crawl on top of our classroom."

The sixth graders were dismissed at 5, an hour before we were. At precisely 5 o'clock, Gershon Lieber raised his hand and asked politely to be excused. He headed straight to the janitor's closet, removed a ladder, and set it up in the sixth-grade classroom. Then he returned to the classroom and nodded to Shmuli.

A few minutes later, Shmuli started humming. "Stop that humming, please," Mr. Miller instructed. Shmuli stopped humming, but after a short while he started again.

"No humming!" Mr. Miller thundered.

Shmuli clapped his hands over his mouth. "Oops," he said blandly.

When Shmuli began humming a third time, Mr. Miller ordered him to leave the room. Shmuli didn't argue; he just stood up and left.

It was not long before I heard noises from the ceiling. I winked at Gershon knowingly.

Mr. Miller turned his back to the class and began writing something on the blackboard. The drop ceiling above him moved slightly to the side, and a finger emerged and started wiggling. The class erupted in laughter.

Mr. Miller whirled around. The finger disappeared, and we forced our faces to be somber. Not seeing any cause for our sudden hilarity, Mr. Miller began looking over his shoulder, trying to see if there was anything stuck to his back. When he was satisfied that there was nothing there, he turned back to the blackboard.

This time, a full hand descended and waved. Once again, we exploded in laughter.

The next day, it was my turn to climb into the ceiling. After asking to be excused, I slipped my eraser into my pocket. I dragged the janitor's ladder into the classroom next door and vaulted myself above the drop ceiling. Then I crawled across the ceiling to where Mr. Miller was standing and dropped the eraser through the opening in the ceiling that Shmuli had made the day before.

Ping! The eraser fell directly onto Mr. Miller's balding head. He looked up, stunned, but he couldn't tell where the eraser had come from. He picked up the eraser, examined it for clues, and then continued with his lesson.

A few days later, Gershon Lieber came up with an even more ingenious plan. "I call it 'The Drip,'" he informed us. "Just wait."

At 5:20, Gershon asked politely to leave the room. About five minutes later, I heard a drip coming from the corner of the classroom. "Oh, dear," said Mr. Miller. "I'd better tell the administrator about this."

Two minutes later, when Mr. Miller was back at his desk, a drop of water landed right in front of him. He looked up, and another drop of water hit him right on the nose. "Hmph," he said, rubbing his nose. "Looks like there's a plumbing problem."

Just then, the drop ceiling moved over a few inches, and a bag of water came sailing down from above, hitting Mr. Miller squarely on the head. By the time he looked up, the ceiling was back in place.

Drenched and furious, Mr. Miller stormed out of the room and headed straight for the office of Mr. Gewirtz, our general-studies principal. In the meantime, Gershon managed to return the ladder to its place and slip back into the classroom.

Neither Mr. Miller nor Mr. Gewirtz could figure out how a water bomb had made its way down from the ceiling. They couldn't punish any of us, because they had no way of proving that any of us had been responsible for the prank. I'm sure Mr. Gewirtz had his suspicions, but he didn't confront any of us directly.

Just to be safe, we waited a few days before continuing to torment Mr. Miller. When we felt confident that the water bomb incident was all but forgotten, we continued where we had left off. We started, once again, with fingers wiggling from the ceiling when Mr. Miller wasn't looking. Shmuli Zimmerman went so far as to put his entire head through the ceiling and stick his tongue out at Mr. Miller, much to the delight of the entire class. Each time the class erupted in laughter at these shenanigans, Mr. Miller would whirl around, trying mightily to figure out what was going on. But he never did.

At one point, he got so desperate that he asked Mr. Gewirtz to sit in on the class for a few days and try to help him pinpoint what was causing the class to go out of control. Needless to say, we were on our best behavior on those days, and Mr. Gewirtz's presence just made Mr. Miller look foolish for accusing us of misbehavior.

After that, Mr. Gewirtz would occasionally stand outside the door to our classroom and watch what was going on inside. He stood at the side of the window in the door so that we wouldn't see him looking in, but Shimmy Fishman's seat was positioned at precisely the right angle to detect any clandestine observers. When Mr. Gewirtz would appear outside the door, Shimmy would let out a loud "Achoo!" and that would be our signal to sit up attentively at our desks and train our eyes on Mr. Miller.

It was shortly before Chanukah, I think, when Gershon got into trouble. That day, he dropped a marble through the ceiling onto Mr. Miller's foot. When he crawled back to the sixth-grade classroom and climbed down the ladder, Mr. Gewirtz was waiting for him.

Gershon was suspended for two weeks, and Mr. Miller gave our entire class detention for a week straight. All that week, we plotted how to get even with Mr. Miller for punishing us.

We settled on a prank that was simple and foolproof, one in which it would be impossible for Mr. Miller to apprehend the perpetrator. Yanky Gartenhaus furnished a tube of rubber cement, and as soon as Rabbi Feldman left for the day, each kid in the class took a turn smearing the teacher's chair with the transparent gooey stuff. Shmuli Zimmerman supervised, making sure that no globs remained. "Even if Geoffrey looks at the chair before he sits down, he won't notice anything unusual," Shmuli assured us.

He needn't have worried. Mr. Miller strode into the classroom that afternoon looking grim and sat down on his chair without even glancing downward. "Take out your literature textbooks, gentlemen," he announced. To his surprise, everyone complied immediately. But when he stood up to write the word 'onomatopoeia' on the board, the chair stood up with him. He struggled to free himself of the chair and then turned slowly to face us, the veins in his temples bulging.

"That's it!" he hissed. "I've had enough of you guys. Good-bye! And good riddance!"

With that, Mr. Miller yanked the chair off his pants, grabbed his briefcase, and fled. We were quite pleased to see that a small piece of his gray slacks remained behind on the chair.

We never saw Mr. Miller again.

Ol' Daddy Dadusc was lured out of retirement, either at gunpoint or with considerable promise of remuneration. From the moment he walked into our classroom, all misbehavior ceased. He kept us too busy reading, writing, and 'rithmetic-ing to even consider pulling any pranks. Besides, you just didn't start up with Ol' Daddy.

———— •◦• ————

It's been a couple of decades since my seventh-grade year. To this day, each time I think back to that year, I am filled with self-loathing at the way my classmates and I tortured Mr. Miller. True, he was inexperienced and perhaps incompetent, but did that give us an excuse to act like savages? And the strangest part is, we weren't bad kids! What possessed us to behave so heartlessly?

I may not have been the instigator or chief executor of most of the pranks we played, but an innocent bystander I wasn't. I don't know how much responsibility I bear now, as an adult, for the way my class behaved back in the seventh grade, but I will forever be haunted by the image of poor Mr. Miller enthusiastically spelling G-E-O-F-F-R-E-Y that first day of school to a class of what he thought were gentlemen.

My own children are young now, too young to know of things like water bombs and rubber cement. But when they get a little older, I think I'll tell them how much I regret quitting the teacher.

Postscript:

After this story was printed, we received this letter from a reader:

> *Could the editor kindly explain the reasoning for printing such a story? Is it to prove that the myths about how chareidi boys treat secular subjects and their instructors are in fact true, and Mishpacha wishes to give its imprimatur on such behavior?*

I'll let another reader's letter answer these questions (bracketed comments are mine):

> *I read last week's LifeLines story with much pain, as I remembered torturing our teachers when we were young [unfortunately, these aren't myths]. We were a very lively class of twenty-eight girls [it's not just boys who do this], and most of us couldn't sit still in class. We were busy with pranks all the time! Poor serious girls in our class, they really suffered.*
>
> *I would like to send a message to youngsters out there nowadays: DON'T DO IT! It's not worth the pain and embarrassment later on! [That was the message of the story, and the reasoning behind its printing.]*
>
> *One story I must mention is about a certain class that recently had difficulties in shidduchim. No one was getting engaged, and they were getting older. Someone remembered that they had tortured a teacher very badly when they were younger. They called the teacher and begged for forgiveness. It wasn't easy for her to forgive, because she was still wounded, but she did, and the girls started to find their basherts from then on!*

Well said.

No Student Left Behind

The mark at the top of my first tenth-grade *Navi* test said 32, and beside it Mrs. Davis had written, "Please see me after class."

I cringed, knowing that I was about to get a lecture, but unsure what she was going to lecture me about. Mrs. Davis certainly couldn't accuse me of not paying attention in class, since I was one of the most avid participants in the classroom, asking questions, raising my hand to answer her questions, and offering my thoughts on the class discussions she initiated.

I was used to being lectured by teachers, especially after the first test of the year. They told me I was irresponsible, that I didn't take school seriously enough, that I didn't study enough, that I was lazy, that if I only *tried* I would be able to get 90's... I'd heard it all. But I really didn't want to be lectured by Mrs. Davis. She was the cutest teacher, and everyone looked forward to her class. I really enjoyed her style of bringing the words of the *Navi* alive, and I desperately wanted her to like me.

To my surprise and relief, Mrs. Davis didn't lecture me when I approached her timidly after class. "I see you had some trouble with the test," she told me matter-of-factly. "Would you like to take an open-book retest? I'll allow you to look inside the *Navi* and your notes."

I nodded eagerly, too overcome with gratitude and admiration to get a word out of my mouth.

Mrs. Davis smiled. "Well, then, come see me in the teachers' room tomorrow during lunchtime, and I'll give you the retest then. Just make sure to study well tonight, okay?"

"Sure," I managed to croak.

That night, I studied like never before. From the minute I came home until the minute I went to sleep I had my *sefer Yeshayahu* and my notes from Mrs. Davis's class open in front of me, trying as hard as I could to cram the information into my head.

The next day I met Mrs. Davis in the teachers' room, and she handed me the retest. "It's the same test as the first one," she informed me. "I'm sure you'll do a great job."

Taking the test with my notes open in front of me made a world of a difference, and I was able to answer almost all of the questions on the test this time around. It didn't help me that much to look inside the *Navi*, because Hebrew was gibberish to me, so there were a few questions that I had to skip. But my test paper this time around looked very different from the half-empty paper I had handed in the first time.

Two days later, Mrs. Davis called me over after class and handed me back my retest. When I saw the mark — 81 — I was thrilled! I *never* got 80's, in any subject.

So why wasn't Mrs. Davis smiling?

"Shira," she said in that teacher's voice I recognized so well, "I'm really disappointed with you. I made this test as easy as possible for you — I let you use your *Navi*, your notes. I even gave you the same test as the first time! There's absolutely no reason you shouldn't have gotten a hundred on this test. All you had to do was study a little.

"You know," she continued, lowering her voice, "I was just like you in high school. In class I listened, I asked great questions, and I knew all the answers. But after school, I wasn't interested in studying, so I got horrible grades. Until at some point I buckled down and started studying. From then on, I did wonderfully — and here I am, teaching *Navi* today!" she concluded triumphantly.

"I did study," I mumbled, my face feeling very hot.

"You'll study better next time," Mrs. Davis said sweetly.

I never raised my hand again in Mrs. Davis's class.

From the time I was in pre-1A I knew I was dumb. All the other kids were catching on to the *nekudos* effortlessly, while I for the life of me couldn't tell the difference between a *kamatz* and a *pasach*. In the first grade, when we started learning to read English, it was no better. How was I supposed to tell a *b* from a *d*? Or a *p* from a *q*? And math? That was the worst! Of course two and two made four, but why all the funny lines and symbols? What did "greater than" and "less than" mean? What was equals? What was minus?

I spent half my school day in the resource room, and my evenings and Sundays were spent sitting at home with tutors while my friends played outside and had fun. I remember my tutors sitting with me and trying to coax the answers out of me. "It's easy!" they used to tell me. *For me it's hard*, I used to think. *So I must be really, really dumb.* Eventually, the tutors would get frustrated and give up, saying that they couldn't work with a kid who didn't cooperate.

I must have gone through dozens of evaluations by educational psychologists, who tried valiantly to find a fancy name for why I wasn't learning the way other kids did. I was tested for dyslexia, for hearing problems, for speech-language issues, but no one could find a label to stick to me. My IQ was above average, I had a good memory, my vocabulary was great. "Your daughter must be suffering from a learning disability that hasn't been discovered yet!" one reading specialist told my mother in frustration.

There were some subjects in school that I liked: art, gym, music. I also liked subjects that involved storytelling, such as *parashah*, *Chumash*, *Navi*, and History. But the rest of school was a disaster for me. Language subjects, in particular, were torture. I couldn't handle English, let alone Hebrew, French, or Spanish. Math was also its own language, the vocabulary becoming ever stranger with each passing year — integers, exponents, isosceles triangles... I couldn't handle science either, what with its talk of monocots and dicots — in second grade! — and things like cytoplasm, vacuoles, and Golgi bodies. It was all Greek to me.

In elementary school, I was a teacher's nightmare. Not only did I fail every test and skip every homework assignment, I also acted out in class and was *chutzpadik* to the teachers. I remember sending pencils flying across the room and going "vroom, vroom" as though I was driving a car. Once, I snuck some bread onto the windowsill during class, and when some birds landed on the windowsill, I opened the window and let them into the classroom.

My teachers didn't know what to do with me, besides sending me to the principal and giving me lots of warnings. Nor did they know what to do about my dismal grades, besides chastising me for not putting in enough effort and telling me that I could do better if I would only put my mind to it.

My parents were pained by my failure in school, and they tried to help me by sitting and studying with me and hiring private tutors for me. But they couldn't understand what I was going through, since everyone else in my family was smart and had no trouble learning, and they alternated between feeling bad for me and being disappointed in me.

When I started high school, I resolved that I was going to be a good student. I listened, I took notes, I asked questions. I even tried to do homework, at least at the beginning of the year, before the teachers started to ignore me.

They typically started ignoring me about a month into the school year, after the first test. Until then, I was an active participant in the classroom, and the teachers would call on me just like anyone else. But when they saw the failing grade on my first test paper, they'd assume that I wasn't serious, that I didn't care, and subsequently, when they surveyed the classroom, their eyes would skip over me as though I didn't exist.

Rarely did a teacher call me aside to discuss my pathetic test scores, and when they did, it was usually to excoriate me for my lack of effort. After all, if a student understands all the material in class and asks great questions, that means that she should do well on the test, right? Especially when they gave me a "special, easy" test. But no test was easy for me; I wasn't born to take tests, it seemed.

The pattern repeated itself every year of high school, in almost every class.

The notable exception was Rabbi Abrams, our twelfth-grade halachah teacher. Halachah was not one of my good subjects; I didn't "speak" the language of halachah, and I could never remember the difference between a *k'zayis* and a *revi'is*. But Rabbi Abrams didn't made me feel dumb, the way most other teachers did.

After the first test of the year, he called me over after class and said, "I see that you're having a hard time. What do you think would help you to improve?"

I didn't know how I could improve, but just being asked made me feel a thousand times better about myself.

Somehow, Rabbi Abrams figured out that I was artistic, and one time, when we were learning about the *melachos* of weaving, he called me up to the board and asked me to draw a loom. "Wow," he marveled when I finished. "That looks *real!*"

I think that what saved me in high school was the fact that I was talented in art and music. If I couldn't solve a quadratic equation to save my life, at least I could paint gorgeous sceneries and sing heart-stirring solos. If I hated every minute of class, at least I could look forward to the school's annual production.

In the twelfth grade, I was head of choir for the production. Occasionally, when Rabbi Abrams would pass me in the hall, he'd ask me, "How's production going?" He did the same for many of the other girls, especially the ones who were academically weak.

I don't remember any of my other teachers complimenting me on my role in the production or showing an interest in my extracurricular activities. It was as though they believed that acknowledging my contribution to the school production would somehow justify my academic underachievement and make me take my schoolwork even less seriously.

I chose to go to a seminary that didn't focus on academics, but rather on *hashkafah* and life skills. I loved the classes, but I was shocked to see where many of the girls were holding in terms of their *frumkeit* and life decisions. Every girl in the seminary had suffered through 12 years of school just as I had — some had low IQs, others were learning disabled, some had family issues that prevented them from focusing on their schoolwork — and their self-esteem was destroyed. Embittered by their school experience, several girls had resorted to drugs or other self-destructive behaviors, while others had thrown away different aspects of their *Yiddishkeit*: Shabbos, *tznius*, *kashrus*, you name it.

I wasn't holding *there*, thank Heaven, but inside I was just as much of a broken vessel as the others. Grade school might be only 12 years out of a person's life, but those years are formative years, and continuously feeling like a loser between ages 6 and 18 doesn't do much for your self-image.

In seminary, where the teachers looked at me as a human being rather than judging me by my grades, I learned to value myself for the things that really mattered, like being kind and compassionate to others, and to look at myself as a success just by virtue of the fact that I was created in Hashem's image.

There was no question in my mind what I was going to do after seminary. I was going to become a teacher, of course. Having suffered so much in school, I felt compelled to right the wrongs I had experienced as a student.

I had always been great with kids, and I loved teaching. Once I managed to learn something, I had a knack for giving it over in a way people could understand. I was going to be the perfect teacher, the one who would truly understand the difficulties her students were experiencing and ensure that each and every student was able to learn.

I started off as an assistant in a first-grade class. If the teacher's job was primarily to stand in the front of the classroom and teach a group of students, my job was to circulate around the classroom, pinpoint the kids who needed help, and work individually with those kids.

When I'd see a kid sitting there with a blank face while the teacher, Mrs. Engel, was talking, my heart would go out to her. I had a soft spot in my heart for one student in particular, Racheli Kantor, who was always struggling to follow Mrs. Engel's instructions and keep up with the class. Remembering what it was like for me in first grade when the teacher started talking about pluses and minuses, I'd go over to Racheli's desk quietly and start telling her stories of how I first had five candies and then someone took away three, so how many was I left with?

I thought Racheli would have an easier time understanding the lesson if I told her a story, just as I had always learned better through stories than through straight information, but she continued to space out no matter how hard I tried to enliven what the teacher was teaching. To my great consternation, I actually found myself becoming frustrated with her for not paying attention. *Why won't she cooperate?* I thought to myself as I gritted my teeth and tried telling my story about the candies yet another time.

When I almost said the words "This is so easy!" to Racheli, I realized that it was time for me to get help. I wasn't going to be like my old tutors who had tried the same old tricks again and again to get to me to understand, until they finally gave up and blamed me for being uncooperative, or made me feel dumb by telling me, "It's easy."

It was very humiliating for me to have to approach Mrs. Farkas, the head of the school's resource room, and tell her that I was having trouble getting through to one of my students. Once again, I was back in the resource room, in need of extra help.

I told Mrs. Farkas about Racheli, and how I was trying so hard to translate the concepts into words that she could grasp. "That was the only way I was able to learn when I was in school," I said, "but it's just not working with Racheli."

"There are two types of teachers," Mrs. Farkas explained to me. "The ones who aced their way through school, and the ones who weren't the greatest students. Each has a particular pitfall in reaching out to weaker students. The ones who were top students often have trouble relating to the weaker students because they never experienced any difficulty themselves, and the ones who weren't top students often assume that the learning strategy that worked for them will work for their students as well. What they fail to realize is that every student learns differently, and that by trying to recreate the remedy that worked for them, they may actually be erecting a learning barrier for their student."

Listening to her speak, I could just hear Mrs. Davis's voice telling me, *I was just like you in high school*, and I could still feel the burning shame of being told that I must not be trying hard enough if I wasn't succeeding the way she did.

I listened eagerly as Mrs. Farkas gave some suggestions for working with Racheli. "Give her short goals, a couple of math problems or words at a time, so she won't be overwhelmed," she said. "And find something to compliment her for, even if the only good thing you can say is that she remembered to bring her pencil case to school."

The next day, when I saw that blank look come over Racheli's face as Mrs. Engel handed out a writing exercise with words starting with the letter *d*, I made my way over to Racheli's desk and whispered, "I see your pencil is sharpened and you're all ready to write! Good for you! Let's see you write the first two words, and after that I'll come back to you."

When I came back a couple of minutes later, I saw that Racheli had written "dot" and "den."

"Great job!" I told her. "Now I bet you can do three more by the time I come back to you again."

Was that a flicker of pride in Racheli's eyes?

———◆———

I worked as an assistant for a couple of years, and today I'm a full-fledged first-grade teacher. I love my job, but I consider it a huge responsibility, and I ask myself every day whether I'm getting through to every single kid in my classroom. If the answer is no, I don't hesitate to consult with the experts, because I now realize that the truly heroic teacher is not the one who *thinks* she understands her students, but rather the one who's willing to admit when she doesn't understand and seeks help in order to reach out to every student successfully.

Postscript:

"Come on, you can do it!" Are those encouraging words or discouraging words? It depends on who you ask. Some people might feel empowered by the knowledge that someone believes they can do it; others might feel irritated, or ashamed, upon hearing that they can do something when they feel they can't.

One of the tricky things about being a teacher is that what works for one student doesn't work for another. What one student appreciates another hates.

The story "No Student Left Behind" didn't advocate any particular approach to dealing with struggling students. Rather, it emphasized the need for educators to tailor their approach to the needs of the individual student. I was happy to see that at least one rebbi took this message to heart. He wrote:

> Thank you so much for printing your story. I am a rebbi who deals with many such cases, but I was having an extremely difficult time getting through to a boy in my class. He felt that I didn't understand him, and I felt that he simply wasn't interested or trying hard enough. But after reading your story I found that I possibly understood him a lot better. When I sat down to speak to him Sunday afternoon, with a new approach on how we would work out a solution so that he wouldn't just let another year of his life go by wasted, he smiled and said, "Thank you, rebbi. You finally do understand me."

Sheva Berachos Eulogy

Have you ever noticed that every *simchah* has a theme? I'm not talking about the color scheme or any other aspect of the decor; I'm talking about the nature of the speeches.

The "theme" at my *aufruf* was pretty typical and serious: "*Chassan domeh l'melech* — A *chassan* is similar to a king." One speaker focused on the special privileges enjoyed by both a *chassan* and a king; another speaker talked about the potential of a brand-new kingdom and a brand-new marriage. A third speaker mentioned that a *chassan*'s sins are forgiven just as a new king's sins are forgiven.

After about three or four of these speeches, I was bored to tears. Everyone else was, too, I'm sure, but I was the only one who had to look genuinely interested and thank each speaker warmly for his sage advice and inspiration. When *shalosh seudos* was over and with it the speeches of the day, I breathed a sigh of relief while bracing myself for the myriad *sheva berachos* speeches that I would be subjected to in a few short days.

The theme of our first *sheva berachos* was again very typical: "*Invei hagefen b'invei hagefen.*" There were about four or five speakers, and each one highlighted a different reason why the *shidduch* between me and my *kallah*, Naomi, was *so* perfect. When Naomi and I left that *sheva berachos*, I commented, "I've heard quite enough about '*invei hagefen b'invei hagefen.*' I hope the theme of tomorrow night's speeches is more original."

Well, my wish came true.

Sheva berachos the next night was hosted by my uncles and aunts, and my cousin Tuli was the emcee. Just after the appetizer was served, Tuli stood up and gave his introductory remarks. "Now that Binyamin's married," he announced, "his *aveiros* are a thing of the past. I'm sure everyone remembers that last Shabbos we talked about how a *chassan* is like a king and how his *aveiros* are forgiven. So now we can reminisce about the good old days."

Tuli's eyes gleamed. I shifted uncomfortably in my chair, wondering which memories he was about to dredge up.

I didn't have to wonder for long. Tuli called up his two younger brothers, Menachem and Zevi, and the three of them proceeded to sing a lively *grammen*.

The beginning of the *grammen* was tasteful and witty, and both Naomi and I were happy to listen to some musical diversion instead of being subjected to yet another speech. But then the tone of the *grammen* changed abruptly.

Binyamin, your aveiros have been forgiven. Now we no longer have to keep them hidden. It's a good thing Naomi didn't know you earlier in life. Because if she had, she would never have agreed to be your wife.

A ripple of laughter spread through the crowd as my three cousins launched into the lively refrain of "na na na na na na na." I forced myself to laugh along, and Naomi tittered, too.

This was the next stanza:

We all remember when you learned to drive. You drove so fast, it's a miracle you're alive. You were almost arrested for reckless driving. But you managed to get out of it with some old-fashioned lying.

I felt the blood drain from my face as I remembered that humiliating incident. I had learned my lesson after my brush with the law, and I've been a safe driver ever since. But the memory of that episode made me cringe. I didn't dare look at Naomi.

I realized that my cousins had paused and were waiting for some sort of reaction from me. "Cheap rhyme, driving and lying," was all I could muster.

"O.K., the next one is better," Tuli declared. He cleared his voice and motioned to Menachem and Zevi to continue.

Naomi doesn't know about your past adventures. How you beat us up so badly we almost needed dentures. You've always been our favorite cousin. Black eyes you must have given us half a dozen.

"How do you like that rhyme?" Tuli whispered triumphantly in my direction. "Adventures/dentures?"

"And cousin/dozen was mine!" 12-year-old Zevi piped up.

"Brilliant," I said grimly as I stole a sidelong glance at Naomi. She was looking a bit green.

I looked around the room. On the women's side, no one seemed to be paying much attention; they were too busy yakking. On the men's side, though, everyone was riveted, and they seemed to be enjoying the *grammen* immensely.

We'll never forget the day the yeshivah kicked you out. Your parents and rebbeim were not very proud. There's no question you deserved to get the sack. But you managed to sweet-talk them into taking you back.

Mercifully, the *grammen* came to an end a few stanzas later. Weak-kneed, I walked up to my cousins and gave them some hearty slaps on the back.

"We worked on it all week," Menachem said proudly. "It's not easy to come up with all those rhymes."

"I'm sure it isn't," I managed to say.

The *grammen* was followed by my Uncle Shmayah's fond recollection of the pranks I used to pull in shul as a kid. That wasn't as bad as the *grammen*, but I found myself squirming in my seat nonetheless and thinking nostalgically about "*chassan domeh l'melech*" and "*invei hagefen b'invei hagefen*."

That *grammen* pretty much set the tone for the rest of that night's *sheva berachos*. Every speaker — even the most serious ones, like my grandfather — had to begin his speech with a reference to a line in the *grammen*. The theme of the *sheva berachos* became "heckle Binyamin." Each of the speakers thought he was being witty and original, but I didn't find their jokes funny at all.

At the end of the *sheva berachos*, my father-in-law came over to wish me *mazel tov*. "A *sheva berachos* is like a funeral," he commented. "They either eulogize you or bury you. This one goes into the second category."

I laughed, trying to sound lighthearted. "It was all in good humor," I assured my father-in-law, hoping that he didn't believe the things he had heard about me. I was even more concerned about what Naomi was thinking. *Was she disturbed by what she heard tonight?* I wondered. *And would I make things better or worse by offering explanations?*

Naomi was very quiet when we left the *sheva berachos*. I didn't know what to say to her, and she said she was tired, so we didn't talk much that night.

The next morning I tried to make conversation as Naomi and I were eating breakfast. Naomi looked uncomfortable, and at some point she blurted out, "What's this with you being kicked out of yeshivah?"

My heart sank. "It really wasn't such a big deal," I said. "When I was 14, I wasn't interested in learning night *seder*, and I played card games with my friends in the dorm instead. The *mashgiach* caught us one night and suspended me and a few other guys for a week."

"Oh," Naomi said. There was silence again.

"You have to understand," I hurried to explain. "Most boys at 14 aren't able to learn all day. It's not unusual at all. Eventually I got used to the yeshivah's schedule and settled down, and I've been learning three solid *sedarim* ever since."

"And what was all that about your adventures and pranks?" Naomi inquired, her voice a bit unsteady.

"They were exaggerating," I said. "It was nothing more than any other *bachurim* do. They say these kinds of things about every *chassan* in my family, don't worry."

"I guess I haven't been to any other *sheva berachos* in your family," Naomi said.

I could tell that she was troubled, but I didn't know what I was supposed to do about it. Should I start making confessions about everything I had ever done as a young *bachur* and give Naomi my solemn assurance that I would never do those things again? Honestly, I didn't think I owed her any explanations. I had grown up since those days, and I was no longer a wild, immature kid. Even if she would be understanding about my past misadventures, I was sure that knowing the details of my every indiscretion would make her lose respect for me.

As the days of *sheva berachos* went on, I saw that Naomi was still very rattled by what she heard at our second *sheva berachos*. Instead of spending the first few days and weeks of our marriage in pleasant conversation and companionship, I found myself making excuses for my past behavior and reassuring Naomi that I hadn't been hiding anything from her during our courtship and engagement. It took quite some time for her to regain the trust and respect we had built up prior to that *sheva berachos*, and my confidence as a new husband was sorely shaken.

Since then, I've thought back many times to the family *sheva berachos* I attended before my own wedding, and I remembered the speeches I had given at those occasions. My speeches had been very funny — or at least I had thought so at the time. Now, from my new vantage point, I wondered whether the *chassanim* I had heckled had suffered as much from my speeches as I had suffered from the speeches at my own *sheva berachos* funeral.

I shudder to think of the damage I may have done to other couples with the good-natured digs I delivered at their *sheva berachos*, and I really have no way of making amends for those digs.

Nowadays, when I'm asked to speak at an *aufruf* or *sheva berachos*, I stick to safe topics like "*chassan domeh l'melech*" or "*invei hagefen b'invei hagefen*," and I make a point of saying something nice about the *chassan*. My philosophy is, I'd rather give a boring eulogy than a brilliant burial.

Postscript:

Writing is a solitary pursuit. No matter how many people ultimately read what you've written, the experience of writing involves one person (you) and a computer screen.

So writing a LifeLines story is like shooting an arrow blindly; I never know whether it's going to strike the target.

Sometimes readers write to let me know that the arrow hit the bull's-eye. (When the arrow misses, they definitely write!) Often, however, a story generates little or no reader feedback, which leaves me to wonder whether the story made its mark.

After "Sheva Berachos Funeral" was printed, I didn't hear from any readers. But then I received this e-mail from a colleague:

> *I was at a sheva berachos and the speaker, a chashuve rav, got up and said he has to be careful what he says because he doesn't want to be like in the Mishpacha story. And everyone got the reference.*

Just how many chassanim were spared a "roasting" because of the story, we'll never know.

Sticky Fingers

"I want to thank you for having me, Mrs. Goldberg," said Jenny, the newly minted *ba'alas teshuvah* we had hosted for Shabbos. "It was really nice getting to know your family. Your kids are so well behaved."

"It was our pleasure," I said, smiling. *And the kids behaved a lot better with a stranger around.*

Jenny zipped up her coat and slung her overnight bag over her shoulder. "Oh, just one thing," she added. "I had a hundred dollars in my wallet, and it seems to have gone missing. If it turns up, can you let me know?"

My blood ran cold. "Sure," I replied, forcing myself to look Jenny in the eye.

I knew exactly what had happened to Jenny's hundred dollars. It was stolen. And the thief was my own son.

———◆———

Fourteen-year-old Meir had been stealing since he was about 10. At first, he would sneak money from the house and buy candy to eat or share with his friends. Then he started "finding" things: fancy pens, little toys from other kids' lunch bags, money. "I found it under a rock in the yard," he'd explain. Or, "It was just sitting on the bench in the park when I passed by."

"How could that be?" I'd challenge him. "No one leaves their pen under a rock in the yard."

"But it's true!" he'd protest, bursting into tears. "That's where it was!"

My husband Sruli and I consulted with *rabbanim, mechanchim,* and professionals and got all sorts of advice — much of it conflicting — on how to deal with Meir's stealing, but nothing seemed to help. We were told that if a kid steals, it means he is lacking something in his life, but, *baruch Hashem,* neither Meir nor my other children could be described as lacking in the material sense.

The only thing Meir lacked was friends, because he was shy and timid, but friends were not something we could have supplied him with. He began stealing as a way to buy friends — literally. We tried giving him a generous allowance, but it didn't help. He continued to steal, while squirreling away his allowance.

Most of the experts we spoke to told us that there really isn't an all-encompassing solution to the stealing issue; it's something kids grow out of (or don't, *lo aleinu*). "You just have to wait it out and do the best you can," we were told. But that was an incredibly difficult strategy to follow.

As Meir got older, he stole more, and perfected the art of deception to the degree that I could no longer tell when he was lying to me and when he was telling the truth. The stories he told became extraordinarily believable, so I felt silly and paranoid each time I confronted him, even as I knew in my heart that my suspicions were well founded.

Once, we discovered that he had bought himself a new bike and hidden it at a friend's house. By the time we found it, we could no longer get back the money he had paid for it, nor did we know where the money had come from. My wallet? The shul's *pushka?* The neighbor's purse?

"Ma, my babysitting money is missing!" my teenage daughter Riva wailed one morning. "And I needed it to chip in for a present for my friend!"

I knew what had happened to the money, and so did Riva. From then on, I told her and all the other children to deposit their money in the bank or give it to my husband Sruli for safekeeping; otherwise, I could not take responsibility for it.

Sruli and I began hiding all of our cash and credit cards in our bedroom safe — until money started to go missing from there, too. We realized with dismay that Meir had found a way to break into the safe. From then on we stopped keeping money in the house entirely; the only cash or credit cards to be had were safely stowed in Sruli's pocket. I couldn't keep a penny in my own purse.

By the time Meir became bar mitzvah, the stealing wasn't for his friends anymore. It was a way for him to get what he wanted *now* without any effort. I hate to use the word "lazy," but that really described Meir's whole gestalt. He was a bright kid, but he kept failing in yeshivah because everything was "too hard." He didn't want to work at his learning, and he refused to do anything at home.

Meir's two older sisters called him "the *poritz*" because of the way he would sprawl out on the couch, his long legs extending well into the living room where the younger kids invariably tripped over them. He couldn't be bothered to pull in his legs even when people politely said, "Excuse me." Instead, he'd holler at them, "I'm resting, get out of my way."

If I'd ask him to take out the garbage, or pick up the screaming baby, or even go answer the door, his face would take on this wounded look. "I worked so hard today," he'd groan. "I can't move."

Meir did have a long day at yeshivah, that was true. But even on Shabbos, or during *bein hazemanim*, he refused to pitch in at all. One Pesach, he walked around all Yom Tov grumbling about how hard he had worked, when the only thing he had done was take some new dishes to be *toiveled*. His younger brother had vacuumed the car, scrubbed half a dozen kitchen cabinets, and babysat the little ones the week before Pesach, but Meir was the one who was too tired to even lift his own plate off the table. He wasn't too tired to go play baseball or basketball for hours every day, though.

———•———

Shortly after Meir began high school, he stole a large amount of money from a classmate. When the heist was discovered, Meir was expelled. "Not for stealing," the *rosh yeshivah* explained to me, "but for all the lies he told when he was apprehended."

Now that the nearby yeshivah had thrown him out, Sruli and I were in a quandary. We would have to find Meir a yeshivah in a different part of town, or perhaps in a different city altogether, but how could we put him in a dorm with his sticky fingers? Besides, the mainstream yeshivos we contacted were not very enthusiastic about taking Meir, and we were advised not to put him in a yeshivah for troubled kids. "You'll only make things worse if you put him together with kids who have serious problems," several *mechanchim* told us.

And so Meir remained at home as we continued to search for a suitable yeshivah for him.

I never thought a mother could hate her own child, but when your teenage son is home all day whiling away his time with a doodling pad and pencil, refusing to even go to the grocery, complaining about absolutely everything, plus lying and stealing regularly, at some point you start feeling a surge of animosity toward him. At least I did. And it frightened me.

"I need to get help," I told Sruli. "This situation is unbearable."

Not knowing where to turn, I joined a forum for *frum* parents of kids at risk, describing my situation and calling out for help. One of the people who responded was Mrs. Ita Kurland, a social worker and certified parent-teen coach. I was impressed with her sympathetic tone and her pragmatic advice, so I began corresponding with her.

Ita introduced me to something called Choice Theory, a psychological theory that posits, among other things, that "the only person whose behavior we can control is our own. All we can give another person is information."

"You can't force your child to stop stealing or any other self-destructive behavior," Ita explained. "All you can do, as Meir's mother, is provide him with a stable, loving environment where his relationship with his parents and his family takes precedence in any discussion you have with him. That means no criticism, no blaming, no asking where things came from, no checking up on him."

"So what are we supposed to do?" I asked. "Let him steal whatever we wants without saying a word?"

"Honestly," she responded, "all the accusations, the suspicious questions, the nagging — are they getting you anywhere? Do they stop Meir from stealing the next time?"

"No," I admitted. "Most of the time Meir makes up a story that we can't disprove, and we've ended up with a *hashavas aveidah* box that's overflowing with expensive gadgets and cash. We've tried to get him to make restitution to the people he steals from, but usually we don't know who they are."

"So what good does all the accusing do for you?" Ita challenged me. "Your confronting, confiscating, and punishing isn't changing his behavior. It only severs your relationship with him. The only way you're going to get through to him — in the long run, I mean — is by giving him unconditional love, trust, and respect."

I had heard a lot about unconditional love in various *chinuch shiurim* and books. But it never translated into action for me, because when your kid is stealing, what are you supposed to say? "I love you unconditionally, but, uh, what about that camera I found stashed away in your drawer?"

"Unconditional love doesn't mean that you like or accept everything the child does," Ita explained. "What it means is that you see the child as basically good and trustworthy and you don't try to change his behavior. At this point, you can't anyway."

That's when it clicked for me: a parent's relationship with any child has a portion that is static and a portion that evolves as the child grows and matures. The static part is "I love you because you're my child, period. It doesn't matter what you look like, how you behave, or what your capabilities, accomplishments, and failures are." The part that evolves is how the parent-child relationship works. By the time the child is a teen, I am no longer his teacher, who makes decisions and ensures they are implemented. If he asks me for advice, I can offer it, but the choices he makes in the end are his own, and whether or not he lives up to my standards, he will have to deal with the repercussions of his own actions.

My *tafkid* now, I realized, was to empathize with Meir's difficulties when he made bad decisions, encourage him when he made good ones, and, most importantly, daven that he mature into a healthy adult who would bring *nachas* to the *Ribbono shel Olam*.

My love for Meir had to be purely unconditional; it was no longer my place to discipline him or attempting to influence his behavior. So I stopped trying to be *mechanech* him. The mantra I chose from Ita's toolbox was "Is this going to build or hurt my relationship with Meir?" I asked myself this question before saying or doing anything to Meir, and if the answer was "It's going to hurt the relationship," I stopped myself in my tracks — even if it meant ignoring unacceptable behavior.

"But how can I ignore unacceptable behavior?" I questioned. "If Meir steals, how do I condone that?"

"You're not condoning anything," Ita replied. "Meir knows that stealing is wrong. Every time he steals, he feels dirty and degraded inside, even though he puts on a 'who cares' attitude for everyone around him. Can you imagine how much he's hurting inside if he's resorting to these behaviors?"

Shortly after I made the decision to shower Meir with unconditional love exclusively, I found a receipt and warranty for $320 in Rollerblading gear, which I later found hidden away in the garage. I knew Meir had stolen the money for the equipment, but I didn't say a word to him. *It's his problem*, I told myself. *All I can do is daven for him with a mother's tears and love him and be as caring and sympathetic a mother as I know how to be.*

My worst fear was that one day Meir would be arrested for stealing — or worse. When I confided this fear to Ita, she helped me to develop a plan of action for that eventuality. Sruli and I debated the pros and cons of bailing Meir out of jail immediately versus letting him stay in a juvenile detention center for a short while. We also found out which connections we'd need to pull if there was indeed trouble with the police. After we decided how we'd proceed in this nightmare scenario, I felt a lot calmer.

When Meir wasn't home, I sat down with the other children and explained to them why I was letting Meir get away with all sorts of negative behavior. "He's like a person in a wheelchair," I told them. "He has a problem, and that's why he's acting this way. In some ways, he's like a handicapped person, so we can't impose any expectations on him. If he does anything helpful, even the smallest thing, we have to be grateful."

Letting go was not easy, and I needed Ita to keep pointing out ways that I was trying to subtly control my son and advise me how to remain consistently warm, supportive, and loving toward Meir, no matter how irritating and infuriating his behavior was. With her prompting, I would smile sweetly at him even as he lay on the couch while everyone else was frantically getting the house ready for Shabbos, or pat him on the shoulder as I led away his bawling younger sister, whom he was teasing mercilessly.

I thought the kids would be resentful of Meir's special treatment, but they weren't. They followed my cues naturally, accepting the fact that Meir was different and had to be handled with kid gloves.

Ita cautioned me that I had to protect the other children, even as I made allowances for Meir. "Even with unconditional love," she said, "there has to be a red line, and that line is where his behavior is dangerous to others. But the point is that you're there for your other kids, not that you're punishing or castigating Meir."

At some point, my correspondence with Ita morphed into something bigger: Ita became my personal parenting coach in dealing with Meir on a voluntary basis. I would call or e-mail her for guidance, encouragement, or a listening ear, crying out my frustration to her instead of turning it on Meir or unloading it on Sruli, who was having as hard a time as I was.

Neither Meir nor the other children knew that my every step vis-à-vis Meir was carefully choreographed with Ita beforehand and analyzed afterward with her. To them, the change was subtle and hardly noticeable, even though for me it was huge.

The results were huge, too — and immediate. It was as though the balloon of tension in the house popped the moment I decided to stop trying to control Meir's actions in any way. Not only did I become more relaxed, but Meir became a different person almost overnight.

Did he stop stealing? No, at least not right away, but his stealing did become a nonissue immediately. His lying also petered out, because when people don't nag you about where you've gone, what you've been up to, and what you have in your pocket, there's not much impetus to lie. Most astonishing to me was how quickly he gave up pestering his siblings and refusing to pitch in at home. It seemed as though these behaviors simply began to evaporate the moment I — and, by extension, the rest of the family — began to accept Meir as he was rather than radiating resentment at him.

———◆———

It took a few more years for Meir to quit stealing and outgrow his other bad habits, but outgrow them he did, thankfully without the involvement of the police.

Hashem works in wonderful ways, and although Meir still has a lot of growing to do, I am confident that he will eventually find himself and settle down. In the meantime, I know that I have done everything I could to lay the foundation for that to happen. The rest of my job is *tefillos*.

Recently, on my birthday, Meir presented me with letter. The end of the letter read:

> *Mommy, there's one small thing I want to tell you: you are the most precious thing that I have in my life. In the last few years we have all changed, and I finally see you differently. I see the delight, the laughter, the love, the happiness, the dreams, and the hopes that you have, and I sit and think about the times that passed and how I have moved forward — how we all have. I know that I have hurt you many times, but you never gave up on me. All of my dreams are in your zechus, Mommy, and only because of your love for me have I pushed myself to keep reaching for them.*
>
> *With love and acceptance,*
>
> *Your son, Meir*

Postscript:

Sometime after the publication of this story, I received the following e-mail from a reader named Devorah Weiss:

As a social worker, I've had personal and clinical experiences with so many of the stories you write and they are so true and compelling. I have quite a collection that I've cut out, scanned, and saved on my computer to share with clients when appropriate.

I treat myself each Thursday night (regardless of how much work I have to do) to LifeLines. Only after licht bentching do I permit myself to sit and enjoy the rest of the magazine!

Sitting at the kitchen table one Thursday night, I was intrigued by the "Sticky Fingers" article. I really related to Mrs. Goldberg's pain, frustrations, and fears, reading each word and sentence twice. Turning the page, I was introduced to Mrs. Ita Kurland. Imagine that, I said to myself. There's someone else who's a social worker, parent-teen coach, and into choice theory. Then I started shaking — the words on the page sounded like they had come out of my mouth! My words, expressions, and insight! But I simply couldn't remember the case or client. I called a few clients who might possibly have been behind the story, even though I wasn't a hundred percent sure the story was about me!

Sitting at work one day, I received an e-mail from Mrs. Goldberg herself. Do I get Mishpacha, and if so did I read "Sticky Fingers"? If not, she'd send it to me.

Yup, it was her and me.

Yeah, confirmation! I quickly wrote back that she had just solved the three-week mystery. She blew me away, revealing that the story was written as hakaras hatov to Hashem for sending me to help her and in the hope that through the article she would be able to give back by helping others. We resumed our friendship, and we both agreed that it was important to share this parenting approach with others.

For years, I had wanted to restart the very successful e-mail support group I had once run, and I approached family service *organizations for assistance. But I never managed to get the group off the ground again — until the "Sticky Fingers" story was printed and about forty new parents contacted me, from all over the U.S., Israel, and Canada.*

Already there have been major changes in many households, and with Hashem's help, the group will grow and grow. All because of the article.

Reading the Riot Act

I was doing *alef-beis* homework with my 5-year-old son, Yossi, listening to him rattle off two-syllable words like *ba-ra*, *a-mad*, *de-ma*, when Yossi looked up at me.

"What does this say?" he asked, pointing to a word spelled *shin-mem-alef*.

"Uh," I fumbled, "uh, it says *shema*. You know, like *Shema Yisrael*."

Yossi's brow furrowed as he studied the word. "*Sheh-muh*," he read. "Not *she-ma*." A puzzled expression crossed his little face. "Tatty, how come I know how to read better than you do?"

I took a deep breath. "Yossele, do you have kids in your class who don't know how to read so well?"

"Yeah."

"And someone helps those kids with their reading?"

He nodded vigorously. "Sure, they go to the resource room."

"Right. But when I was your age, and I was having trouble reading, we didn't have such a thing as a resource room. So I never learned to read Hebrew." *And believe it or not, kid, I attended a mainstream, in-town cheder just like yours. Back then — and this was only 25 years ago — there were programs for special-needs kids, but zero in the way of remedial.*

Yossi eyes widened. "Tatty, you always tell me, 'You can do it!' So why don't you learn to read now? You can do it!"

Me? Learn to read? At the age of 30?

The challenge was on.

———— • ————

The first time I realized I had a reading problem was when I was in the third grade. My parents had hired Rabbi Pollack, one of the *rebbeim* in my *cheder*, to tutor me privately, and he had opened a siddur to *birchos Krias Shema* and asked me to read the paragraph of *"HaMeir LaAretz."*

Easy, I thought. I recited the paragraph smoothly, concluding confidently with the words *"Al kol shevach ma'asei yadecha v'al me'orei ohr sheyatzarta heimah yefa'arucha sela."*

Rabbi Pollack eyed me strangely and pointed to the last line of the paragraph. "Read this again," he instructed.

"Starting from which word?" I queried. How was I supposed to know what to read if he didn't prompt me aloud?

"From *'v'al me'orei ohr,'*" he said.

"*'V'al me'orei ohr sheyatzarta—'*" I began.

"No," he corrected me. "You're saying the Sephard davening. This is an Ashkenaz siddur. Look inside and *read* the words. Don't just say what you daven in school. Let's go: *'v'al me'orei ohr she'asisa...'*"

I was officially busted.

Until then, I had fooled everyone: my *rebbeim*, my parents, my friends, even my own self. I listened carefully when the rebbi read something, or when he called on one of my classmates to read something, and then, when he called on me, I simply parroted back what I had heard. If I happened to be the first one called on, with no advance prompting from the rebbi, I'd suddenly have a coughing fit or jump out of my seat and start acting like a clown. If necessary, I'd throw my pencil or some other handy projectile at the rebbi. These behaviors were guaranteed to get me kicked out of class, which was a relief. Better to be outside in the safety of the hallway than to have to stammer my way through a *pasuk*.

In the younger grades, this process was totally subconscious. I didn't understand my own reluctance to read a *pasuk*; I just knew that I needed to hear something read before I could repeat it back. Only when I was confronted with those unfamiliar words at the end of "*HaMeir LaAretz*" did it dawn on me that I was illiterate, at least in Hebrew.

My parents talked to my *rebbeim*, my tutor, my principal, but no one had any solutions other than to move me ahead grade after grade and hope that I didn't make too much trouble.

Having no recourse, my parents tried hard to convince themselves that I was O.K., that my problem wasn't really so serious. Occasionally, on Shabbos, they would test me by opening to *Kiddush* and telling me to read. That was a cinch; I knew *Kiddush* by heart. Things got tricky when they pointed to a random word in the middle of *Kiddush* and told me to start reading from there. But I had a clever solution to that, too. I'd look at the word they were pointing to and find an easy, familiar "bookmark" word nearby that I recognized by sight, like "Shabbos" or "Mitzrayim." Then I'd start talking about something else, while furiously scrolling through the text of *Kiddush* in my head until I got to my bookmark word. After that it was easy; I just had to figure out how many words away from the bookmark I was supposed to start, and then I could rattle off the rest.

So I was able to fool them, and they were happy to be fooled. After all, who wants to have a son who can't read? As a *frum* Jew, if you can't read, you're a goner; you can't daven and you can't learn.

I fooled my *rebbeim*, too, with an array of diversionary tactics. Any time I smelled trouble on the horizon — trouble meaning that I'd be exposed as illiterate — I preempted it by getting myself thrown out of class or simply walking out unbidden. At some point every year, the rebbi would just give up on me and leave me alone, realizing that the less attention he gave me, the less I'd misbehave.

In English and secular studies, I was an O.K. student, with no academic problems. I didn't have any social problems either, because I belonged to a great *chevrah* and my friends thought I was a riot. Besides, I compensated for my reading woes so well that my friends didn't consider me dumb. I could explain the *Mishnayos* or Gemara reasonably well, as long as I had heard it explained in English, as opposed to word-by-word *tietch*. I could even ask or answer questions in class on material the rebbe taught "outside."

When I was in the sixth grade, my rebbi called over each boy separately and asked him to read the *Shir shel Yom* of Wednesday, which is full of hard words like "*sarapai*" and "*hayechavrecha*." Never having learned the *shir* by heart, I made a whopping 32 mistakes in as many words before the rebbi mercifully let me go. At the end of the testing session, the rebbi announced to the class, "Can you believe that one boy in this class made *32* mistakes in one *Shir shel Yom*?"

No wonder, then, that I often didn't want to get out of bed and go to yeshivah.

High school was pure misery. *Everything* was about reading the Gemara, and the tests were in Hebrew, so I didn't understand any of the questions. I couldn't learn with a *chavrusa*, and no one wanted me as a *chavrusa* anyway, so I usually became the third wheel of another *chavrusa* partnership, listening in without ever attempting to decipher the mysterious words on the page.

In the ninth grade, I got caught — almost. One day, my rebbi handed me a photocopied page of the Gemara and told me to put in the appropriate *nekudos* and bring it back to him the next day. *This is it*, I thought. *When I hand in a blank page tomorrow, the game's over*. I was terrified, but overwhelmed with relief at the same time: *Finally, I won't have to carry around this terrible secret anymore*.

"I'm dead," I told my father when I got home that night. "The rebbi gave me this assignment, and I can't do it."

"Sure you can," my father said. "Come on, sit down and give it a try."

I sat with the paper for five minutes, and then I said, "Nothing doing. I'm going to bed."

When I awoke in the morning, the page was on my night table, complete with all of the *nekudos*. My father had done me a "favor" and filled in the sheet for me.

After that, the rebbi never bothered me again.

In yeshivah, there was a rule that you weren't allowed to eat in pizza shops. I didn't pay particular attention to rules, especially silly rules like that one. Rabbi Schiff, the principal, confronted me several times after I had been spotted in nearby pizza shops, warning me that I'd better shape up.

Eventually, after my umpteenth pizza outing, Rabbi Schiff told me that I was being expelled from yeshivah. Knowing that no other yeshivah was going to accept a guy who couldn't read, I viewed this expulsion as a death sentence.

"Rabbi Schiff," I challenged him, "are you telling me that I'm being thrown out for going for *pizza*?"

"It's not the pizza," he explained, "it's the rules. The yeshivah has rules for a reason, and you broke the rules enough times to earn yourself a one-way trip out the door."

"I'm not going to argue," I told him, "but the bottom line is I'm getting thrown out of yeshivah for going for pizza. If that's the case, this system is not for me."

With that, I hurled my hat, jacket, *tefillin*, and yarmulke on his desk and then reached under my shirt and whipped off my tzitzis. "Here," I said, "you need this more than I do. I'm finished with all this stuff."

Rabbi Schiff was a smart man, and he realized that I was serious. "O.K.," he said. "If that's the case, I'm sorry. You can stay."

From then on, there was an unspoken understanding between us: I could do whatever I wanted, as long as I didn't embarrass the yeshivah by flouting the rules publicly. If I drove to yeshivah, for instance, I'd park a few blocks away so as not to flaunt the fact that I had gotten my driver's license, which was against the yeshivah's rules.

I coasted through the rest of high school, not learning much but not dropping *Yiddishkeit* either. There were actually some areas in which I was unusually *makpid*: I never, ever spoke while wearing my *tefillin*, for instance. I was also involved in *bikur cholim* and other forms of *chesed*, and everyone knew that if he needed something, he could turn to me.

Some parts of *Yiddishkeit* are very difficult for a person who can't read, but I found ways to observe even the halachos that I found challenging. When I'd go to do *hataras nedarim* before Rosh HaShanah, I'd be an *eid* 50 or 60 times before saying the tongue-twisting words: "*Kol neder o shevuah o issar o konam o cherem…*" When I'd finally step up to do my own *hataras nedarim*, I could say the words in my sleep.

After high school, I went to learn in Eretz Yisrael, where I attempted to really learn. I found *chavrusa*s who were willing to do all the reading, and I followed along carefully as they explained what the words meant, taking copious notes in the margins of my Gemara. Still, learning was a gigantic struggle, because I exerted so much of my energy trying to piece together the words.

I did grow a lot as a person in Eretz Yisrael, though, and by the time I was in *shidduchim*, I had a reputation as a solid boy, if not a great learner.

My wife didn't know anything about my reading problems when we got married, but once I confided to her how hard it was for me to read, she was very understanding. She encouraged me to go to *shiurim* and to find someone who could teach me how to read, but when she saw I wasn't interested, she didn't push me. She respected me for who I was — an *ehrliche* person, a *ba'al chesed* — and never did I feel that she was judgmental or condescending.

I opened a business and became involved with many different *tzedakah* and communal causes, proving to myself that I *could* be a good Jew even if I couldn't read.

Until my son Yossi challenged me to do it.

———◆———

Carrying the mental image of his innocent face telling me, "You can do it," I went to have myself evaluated, and discovered that I had an issue with processing and retrieval, not with reading per se; I *was* able to read English, after all. My problem was that the traditional system of "*kamatz alef ah*" involved too many different elements — the name of the letter, the name of the *nekudah*, and their respective sounds. Basically, I couldn't pair the *kamatz* with the *alef* and squeeze out the "*ah*"; there was too much going on for my brain to handle. To finally learn to read, I had to ignore the names of the letters and *nekudos* and just blend the vowel with the letter sound, as I did naturally in English.

It was deeply embarrassing to be learning the same thing as preschoolers, and at times I couldn't bring myself to look at my babyish *Alef-Binah* book. *I'm pathetic*, I thought to myself. *Imagine if anyone gets wind of what I'm doing.*

There were times when I couldn't face my *kriah* rebbi, whether out of embarrassment, frustration, or despair. But Yossi's challenge spurred me onward, and I did eventually learn to read Hebrew, when I was nearing my 31st birthday. To this day, however, the energy I expend on sounding out the words precludes any meaningful comprehension, and *kriah* remains for me a technical exercise, not an experience of learning or understanding. Yet I did progress to the point that I'll actually agree to daven for the *amud* on occasion, even though I still stammer and make lots of mistakes during the less familiar parts of davening.

Thanks to my wife's support and encouraging acceptance, I do go to a *shiur* most days, but I try to focus on listening to what the Gemara *means* rather than deciphering what the words *say*. If I look at the Gemara inside, I hear nothing.

So I'm still not the best reader, even if I *can* read. But contrary to the fears of my parents and *rebbeim* — fears that I believe paralyzed them into denying or ignoring my problem — I *am* a successful person and an upstanding Jew. I don't blame anyone for their inability to help me; I understand that they simply didn't have the tools back then, and I know they did the best they could with the limited resources at their disposal.

Now that I've learned to read Hebrew, I've become much more open about my reading impairment. As a result, I've been contacted by a number of parents whose children are suffering from similar problems. One father of a teenage boy told me that he was at his wit's end: "My son can't even sit through *leining*!"

"So what do you do?" I queried.

"I *make* him sit," the father responded indignantly.

"There's no point in doing that," I told him. "If anything, give him an English *Chumash*, maybe with some *mefarshim*, like *Ramban*. But don't force him to follow along with the *ba'al korei* — that's torture."

I often advise parents to get their kids evaluated *outside* the school, because *rebbeim* and resource room staff can become too frustrated with a kid to remain objective about remediation. I also tell parents of reading-challenged kids to focus on the subject matter, not on the words, so that their kids can develop a positive association with learning rather than becoming hopelessly entangled in the words and the *tietch*.

Mostly, I tell parents of kids with reading troubles not to focus too heavily on the reading. "Let the kid feel that he's intelligent, that he can succeed in life and as a Jew despite his reading difficulties," I say. "Get him the help he needs, but more important, get him to feel good about himself. That feeling, more than anything, will propel him past his reading issues."

Postscript:

After this story was printed, the narrator sent me this e-mail:

> *I was at shalosh seudos yesterday and two rebbeim in one of the yeshivos here were talking about the article. One had read it and was telling the other about it. I introduced myself as the narrator. They are both having meetings with their various staff about it.*

In subsequent correspondence, the narrator told me that over 40 people contacted him as a result of the story — including parents, siblings, rebbeim, kriah teachers, bar mitzvah teachers, and older boys who learn with younger high school boys. For this narrator, as for many others who courageously shared their stories in LifeLines, the struggle of a lifetime suddenly became a source of inspiration for others and a springboard for countless chesed opportunities.

Part 7

חַיִּים שֶׁתְּהֵא בָּנוּ אַהֲבַת תּוֹרָה

A Life in Which We Will Have Love of Torah

Building My Rabbi Akiva

The sight of a newlywed couple — young, starry eyed, nattily dressed, oblivious to anyone but each other — inspires a twinge of envy in almost anyone, even those who have been happily married for years. I can tell you, though, that in some instances, the carefree, blissful newlywed picture is nothing but a facade.

I know, because my *shanah rishonah* was one of starry-eyed misery. I was starry-eyed, all right, infatuated with the husband of my dreams, but the husband I married didn't quite match my dreams. Hence the misery.

Simcha was a good boy, with a good personality, from a good family. I had been in *shidduchim* for several years, and when he came along, my parents urged me to go ahead with the *shidduch*.

Simcha wasn't a star *ba'al kishron* or even a legendary *masmid*. He was just a solid, all-around boy. I felt comfortable with him, and I knew he'd make a great husband.

When I complained to my parents that Simcha wasn't anything special, they told me that it's the *penimiyus* of the person that counts, not externalities like where he happens to rank among his peers. "He's a *ba'al middos*, he has a *leiv tov*, he's a *ben Torah* — what more could you want?" my father asked.

I wasn't getting any younger, and Simcha was by far the most suitable candidate I had met, so I got engaged to him.

Throughout my engagement, I drowned in the disappointment of my lost fantasy *chassan*. I couldn't see Simcha's good qualities; I was blind to everything but my shattered dreams. Where was the *chashuve* family I was supposed to join? Why was I engaged to a "very good boy" and not the *best* boy? And couldn't he have learned in a more prestigious yeshivah?

After the wedding, all the smaller things that were wrong with him started to bug me, too. He didn't have *peyos*. He pronounced my name Sa-rah instead of Sorah. He thought a *pulka* was called a drumstick. Friday afternoons he went out to play basketball — in a T-shirt. I couldn't get used to the way he talked, ate, walked, slept, made *Kiddush*, or even sneezed.

These things may sound petty, but once they start to bother you, they can color your entire perception of the person you're married to and sour your whole relationship. I wasn't dumb — I knew that there were a lot of husbands out there who were much worse than Simcha — but that knowledge didn't turn me into an adoring wife.

Viewed through the prism of my disappointment, Simcha couldn't do anything right.

If he came home late from *kollel*, he was inconsiderate; if he came home early, he wasn't learning enough.

In the early days of our marriage, I had to be out of the house at 7:30 in the morning in order to be on time for my teaching job. Simcha was never up when I left the house, and that killed me. Here I was, dragging myself out of the house at 7:30 to go to work so that Simcha could learn, while he was blissfully snoring. My father, who was a businessman, had never in his life slept past 7 o'clock — and a *kollel yungerman* gets up at the leisurely hour of 8 o'clock every day?

Thankfully, I wasn't the type to fight, and neither was Simcha. We got along well, and we made a picture-perfect couple to the rest of the world. It was only inside that I was grieving, tormented by the image of the future *gadol hador* I had hoped to marry.

I never thought that our marriage wouldn't work out. My only question was, how could I succeed at molding Simcha into the person I wanted him to be?

Many times in high school and seminary, I heard my teachers declare that it's the woman's job to build her husband into a *talmid chacham*, and that by encouraging your husband to learn, you can turn him into a Rabbi Akiva even if he's just a simple shepherd.

Emboldened by this knowledge, I set about the holy task of building the next Rabbi Akiva. I nearly destroyed my husband in the process.

What my teachers neglected to mention when they taught us about building Rabbi Akiva was that a woman's power is in changing *herself*, by working on herself to respect and cherish her husband as he is rather than attempting to mold him into someone he's not.

Politely (or so I thought), I reminded Simcha to use his knife when he ate, I asked him whether he had come on time to *kollel*, and I corrected him when he sang *zemiros* in what I thought was the wrong order. He would listen quietly to my reminders and inquiries, and he always answered respectfully. But I noticed that he rarely followed through on what I asked of him. This only made me more intent on "motivating" him to do what he was supposed to, from buying flowers for Shabbos to finding a *chavrusa* for night *seder*.

Instead of my husband becoming the star of my life, I was treating him like a little child, trying to fashion him to my liking as though he were a lump of clay. But I was oblivious to what I was doing — until that fateful visit to my in-laws.

My in-laws had made *aliyah* several years earlier, and the first time I visited their house in Israel was for Pesach, about a year after my husband and I were married. I was horrified by the way they lived — their kitchen was a sink and a bare-wood table without any cabinets, their dishes were mismatched, their apartment was tiny — but I was deeply impressed by their *shalom bayis*. My father-in-law was nothing special, at least in my eyes, but my mother-in-law treated him with the utmost respect.

The morning of *erev Pesach*, when every Jewish home is in a state of turmoil, I came into the kitchen to see my mother-in-law calmly frying eggs for my father-in-law's breakfast. As her boys were frantically collecting the last bits of *chametz* for burning, she removed her apron and sat down at the table while my father-in-law ate. "Mommy!" one of the boys yelled. "I can't find the 10 pieces of bread from last night!"

"You'll have to wait, darling," she replied. "I'm serving Daddy breakfast now."

My jaw dropped. *This is how a wife is supposed to treat her husband*, I suddenly understood. I looked at my father-in-law, who to me seemed like a regular Joe, and I realized that in my mother-in-law's eyes, he was a prince. He was a prince because she chose to see him that way.

When I left Israel after Pesach, I promised myself that I would have a marriage just like that of my in-laws. But I realized that if I wanted the type of marriage my in-laws had, I'd have to respect Simcha for who he was and completely erase my mental image of what he should be. And I realized that if there was someone who had to change in this marriage, it wasn't Simcha: it was me.

I made up my mind that Simcha's davening and learning were not my responsibility or my business. I would make sure not to delay him from going to shul or *kollel*, or disturb him when he was learning, but I forced myself to stop monitoring what time he left the house, how much he talked on the phone, and exactly how much he learned on any given day.

Instead of comparing him to my father, or to my friends' husbands, or to the star *bachur* of my dreams, I began to pay attention to what was right with Simcha. What sterling *middos* he had! If I was cross with him, or criticized him for not picking up a *sefer* all Shabbos, he'd respond with a nod and a patient smile. If that wasn't true *gadlus*, what was?

Instead of fussing about how Simcha was falling short of my lofty spiritual aspirations, I busied myself doing things for him

— cooking meals he liked, giving him my undivided attention when he spoke, listening to his *divrei Torah* with interest and without offering my critique, being ready on time when we had to go somewhere together, taking care of errands or tasks that he needed me to handle, and, most importantly, acting pleasant and happy when I was around him. It was a huge shift in the way I related to Simcha, and I felt myself becoming a completely different type of wife.

It didn't happen overnight, though. Whereas destruction was thoughtless, construction required much thought and energy. Simcha was wary of this new wife, and he felt too unsure of my respect and admiration to confidently step into the role of master of the house. It took many months of conscious effort on my part to build what I had destroyed with my foolish, childish, selfish dreams.

It's been over three decades since my wedding, and I'm a grandmother many times over already. Simcha and I have beautiful *shalom bayis*, and I couldn't possibly be married to a more wonderful person. He's grown into a respected *talmid chacham*, and he's been a successful *mechanech* for over 20 years. All this happened not because I built him into a Rabbi Akiva with my own two hands, but because I taught myself to see the good in him and look up to him while working on myself to create the conditions in which a healthy marriage could flourish.

I look around me, at the unmarried girls hoping to land the next *gadol hador*, at the young wives trying to create another Rabbi Akiva, and at the newlywed *kallah*s trying to project an air of bliss while struggling with the considerable challenges of *shanah rishonah*. And to all of them I say, "Forget Rabbi Akiva for now, and just work on becoming Rachel, his wife."

Postscript:

I consider this story the opposite bookend to "Crowning the Queen" (the story that follows). In both stories, the husband's Torah learning didn't quite match up to his wife's expectations. In this story, the husband didn't learn as much as his wife thought he should; in that story, the husband learned more than his wife thought he should.

My guess is that most young husbands don't learn exactly as much Torah as their wives think they should. It follows, then, that most young wives will have to tailor their expectations in this regard one way or another. The trick is for each wife to read the story that's right for her: "Crowning the Queen" for the wife whose husband learns more than she anticipated, and "Building My Rabbi Akiva" for the wife whose husband learns less than she would have liked.

That's why, when I got the following e-mail, I felt a mixture of gratification and alarm:

> I'm in twelfth grade, and one of my teachers read "Crowning the Queen" to the class. We were all captivated. After four years of high school, a group of indifferent teenagers is not really the best audience for any class or any teacher, and yet we all listened to every word open mouthed. We just couldn't get enough.

It's wonderful that this young lady and her classmates are enthused about doing everything they can to help their husbands learn, but how many of those husbands are going to want to learn as much as their wives want them to? If a teacher is reading "Crowning the Queen" to the class, she should really be reading "Building My Rabbi Akiva" along with it.

I e-mailed the story "Building My Rabbi Akiva" to this young lady, in the hopes that her teacher would read it to the class. I wonder if she did.

Crowning the Queen

On *erev Succos*, after snapping the *succah* panels into place, unrolling the bamboo across the top of the *succah*, hanging up the decorations, and stringing the lighting through the *schach*, I discovered that the splitter — the little piece that converts our porch light into a de facto electrical outlet for the *succah* — was gone. Three hours before Yom Tov, when most other *frum* women were bustling about their kitchens, I piled all the kids into the car and raced to the hardware store to pick up another splitter.

When I came home, I expertly twisted the wires of a converted extension cord into our new splitter, and voilà — the lights in the *succah* flashed to life. Now I could dash back into the kitchen and finish my cooking, then bathe and dress the kids and quickly mop the floor.

My husband, Aryeh, walked through the door just minutes before candle lighting. He headed straight to the *succah* to move around the *schach* so that he could personally perform the mitzvah of building a *succah*. As I watched him shift the bamboo mats from side to side and murmur, "*L'sheim mitzvas succah*," I wondered how many other Jewish wives even knew what a splitter was.

In past years, I had felt a knot of resentment in my stomach as I single-handedly put up our family's *succah*, the same knot of resentment that made its appearance when I changed lightbulbs, mowed the lawn, took out the garbage, and emptied mousetraps.

But now things were different. Now, when Aryeh came home with just enough time to get himself ready for Yom Tov, I felt a surge of pride rush through me, even as my arms ached with exhaustion.

———————•———————

When I entered *shidduchim*, I knew that I had very little going for me. My father was a *ger*, my mother a *ba'alas teshuvah*, and my family belonged to an out-of-town Modern Orthodox community. I had attended a coed Jewish high school, but I became involved with NCSY as a teenager, and by the time I graduated high school, I was far more observant than my family, insisting on covering my knees and elbows and refusing to watch television on Shabbos even though the TV was left on from Friday.

After studying at a seminary in Israel for two years, I returned home determined to marry someone who was serious about *Yiddishkeit* and who wanted to build a Torah home. But my *shidduch* "market value" was pitifully low, especially since my parents were hardly supportive of the lifestyle I had chosen and were neither able nor willing to advocate for me in *shidduchim*.

I realized two things right from the start: one, that only Hashem could bring about my *shidduch*; and two, that I could not be fussy at all about what I was looking for in a husband.

In addition to davening for a *shidduch* in Shacharis, Minchah, and Ma'ariv, I whispered countless personal prayers to Hashem throughout the day. My wish list for a husband was short: "Please send me someone who has *anavah* and *yiras Shamayim*," I would beg Hashem each time I davened. That was all.

I never told anyone that these were the two qualities I was looking for in a husband. Yet when Rebbetzin Levenberg, one of my teachers from seminary, suggested Aryeh Moses for me, the words she used to describe him were "*anav*" and "*yarei Shamayim.*"

On my first date with Aryeh, I could barely understand a word he said. English was not his first language, and he had a heavy stutter to boot. He was seven years my senior and was working as a pharmaceutical engineer. The product of a traditional family, Aryeh had not attended yeshivah in his youth, and he had only recently begun studying Torah seriously.

Culturally, we were miles apart. My family was very American and laid back, while Aryeh's parents were European, very stiff and proper.

My reaction upon discovering all these things about Aryeh was, *Great!* I had known all along that I was going to have to compromise on something, probably on a lot of things, and I felt relieved that Aryeh's "flaws" were purely external. As we dated, I started to have an easier time understanding him, and I realized that behind the stilted speech was a person of sterling character, whose commitment to *Yiddishkeit* and Torah learning was rock solid. He was gentle and unassuming, eager to learn and ready to admit when there was something he didn't know.

When I agreed to marry him, I harbored no illusions about what the future held in store. It was going to take work, hard work, to overcome the communication barriers between us and bridge the differences in our respective backgrounds. But we had *rabbanim* and *rebbetzin*s to guide us, and we resolved to consult with them on a steady basis to ensure that the relationship we were building was healthy and *Torahdik*.

After our marriage, Aryeh took a leave of absence from his job, and we moved to Israel, where Aryeh enrolled in a yeshivah for beginners and I took a job as an English teacher. This arrangement worked nicely until my second child was born, at which point we could no longer subsist on my earnings and Aryeh's savings. Both Aryeh and I wanted me to be able to raise our children rather than go out to work, so we moved back to America and Aryeh rejoined his old company.

I sort of assumed that now that Aryeh was working full time, he would cut down his learning schedule to an hour or two a day, like most of the *frum* working men I knew. But Aryeh had other plans. "Just because I'm working, I don't have to learn anymore?" he asked rhetorically.

On his very first day back to work, he awoke at 5 a.m. and hurried to shul to learn. He came home to eat a quick breakfast and then drove off to work. After work, he headed straight to a nearby *beis midrash*, returning home for supper at 8, after the kids were in bed, and then leaving the house again to learn until midnight.

And that has been his schedule for the past eight years.

By now, we have six young children, the oldest of whom is 10, and although I don't work out of the house, I'm busy all day with housework, child care, and errands. Aryeh does literally nothing in the house. On the contrary, I have to take care of everything for him, from laying out his clothes on the dresser at night to packing his lunch in the morning.

In the beginning, the burden of running the house and caring for the kids all on my own was crushing. It wasn't only that I was working hard all day (and much of the night as well); it was also the psychological strain of knowing that I was carrying the entire load alone. I couldn't even unburden myself to Aryeh at the end of a long day, since by the time he came home at night he was so exhausted he'd collapse straight into bed.

My resentment was exacerbated by the culture gap that existed between us. My father was the all-American dad, playing baseball with my brothers, driving us to school, doing the grocery shopping, and cooking supper when my mother wasn't in the mood. In Aryeh's family, the gender roles were much more traditional: his mother had handled all child care and housework, and his father had been the sole breadwinner. Leisure hardly existed in their lexicon.

One day, I picked up the phone and called Rebbetzin Levenberg. "This is too much for me," I cried to her. "I feel like a single parent! I can't manage all by myself!"

"Devora," she said gently, "you *can* manage. Maybe you need help, but you don't necessarily need your *husband's* help. You can get a mother's helper, or some extra cleaning help, or hire a babysitter so that you have some time to yourself. It's not fair to expect your husband to help in ways that he's not comfortable with or capable of. I know you think fathers should play ball with their kids, but if he never played ball in his life, how's he supposed to know how to do that? You have to let go of your vision of what a man is supposed to do and adjust to his prototype.

"I know you're feeling very overwhelmed," she added, "but do you realize what a great privilege it is to be married to a person who's such a *masmid* and *talmid chacham*? It's not that your husband is neglecting you; he's giving you the opportunity to support his Torah learning in a way that not too many women today are *zocheh* to."

"But what's going to be with my family?" I protested. "My kids hardly see their father! Even on weekends, he's busy learning all day. I don't want my children to be deprived."

"You know that my father was a great *rosh yeshivah*," Rebbetzin Levenberg half-asked, half-stated.

"Yes," I replied.

"Well, when I was a kid, my siblings and I looked forward to Shabbos because that was the only time of the week we'd see our father. During the week, he came home late at night, after we were sleeping, and he left the house early in the morning, before we awoke. My mother did everything herself — my father never even learned how to drive! — but she was so happy to do it that we kids never felt that there was anything strange about the way we were raised.

"Whether or not your children are resentful will depend on your attitude. If *you* feel deprived and unhappy, your children will mirror those feelings. But if you view it as your privilege to support his Torah learning, and you find alternative ways to get the help you need so that you don't feel like a *shmatte*, your children will grow up just fine — and they'll want to devote their lives to Torah, too."

It took time for me to digest the *rebbetzin*'s words and make the paradigm shift from the neglected, overworked wife to the lucky *eishes chaver*. I kept reminding myself that when I had been looking for a shidduch, I hadn't asked for a husband who would mow the lawn or take the kids to amusement parks. I had asked for someone who was humble and G-d-fearing — and that, I certainly had, plus a whole lot more.

For the first 25 years of his life, I reasoned, *Aryeh never opened a Gemara. Now he's on his way to making his third siyum on Shas. If I have to put the kids to bed all by myself every day to make that happen, isn't that a small price to pay?*

Having made the switch in my mind, I now had to adjust some of the logistics of my life to reflect my new outlook. I couldn't afford much in the way of hired help, but I decided to cut back on other things — like clothing — in order to pay for more cleaning help. I also hired a babysitter to come to the house Shabbos morning so that I could go to shul. I rarely went out during the week when my kids were home, so I figured I could allow myself the luxury of davening in shul on Shabbos, which gave me a huge spiritual boost. I also started listening to *shiurim* over the phone, and that helped me maintain my composure and be *b'simchah* even when things got hectic and stressful.

In order to build my children's relationship with their father, despite their lack of time together, I started making a point of complimenting the kids in front of Aryeh, capitalizing on the few moments a day that he was home to tell him all the good things the kids had done that day.

"Abba," I'd say as soon as he walked through the door at night, "did you know that Elisheva did all her homework by herself today?"

"Really?" Aryeh would say proudly, tousling Elisheva's hair. "What a big girl!"

"Yup! And Pinchas helped me set the table!"

Aryeh would then swing Pinchas in the air before hurrying to eat the supper that was waiting for him on the table — served on china, the way his mother always did, and plated individually, the way he liked it.

In the past, I used to beg Aryeh every *chol hamo'ed* to come along with us on family trips, since he takes vacation the weeks of Succos and Pesach (and no other time). By now, however, I've made peace with the fact that Aryeh's *simchas yom tov* is to spend his days in the *beis midrash*, and I'm able to take my kids on trips by myself and actually be happy that my husband is *shteiging* while I'm giving the kids a good time.

Both my family and Aryeh's family live far away from us, and when we go to visit them, we drive through the night there and back, so that Aryeh doesn't have to take off more time from work and learning than absolutely necessary. In most families, the husband drives while the wife dozes off in the passenger seat; in our family, it's the opposite. Aryeh needs his rest so that he can head straight to the *beis midrash* in the morning when we arrive home and then go to work; I, on the other hand, can sleep during the day while the baby naps.

Although I very much wanted to live a Torah life, I didn't dream that I'd be the one driving through the night, putting up the *succah*, and being both mother and father to my children in many ways. Then again, neither did I dream that I'd have a husband who would push himself beyond human limits to reach ever-greater heights in Torah learning.

Some time ago, when Aryeh finished *Shas* for the third time, he invited 10 men to the house for a modest *seudah*. The day after the *siyum*, I got a delivery of chocolates from Esther Krauss, the wife of one of the men who had come to the *siyum*. The chocolates were arranged in the shape of a crown, and the accompanying note said, "To the woman who wears the crown of Torah."

I hardly know Esther, but the words she wrote on the note have remained engraved on my mind ever since, making me feel like a queen even when I'm taking out the garbage, playing ball with my kids, or putting up the splitter in my *succah*.

Postscript:

This story generated a few letters to the editor excoriating the husband for his lack of involvement in the family. Here's an excerpt from one of them:

> *I found the LifeLines story about the husband who was devoted 24/7 to his Torah learning heartbreaking. Much as the husband*

who learns Torah each and every waking moment is to be praised, the effects of Torah should be to make him sympathetic and aware of his wife and children and their needs. We are blessed with many talmidei chachamim and they — at least the ones I know — are devoted and caring spouses and fathers... A well-rounded scholar will always have room for others in his life.

In response, the narrator sent the following letter:

Two weeks ago I had my story printed in LifeLines, about my husband who loves to learn and how I changed my perspective from needing him to be the all-American dad to appreciating his long learning hours. Last week a woman responded to my story and said that it was "heartbreaking" and that "the effects of Torah should be to make him sympathetic and aware of his wife and children and their needs."

I would like to respond to her by saying: You entirely missed the point of the story! The story was written by me, not by my husband. Yes, I tried to change my husband many times, but it just left both of us frustrated because I was trying to make him into someone that he isn't. When I began to appreciate him for who he is we both became much happier with ourselves and each other. The point of life is to look at the person in the mirror — and change yourself! After 120 years we come up to Shamayim and are responsible for ourselves. Yes, I've been gently encouraging my husband over the years to be more accepting of the American lifestyle and he's adapting more and more, but the major transformation that changed our life was within me.

I used to be so overwhelmed and resentful toward my husband, and now I sing and dance all day, thanking Hashem for the wonderful life I have. We wives and mothers need to look at the members of our family and see their abilities and try to help them to develop into who they are — not who we wish they were. That's the point of the story! It doesn't matter what it is that I'm appreciating in my husband (or child) — whether it's his learning, his chesed, or whatever —

it's that I am supporting him to become who he can become.
And by changing myself to appreciating his good qualities and
supporting him and feeling that he is chashuv, I'm becoming
who I need to become.

"Devora Moses"

Filling the Cup

My daughter Chayala got married a few months ago, and for the first time ever, I fell behind in my tuition for my two youngest sons. The repercussions were swift, in the form of a summons to a meeting with the yeshivah's tuition committee.

"I have one question for you, Mr. Farber," said Rabbi Edelman, the committee's head. "Are you supporting your married kids?"

"Yes, I am," I said.

He folded his arms. "Well, I'd like to inform you that tuition for your younger children comes first, before support for the married ones."

"That may be true," I replied. "But I'm planning to do both: pay my tuition *and* support my married kids. I just made a wedding, so the past few months have been very stressful financially, but you'll get your tuition very soon, right after Hashem refills my cup."

I don't know if Rabbi Edelman and his compatriots appreciated my answer, but that didn't matter, since I was up to date with my tuition — and my *kollel* support checks — within a couple of weeks of that conversation.

Hashem had refilled my cup.

———◆———

When I got married some 35 years ago, I was already working. In those days it was relatively unusual for married men to learn in *kollel* and practically unheard of for parents to support their married children. Having seen my own Polish-born father rise before dawn every day to learn and reopen his Gemara in the evening immediately upon returning home from his dry-goods store, the value of being *kovei'a ittim laTorah* was in my blood without my father ever having to give me a *derashah* about it.

The value of full-time *kollel* learning, on the other hand, was hardly one I imbibed with my mother's milk. My father managed to learn six to eight hours a day plus run his store, and he was dismissive, even scornful, of the newfangled notion of *kollel*. "In *der heim*," he pronounced, "we didn't know of such a thing."

I didn't have the luxury of sitting and learning a full day past the age of 19. At that point, I started helping my father in his store, and I worked there for a few years before going off on my own and opening a textile manufacturing business.

When I opened the business, my father gave me a modest start-up loan, which I repaid to the last penny. I never expected my father to *give* me the money, even though by that point he and my mother were no longer the impoverished greenhorns they had been when I was a child.

Times were changing, though. My generation wasn't rising before *neitz* to pore over our Gemaras, even if many of us — myself included — did attend a pre-Shacharis *daf yomi shiur*. And the next generation...well, from what I could see, most of the *bachurim* were going in one of two directions: they were either devoting themselves to full-time learning, or they were devoting themselves to full-time moneymaking, punctuated by trips to Florida or visits to the golf course.

This wasn't Europe, where you worked because you needed to eat, but your heart was so drawn to the *beis midrash* that you were able to learn by candlelight for hours after you finished your work. This was America, the land of Hollywood and Fifth Avenue and Carvel.

Mine was a hybrid generation. We had enough voltage left over from our European parents that we could recharge our spiritual batteries with the power of a daily *shiur*. We had seen what it meant to be a real Jew, to live and breathe *Yiddishkeit*, to be *moser nefesh* in the literal sense.

We had absorbed, yes, but we weren't *tofei'ach al menas l'hatfiach*; we didn't hold enough spirituality to flow over to the next generation. Working as lawyers, accountants, and businessmen, we weren't going to be able to propel our children to be *ehrlich*, G-d fearing, and *Torahdik baalebatim*.

That's why I enrolled my sons in yeshivos, where I knew they'd be encouraged *not* to be like me, where they'd be urged to put Torah study first, and where they wouldn't view the *baalebos* who is *kovei'a ittim* as the paradigm of a successful Jew. I knew that this meant they wouldn't have a natural source of income down the line. But given the choice, I preferred to invest in their spiritual bank accounts at the expense of their future financial security.

Many of my friends sent their kids to other yeshivos and schools, places where secular studies were at least as important as — or even more important than — Gemara and *Tosafos*. "What are your kids going to do for a living?" my friend Boruch Plotkin challenged me once. "Are they going to sponge off you or their *shver* forever?"

"*Parnassah* is from *Shamayim*," I replied, "but Torah is '*lo baShamayim hi*.' I'll take care of my kids' *ruchniyus*, and Hashem will take care of their *gashmiyus*."

"Don't be a fool, Heshy," Boruch warned me. "This is going to cost you, big time. How many daughters do you have? Three?"

"Four," I said. "And four sons, too. My boys are as much my kids as my girls are, and I'm not auctioning them off to the highest bidder."

Boruch cocked his head. "And where do you plan to get the money to support all of them?"

I pointed upward. "Hashem fills everyone's cup. The bigger your cup, the more it gets filled."

"Heshy," he said, shaking his head, "you really are crazy."

He wasn't the only one who thought I was crazy. My own parents thought I was out of my mind when I told them I was hoping to support my kids in *kollel*.

"What kind of *narishkeit* is that?" my father fumed. "The Torah says that first you build a house and a vineyard, then you marry a wife. '*Katan someich al shulchan aviv*' — a baby, you support. A man supports himself."

"It's a different generation, Daddy," I responded. "Nowadays, if you want your kids to have *yiras Shamayim* and know how to learn, they have to start their married life in *kollel*. That's just how it is."

The only one who enthusiastically agreed with me was my wife, Chani. "I don't care if I have to sell every piece of jewelry I own," she told me. "I want our kids to be able to sit and learn. We didn't have that opportunity, but I want them to have it."

When our oldest son, Elchanan, became engaged to his *kallah,* Rivky, her parents said they would give the couple a certain sum every month. "With what Rivky earns, that should be enough for them to live on," her father told me. But Rivky didn't find a job right away, and even when she did, she wasn't earning enough to close their budgetary gap — even without a car and on a no-frills budget. So I sent the couple a check every month to supplement their income.

Shortly afterward, my daughter Leah got married, and we committed to supporting her fully; she was in school at the time. Helping Elchanan had hardly made a dent in our bottom line, but adding full support for an additional couple was a serious financial burden. Until Leah got married, Chani worked part-time as a teacher, but at that point, our youngest son was already in school, so she took on a second teaching job to help with the finances.

When our next daughter, Nechama, got married, we had to make some lifestyle changes in order to support her and her husband, Ari. We got rid of our second car and closed off our basement so that we could rent it out. Chani all but stopped shopping for herself. I often urged her to go out and buy herself something new to wear, but she'd say, "I'd rather give Rivky the money to buy herself a nice robe. And Leah could use a new pair of shoes."

I remember sitting at the Pesach Seder one year and looking around the table. Chani had made sure to get new clothing for every member of the family, and she had slipped Elchanan money to buy Rivky a new pair of earrings. At my insistence, Chani had bought herself a new necklace for Yom Tov — for $35. When I protested that she deserved better than costume jewelry, she responded, "Elchanan and Rivky are still young. They need gold and diamonds. But what I have is more precious than gold and diamonds."

I felt blessed to have such a wife.

Chani did have her limits, though. One year we decided not to go up to the country for the summer, and send the kids to local day camps instead. A few weeks after we made this decision, I came home to find Chani on the verge of tears.

"I can't do it, Heshy," she said. "I know we can't afford a bungalow because we're shelling out thousands of dollars for the couples, but I really need a vacation. I work hard, and if I don't get to recharge my batteries a little, I'm going to burn out.

"I don't want to become one of these dried-up, bitter people who gives everything to their kids and withers away," she added. "I don't mind working hard, but I can only do it up to the point where I start feeling resentful. Giving up my summer is too much."

I didn't know how we were going to pay for the bungalow and keep up our commitment to our three couples over the summer. But the day before I wrote out the check for our summer bungalow, I got a large order from a new customer that covered the price of the bungalow and then some.

"You see, Heshy?" Chani remarked. "Hashem knows how big our cup is, and He fills it."

If not for Chani's rock-solid belief in the value of supporting our children in learning, I don't know if I would have been able to commit to supporting our next daughter, Gitty. We were still helping the older three, and adding a fourth support check to our monthly expenditure — on the heels of making a wedding — was unquestionably beyond our means.

"So let's sell the house," Chani suggested.

"You're joking, right?" I asked.

"Not at all," she replied. "Our house is worth triple what we paid for it 20 years ago. It's too big for us now anyway, and we're getting too old for the neighborhood. We can find a cheaper place to live that's close to the married kids and still keep our jobs."

My friend Boruch thought I should be committed for selling my house. "You know, Heshy," he lectured me, "you're not getting any younger. To sell a house at this age is suicidal! Instead of leaching all your money to your kids, you should be doing some serious retirement planning."

Boruch knew a thing or two about retirement planning, having carefully invested his money in stocks and mutual funds over the years. He was proud of his oldest son who had an MBA, his second son who was in law school, and his daughter who was becoming a psychologist. Much to his consternation, his second daughter had "flipped out" during her seminary year in Israel and was now living hand to mouth in what Boruch described as a ratty *kollel* apartment in Yerushalayim.

"And I'm stuck supporting her," he grumbled.

"You're not stuck," I said. "You have a choice."

"What, to let my daughter starve?" he retorted.

A few months after that conversation, the real-estate market crashed, along with the stock market, and the value of our old house plummeted to a fraction of what we had sold it for.

The next time I bumped into Boruch, he looked terrible. His shirt was unkempt, and he seemed a lot grayer than the last time I met him.

"Is everything O.K.?" I asked in concern. "No one's sick, I hope."

"Nah, everyone's fine," he said dolefully. "It's just that I lost close to half a million dollars on the stock market."

I made a quick calculation. In the years since Elchonon's wedding, I had paid out close to half a million dollars in support — and that was besides the little extras that Chani slipped the kids for clothing, *sheitels*, baby furniture, or "just because."

"Look at the bright side, Boruch," I said. "The money you sent your daughter in Israel is still securely invested in *Olam Haba*."

He sighed. "Whatever."

Even after losing half a million dollars, Boruch is still in a better financial position than I am. He still has a house, and he still has some money left in his retirement funds. Besides, if things go really sour for him, he can always turn to his hotshot lawyer son for a loan.

I, on the other hand, recently made my sixth wedding, and I'm still helping all of my married children. Elchanan, my oldest, recently took a job as a rebbi, but even with Rivky working, they're struggling, and I try to help them out here and there. My second son-in-law, Ari, is completing some courses now and starting to look for a job. I'm committed to helping him and Nechama until they're solidly on their feet, though.

Then there's my son Duvi, whose wife Chaviva comes from a very wealthy family, the type that gets honored every year by a different organization or *mossad*. Everyone thinks that I got off scot-free with Duvi, but I know — and only I know — that he often doesn't make it to the end of the month on the money his in-laws give them. So every month, I ask him whether he has enough money to pay his rent and utilities. If not, I transfer money into his account. That's my *mattan b'seiser*.

Is it easy to dole out so much money to my married kids? No, not at all. Harder than the financial strain is the psychological burden of knowing that there are six families depending on me to some extent — and that's besides the two teenage sons whose tuition I still have to pay.

My kids don't know that I was called down by the tuition committee recently. Why should I tell them? That would only make them feel bad about taking money from me, when the truth is that I'm really happy to give it to them.

I give them their money quietly, without fanfare, and I try not to look at how they spend it. Thankfully, none of my kids are high rollers; they live simply, and they spend their money responsibly, for the most part. My daughters and daughters-in-law work hard, too.

I'm also very fortunate to have sons and sons-in-law who are serious about their learning; none of them waste their *seder* time.

When Ari, my second son-in-law, felt that the time had come to leave the *beis midrash*, he was honest enough with himself to enroll in a course and start looking for a job.

It worries me sometimes that I have no equity outside my business: no house, no investments. But I tell myself that financial security is an illusion. Money comes and goes, and the only equity we hold onto are the *zechuyos* we ship ahead of us to *Gan Eden*.

In my office at work, I have a little paperweight engraved with the words "*Eitz chaim hi lamachazikim bah v'somcheha me'ushar.*" I feel fortunate to have the privilege of supporting Torah, and I believe that Hashem will continue to fill my cup no matter how big it becomes.

On the outside, it looks as though I'm the one supporting my kids. I'm convinced, however, that they're the ones supporting me.

Postscript:

"We had absorbed, yes, but we weren't 'tofei'ach al menas l'hatfiach' — we didn't hold enough spirituality to overflow to the next generation."

There are two ways to fill one cup from another: one is by pouring from the first cup into the second cup, and the other is by continuously filling the first cup so that it overflows into the second cup. The first way is direct, while the second is indirect. The difference is that when you pour from one cup into another, the contents of the first cup are depleted, whereas when you keep pouring into the first cup until it overflows, the cup remains full.

I've heard it said that the same is true of ruchniyus. A person can try to directly influence others by pouring from his cup into theirs, so to speak. This approach favors lectures, instructions, dos and don'ts: proselytizing, essentially. But the end result is that the person's spiritual energy is depleted; he's too busy influencing others to focus on refilling his own tank.

Alternatively, a person can influence others indirectly, by filling his own spiritual cup to the point that it overflows onto the people around him, whether they are his own family, his friends, or his students. Who he is then becomes the inspiration, not what he says.

The more Torah he learns, the more fervently he davens, the more he works on his middos — all things that may seem spiritually self-centered — the more he impacts the world. He may not even realize the extent of the impact he is having, because his goal is to improve himself, not to fix others.

The primary way that a Jew is meant to accomplish tikkun olam is not by proselytizing, but by overflowing. We don't "fix" other people; we improve ourselves, and that automatically fixes the world. Any kiruv professional will tell you that personal example goes a lot further than the most inspiring lecture.

The narrator of this story used the metaphor of "filling the cup" to refer to the way Hashem steadily provided for him even as he extended himself to support additional couples in Torah learning. More significantly, however, his own value for Torah learning clearly overflowed onto his children, whom he now has the privilege of supporting.

Ice Cream for Breakfast

When my parents moved to the frigid Canadian city where my father was to serve as rabbi, they didn't know that only three kids out of 60 in my kindergarten grade would be *shomer Shabbos* or that two of those three would be my twin sister and myself.

As inspired *ba'alei teshuvah* who were looking to spread *Yiddishkeit* and love of Hashem, my parents relocated every few years. After moving to Canada, they realized very quickly that if they wanted to raise *frum* kids in that spiritual tundra, they would have to get creative.

There wasn't much going on where we lived, other than ice hockey. It was 30 degrees below zero six months out of the year, and with nothing to do, lots of teenagers — and their parents — sat around and smoked. Or worse.

My parents, Rabbi Yitzchak and Rebbetzin Robin Meyerowitz — deep, passionate people with a huge sense of responsibility to *Klal*

Yisrael — lit a fire of *Yiddishkeit* in that hockey town of Winnipeg, Manitoba, inspiring some 200 families to keep Shabbos.

To raise us Orthodox in an environment that was at best apathetic, at worst hostile, my parents had to resort to some unorthodox, do-it-yourself strategies. Which parents give their kids ice cream for breakfast Shabbos morning, and invite all the neighborhood kids to join the fun and experience the sweet taste of Shabbos? Which parents sing and dance with their kids until 3 a.m. Friday night? Which parents have a "date night" with each of their kids once a week?

Our home was an open house where all sorts of lost souls gravitated: at-risk teens, searching adults, inquisitive university students, lonely orphans... In addition to my three sisters, I have loads of other "siblings" that my parents adopted along the way, helping them emotionally, physically, financially, everything.

We often had 20 to 30 guests at our Shabbos meals. I was a hyper kid, not the type to sit at the table, but that didn't matter. "Shai, get your Rollerblades on," my father would tell me. All through the *seudah*, I'd skate around the table, scoring imaginary hockey goals and smashing into the walls just for fun. The guests loved it.

There were no kosher stores around, so we had to have food shipped in for our family, and for all our guests, too. I didn't even know there was such a thing as buying fresh kosher bread. We either made our own, or managed with the frozen stuff that we imported.

Every *chag* was an experience, an opportunity for my parents to share the joy of *mitzvos* with the community, and, most importantly, with their own children, who weren't going to learn about it in school.

Before we arrived, most of the community had never seen a *succah*. My parents built a *succah* out of thick cedarwood to keep out the driving winds and snow, and they invited each of their kids' classes to come over and paint one wall. Year after year, my friends and my sisters' friends would come back to visit our *succah* and locate their artwork and handprints.

Purim was another forgotten holiday that we brought to life. We'd spend Purim night preparing *mishlo'ach manos*, and then get dressed up the next day and go around delivering our packages to all our friends, our car blaring lively music. Our friends knew little to nothing about Purim, so as part of our visits we'd tell and retell the Purim story, explaining how G-d saved the Jewish people on this day and that we were coming to share the joy with them.

My parents wanted me to have healthy outlets for my energy, and not spend my time watching movies or playing mind-numbing computer games, so they sent me for rock-climbing lessons and signed me up for hockey and baseball leagues. My father was always the coach of my baseball team.

When I was in the third grade, my father and I were playing baseball out in the yard. I was always a pretty good hitter, but this time I was a little too good and the ball hit the living room window, shattering it. I anxiously watched my father's face to see his reaction, thinking that he would reprimand me. But instead of registering irritation, his face lit up with joy. "Wow!" he exclaimed. "I can't believe you're strong enough to hit a ball through a window!"

Even so, my father drilled into me that Torah was much, much more important than hockey or baseball. Sports were a diversion; Torah was the real thing. I didn't do much formal learning as a kid, but my father and I had meaningful discussions, and I loved the way he listened to my weird 8-year-old views on life.

During and after the Shabbos meals, my father would pepper me and my sisters with questions on the *parashah*. After saying a *devar Torah*, he would ask us, "What do you say?" and we would all discuss and debate the points that had been raised. To us, the Torah was alive, vibrant, and exciting.

Still, since we were practically the only *frum* kids in town, *chinuch* was an uphill battle. The Jewish school we attended had Hebrew studies in the afternoon, which meant that Shacharis happened at 3 p.m. To my parents, davening was very important, so they would sing davening with us spiritedly in the car on the way to school each morning. One day, as we were saying *Shema*, a car speeding from the other direction cut us off and narrowly missed us.

"Does anyone realize what just happened?" my mother exclaimed. "You were saying *Shema*, and your *tefillah* saved us from a car accident!"

Our davening may have lacked decorum, and may not have been as formal as that of a yeshivah or Bais Yaakov, but we certainly felt connected to Hashem. How could we not? My mother was constantly talking about Hashem. When she left our rooms after kissing us good night, she would turn to us and say, *"Hashem li v'lo ira* — Hashem is with me, and I'm not afraid!"

Whenever we davened, my mother would tell us, "Now is your time to talk to Hashem. You can say whatever you want and Hashem wants to hear it." The love that she and my father had for Hashem and his *mitzvos* was palpable and contagious, and Hashem's presence was clear and obvious in our lives.

When my sister Ayelet was in the second grade, she had a teacher who spewed venom against Orthodoxy. "Why should women sit separately in shul?" she shouted at my sister one day. I don't know what exactly Ayelet answered, but what she felt like saying was, "I'm, like, 8 years old. Like, leave me alone?"

My oldest sister, Yael, had it the hardest. She was the only one in her class wearing skirts, and among her friends she felt like an alien from a different planet. She went through a rebellious phase, but she had a hard time figuring out how to rebel. She didn't want to do drugs, because she didn't want to hurt herself. She didn't want to hang out with boys, because growing up in our house and seeing the phenomenal *shalom bayis* my parents had, she didn't want to jeopardize her chances at a great marriage. So she had a problem: She didn't know how to rebel.

Any time one of us had a problem, we turned to our parents. It was only natural, then, for Yael to confide in my mother. She and my mother discussed the issue at length, exploring various possibilities for how to rebel, until they finally settled on a suitable teenage rebellion: she would pierce a few holes in her ears.

"Would you like me to tell you that you can't do that so you'll feel rebellious?" my mother asked.

"No!" Yael replied. "I want you to come with me and hold my hand while I get my ears pierced. I'm scared!"

"Okay," my mother agreed. "But then I should probably act mad at you when we get home, no?"

"Of course!" Yael said. So they went together to have Yael's ears pierced, and when they came home my mother pretended to be upset, and that was the whole rebellion. Later, when we moved to the East Coast and Yael began attending a mainstream Bais Yaakov high school, she tucked away the extra earrings.

The reason my parents decided to move was actually because of me, not because of Yael. I loved playing hockey, and my parents were concerned that it would be hard for me not to play on Shabbos. I wasn't asking to play on Shabbos, but they read the handwriting on the wall, and they decided that they'd better get out of Winnipeg before it was too late.

My parents were immensely successful and popular in Canada, yet my father traded his position as rabbi of a shul of 1,200 members for a far less prestigious and far less lucrative position in the States. But it's a good thing they left when they did. Back then, my friends were into hockey. A few short years later, many had non-Jewish girlfriends.

My parents did everything they could do ensure that the move from Canada to the States would be as smooth as possible. Each time we moved to a different city — which happened every four or five years — we were each allowed to redecorate our bedrooms. We didn't have a lot of money, but my parents made our emotional stability a spending priority. Every move was an exciting adventure, and I remember being thrilled to be able to go on yet another road trip.

The first time I attended a yeshivah was when I was in the eighth grade. I sorely lacked text skills and could barely read a Gemara, but the heart and soul of *Yiddishkeit* I did have — unlike many of my classmates, who had solid text skills but little feeling for Torah and *mitzvos*. I thought the other boys were so lucky to have grown up in a *frum* environment and have spent so much time learning *Chumash*, *Mishnayos*, and Gemara, but for some strange reason they didn't seem as enthusiastic as I was. I was put into a lower class, and I had to work really hard just to keep up.

The first few times I heard boys in my class speaking disparagingly about other Jews, I was genuinely shocked. How could a *frum* person speak *lashon hara*? Never having been part of a *frum* community before, I had idealized *frum* people, thinking that they must all be as passionate about *Yiddishkeit* and as loving of other Jews as my parents were. It was quite a disappointment to discover that *frum* boys could sometimes bully other kids or be insolent or nasty.

Before my bar mitzvah, my Gemara skills were still weak, but I did win an award from Torah U'Mesorah for having good *middos*. I used the money from that award to buy my first black hat. My father had never worn a black hat, and everyone in my family was abuzz with excitement over this purchase. It was a sign of belonging, finally, to a real *frum* community. In Canada, I had worn Power Ranger tzitzis and a yarmulke with a customized Washington Capitals logo that let my friends know which NHL team I favored. But now I was proud to be a bona fide *yeshivah bachur*, even if it meant that I had to work really hard to catch up to my classmates.

I'm now a *kollel yungerman*, and my three sisters are all married to *bnei Torah*, much to the delight of my parents. We were raised to share our feelings openly — my mother always listened to us and allowed us to express what was bothering us, without judging or condemnation — and my sisters and I have carried that emotional honesty over into our relationships with our spouses and children as well. I don't know too many other guys who can talk about their feelings as comfortably as I can, and it certainly makes for much smoother *shalom bayis* and a much easier time getting along with *chavrusa*s.

People often wonder how my parents succeeded in raising *frum*, well-adjusted kids without ever being part of an organized *frum* community. I think the answer lies in a statement my father often makes: "I never thought I could meet anyone who was better than my kids — and then I met their spouses."

When we were kids, my parents thought that my sisters and I were the greatest people in the world. They always wanted to be with us, and they not only loved us, they *liked* us. They enjoyed our company, and looked for ways to make life and *Yiddishkeit* fun for us.

Sure, there were times when they disciplined us, and times when they didn't allow us to do things that we wanted to do. But those memories are a blur. My childhood wasn't perfect, but when you're showered with positivity and you know that your parents value you enormously, it doesn't matter if there are some mistakes along the way. When we saw the beautiful relationship my parents had and the fabulous life we had at home, we knew instinctively that anything outside Torah was meaningless and hollow. Bottom line: I grew up thinking that Torah is a celebration, that Hashem is real, and that my parents are the greatest.

Postscript:

In the course of writing this story, I was in touch with three out of the four siblings in this unique family. These are some points the siblings e-mailed me that didn't make it into the article (I condensed and lightly edited them for inclusion here):

- *My father was and still is my best friend. I remember that he would always listen to my weird 8-year-old views on life. I loved those talks we had.*

- *My father was and is such a large part of my life. His demeanor, his motivation and simchah, permeated our home, and his character is something I try to emulate throughout all my roles in life.*

- *My parents always instilled in us a very deep bond with each other as siblings, we were (and still are, baruch Hashem!) each other's best friends and support systems.*

- *My parents spent a lot of money for us to go to frum camps in the summers; they wanted us to be in a frum environment and get in the summer what we couldn't get during the year (frum friends, inspirational moments, rabbis to look up to). Specifically, my sisters were sent to Israel a few times to get the inspiration a teenager needs. My parents also spent money on after-school lessons, like piano, skating, voice, sports, and art lessons. I was always very creative and they understood my need to have an outlet.*

- *My brother is one of the hardest working, most dedicated people I know. I think the seeds my parents planted within him as a child were able to come out when he was put in a Torah environment. He worked so hard to be a ben Torah because he was trained from a young age that that is our goal. There was never pressure, and he was always encouraged to be a regular boy who played sports and had a good time.*

- *When I asked my mother how to keep children frum and inspired, she said, "Treat every child as a ba'al teshuvah, make Torah exciting, make Torah about saying yes (especially on Shabbos)." Also, once she told me, "For 18 years I was obsessed with you being frum." She made it her whole life to keep me inspired and connected. So baruch Hashem it worked! Even though I was never a hard child, she never just assumed I would be frum or be close to Hashem. It was their entire focus.*

One of these four siblings is a kollel yungerman, one is a therapist, one is an accountant, and one is a teacher, but what they all had in common was their love of Torah and the feeling that "our parents are the best."

Glossary

a"h — acronym for "*alav* (or *aleha*) *hashalom*," literally, *peace be on him/her.*

abba (l.c.) — father; Abba (u.c.) — Father.

achdus — unity.

agurah — Israeli coin of the smallest denomination, equivalent to one-tenth of a shekel.

ahavah — love.

ahavas Yisrael — love for other Jews; love of Jews.

al pi teva — occurring naturally; in the course of nature.

alef — the first letter of the Hebrew alphabet.

alef-beis — the 22 letters of the Hebrew alphabet; the Hebrew alphabet.

Alef-Binah — a Hebrew reading primer.

aliyah (pl. *aliyahs*) — lit., *going up.* 1. spiritual elevation. 2. act of being called to recite a blessing at the public reading of the Torah. 3. immigration to Israel.

Am Yisrael — the Nation of Israel.

amud — 1. lectern or podium. 2. one folio of the Talmud.

anav — a humble person.

anavah – humility.

Ashkenaz — referring to Jews of European descent.

askan (pl. *askanim*) — a community activist.

assur — forbidden by halachah.

aufruf — act of being called to recite a blessing at the public reading of the Torah, esp. of a bridegroom or a boy on his bar mitzvah.

aveirah (pl. *aveiros*) — sin; transgression.

avodah — 1. the service of God, whether in sacrifice, prayer, or self-refinement. 2. work, effort, service.

Avraham Avinu — our forefather Abraham.

b'ezras Hashem — with Hashem's help.

b'simchah — with joy and happiness.

ba'al kishron — gifted Torah scholar.

ba'al korei — person who reads the weekly Torah portion aloud on behalf of the congregation.

ba'al middos — one who exhibits proper behavior and character traits.

ba'al teshuvah (pl. *ba'alei teshuvah*) (f.) *ba'alas teshuvah* — one who repents; one who returns to Torah-true Judaism.

ba'al tzedakah — one who is a generous donor to charity.

baalebos (pl. *baalebatim*) — lit., *householder*; layman.

baalebusta — a housewife.

bachur (pl. *bachurim*) — young man; an unmarried young man, used to denote a student in a yeshivah.

balebatish — respectable, of good standing.

baruch Hashem — lit., *Blessed is Hashem*; an expression of appreciation of Hashem's goodness.

bas — daughter.

bas/bat mitzvah — 1. a 12-year-old girl. 2. ceremony marking the coming of age of a Jewish girl.

bas kol — a Heavenly voice.

Bas ploni l'ploni — the daughter of so-and-so is destined for so-and-so.

bas yechidah — an only daughter.

bashert — 1. fated. 2. the person one is fated to marry.

bechor — firstborn.

bein adam laMakom — between man and God.

bein adam l'chaveiro — between man and his fellow.

bein hasedarim — between daily study sessions.

bein hazemanim — vacation time preceding Elul; intersession.

beis din — a Rabbinical court.

Beis HaMikdash — the Holy Temple in Jerusalem.

beis midrash — a study hall where Torah is learned, often used as a synagogue as well.

ben — *son.*

ben bayis — a person who, though not related, is considered part of the family.

ben Torah (pl. *bnei Torah*) — 1. one who studies and observes the teachings of the Torah. 2. a yeshivah student.

bentch — (Yiddish) 1. recite Grace after Meals. 2. to bless someone.

bentch licht — (Yiddish) light Shabbos or Yom Tov candles.

berachah (pl. *berachos*) — a blessing recited before performing a mitzvah and before and after eating; a formula for acknowledging a gift from G-d, whether material or spiritual.

Bereishis — the Book of Genesis.

bikur cholim — lit., *visiting the sick*, referring to the Torah commandment to care for the ill.

birchos Krias Shema — the blessings in the daily liturgy preceding and following the *Shema.*

bitachon — lit., *trust*; trust in Hashem.

blatt — a page in a Talmudic tractate.

bris — circumcision.

bris milah/brit milah — circumcision.

Brit Yitzchak — ceremony held in Sephardic communities on the night before a circumcision.

bubby (pl. bubbies) (l.c.) — (Yiddish) grandmother; Bubby (u.c.)— Grandmother; Grandma.

chaf — a letter in the Hebrew alphabet.

chag — a holiday.

chagigah — a celebration.

chai — lit., *eighteen*; life.

chaim — life.

challah (pl. *challos*) — 1. colloquially, loaves of soft wheat-bread traditionally eaten at a Shabbos meal. 2. the portion separated from the dough and given to a *Kohen* (today it is burnt).

chametz — leavened foods prohibited during the Passover festival.

chareidi — strictly religiously observant.

chas v'shalom — Heaven forbid.

chashuv/chashuve — important; prominent; renowned.

chassan/chattan (pl. *chassanim*) — a bridegroom.

chassid (pl. *chassidim*) — 1. pious man. 2. the follower of a Rebbe.

chassidish — Hassidic.

Chassidus — the study of Hassidic thought.

chasunah — a wedding.

chavrusa (pl. *chavrusas*) — a study partner.

Chayei Sarah — lit., *the life of Sarah*; one of the Torah portions in *Genesis*.

Chazal — acronym for *chachameinu zichronam livrachah*, "Our Sages of blessed memory."

chazzan — a cantor; one who leads the prayer service in the synagogue.

chazzanus — cantorial singing.

cheder — school, usually an elementary school (spec. for Jewish studies).

chesed — kindness; acts of beneficence; charitable giving.

chevrah — a group.

chevrah kaddisha — burial society.

chillul Hashem — desecration of Hashem's Name.

chinuch — Jewish education; Torah education (of minors).

chiyuv — obligation.

chizuk — encouragement.

cholent — (Yiddish) a stew prepared before Shabbos, simmered overnight, and traditionally eaten at Shabbos day meal, often consisting of meat, potatoes, beans, and barley.

chol hamo'ed — the intermediate days between the first and last days of Pesach and Succos.

Chovos HaLevavos — *Duties of the Heart*, a classic work of Jewish thought written by Rabbi Bachya ibn Pekudah in the 11th century.

Chumash — one of the Five Books of the Torah; the Five Books collectively.

chuppah — 1. wedding canopy. 2. the marriage ceremony.

Churban — destruction of the Holy Temple.

chutz la'aretz — outside of the Land of Israel.

chutzpadik — rude.

da'as Torah — Torah viewpoint; one who assesses situations solely through the perspective of Torah.

daf — lit., *page*; one folio of the Gemara.

daf yomi — daily study of one folio of the Gemara.

dalet amos — lit., *four cubits*; refers to one's personal space.

dan l'kaf zechus — the obligation to judge others favorably.

daven — (Yiddish) to pray.

David HaMelech — King David.

Dayan ha'emes — the true Judge.

dayeinu — "it is enough for us."

der heim — lit., *the home*; referring to one's traditions originating in one's home or country of origin.

derashah — a Torah lecture; sermon or Torah discourse.

derech — 1. path. 2. method. 3. a way.

derech eretz — proper conduct; respect; courtesy.

devar mitzvah — a matter relating to performance of a *mitzvah*.

dreidel — a four-sided top marked with the Hebrew letters *nun, gimel, hei,* and *shin,* used chiefly in a children's game traditionally played on Chanukah.

dvar Torah (pl. *divrei Torah*) — a lesson from the Torah; a Torah thought.

ehrliche — (Yiddish) upright; honest.

eid (pl. *eidim*) — a witness.

ein od milvado — "There is nothing besides Him (Hashem)."

einekel — (Yiddish) grandchild.

eiruv — lit., *mixture*; refers to several halachic procedures or devices, most commonly used to refer to a string surrounding the perimeter of an area to allow people to carry within that place on the Sabbath.

eishes chaver — the wife of a Torah scholar.

Eitz chaim hi lamachazikim bah v'somcheha me'ushar — "It is a tree of life for those who grasp it, and its supporters are praiseworthy" (*Mishlei* 3:18).

eltere bachur (Yiddish) — an older unmarried man.

Elul — one of the Jewish months.

emes — truth; truthfulness.

emunah — faith.

Eretz HaKodesh — the Holy Land.

Eretz Yisrael — Land of Israel.

erev — eve of.

Esther HaMalkah — Queen Esther.

farchenyukt — overly pious; sanctimonious.

FFB — (acronym) *frum* (religious) from birth.

frum — (Yiddish) religious; Torah observant.

frumkeit — (Yiddish) the state of being religious.

gabbai (pl. *gabbaim*) — person responsible for the proper functioning of a synagogue or other communal body; sexton.

gadlus — greatness.

gadol (pl. *gedolim*) — lit., *great;* a great Torah scholar; a term used to refer to a person of great stature.

gadol hador — spiritual leader of the generation.

galus — exile; (cap.) the Diaspora.

gan — kindergarten.

Gan Eden — the Garden of Eden.

gashmiyus — materialism; physical, material.

gemach (pl. *gemachim*) — a free-loan society.

Gemara — the Talmud; (l.c.) a Talmudic passage.

gemilus chasadim — acts of loving-kindness.

ger — a convert.

geshikt — (Yiddish) handy; capable.

get — bill of divorcement.

geulah — redemption; the redemption.

gezeirah — an edict; a decree.

grammen — lighthearted verses recited at a wedding or other celebration to amuse the bride and groom.

gut Shabbos — *(Yiddish)* Sabbath greeting: "Have a good Sabbath."

HaKadosh Baruch Hu — The Holy One, Blessed Is He (i.e., Hashem).

hakaras hatov — gratitude; expressing gratitude.

halachah (pl. *halachos*) — law; (u.c.) the body of Jewish Law; Torah law and practice.

hanhalah — school administration; administration.

harei at mekudeshes li — "You are hereby sanctified to me"; integral part of the marriage service.

hashavas aveidah — returning lost articles.

Hashem — lit., *the Name*; a respectful way to refer to G-d.

Hashem Hu haElokim — Hashem, He is the Lord.

hashgachah — rabbinic supervision on food; supervision.

hashgachah pratis — Divine Providence.

hashkafah (pl. *hashkafos*) — outlook; ideology; worldview; a concept of *emunah;* perspective.

hashpa'ah — influence.

hataras nedarim — negation of vows.

HaTikvah — lit., *the hope*; the Israeli national anthem.

hatzlachah, hatzlachah rabbah — success, "have great success."

Hatzolah — a team of Jewish paramedics who respond to emergencies.

Havdalah — lit., *separation*; prayer recited as the Sabbath or Festival comes to an end.

heter — permission; something permitted.

hilchos Shabbos — the laws pertaining to Sabbath observance.

Hodu laShem ki tov — "Give thanks to Hashem, for He is good" (*Tehillim* 118:1).

ima — (l.c.) mother; (u.c.) Mother; Mommy.

invei hagefen b'invei hagefen — lit., *the grapes of the vine in the grapes of the vine*, referring to a well-suited marriage match.

Isru Chag — the day after a Yom Tov.

k'zayis — the volume of an olive or half an egg (somewhat more than the volume of one fluid ounce).

kabbalah (pl. *kabbalos*) — (u.c.) the body of Jewish mystical teachings. (l.c.) lit., *acceptance*; the act of taking on a specific action to elevate oneself spiritually; an obligation taken upon oneself.

Kabbalas Shabbos — the traditional prayer recited at the beginning of the Sabbath service on Friday evening.

Kaddish — prayer said in memory of the dead.

kallah — a bride; an engaged girl.

kamatz — a diacritical mark.

kapitel — chapter of Psalms (*Tehillim*).

kasher — to make fit for use according to Torah law; purified; purged (of a utensil) of absorbed nonkosher taste.

kashrus/kashrut — Jewish dietary laws.

katan someich al shulchan aviv — lit., *a child depends on his father's table*; halachic description of a minor.

kavanah (pl. *kavanos*) — intention, esp. when reciting a prayer or performing a mitzvah.

kehillah — a congregation; a community.

Keili Keili lamah azavtani — "My G-d, my G-d, why have You forsaken me?" (*Tehillim* 22:2).

kein ayin hara — without an evil eye; used to forestall the evil eye.

kelipah (pl. *kelipos*) — 1. a negative force. 2. a thin removable surface; shell.

Kesser — 1. a crown 2. *Kedushah* service of the Mussaf prayer in some communities.

kesubah — a marriage contract.

kever (pl. *kevarim*) — a grave.

Kever Rachel — Rachel's Tomb.

kibbud av — honoring one's father.

Kiddush — a. mandatory blessing over wine expressing the sanctity of Shabbos or Festivals. 2. (l.c.) a reception after Sabbath-morning prayers at which *Kiddush* is recited and refreshments are served. 3. the blessing over wine recited before the Shabbos and Yom Tov meals.

kiddushin — *part of the marriage ceremony.*

kinderlach — (Yiddish) an affectionate term for children.

kippah — a yarmulke; a skullcap.

kiruv — outreach; outreach movement drawing people to Torah observance.

kirvas Elokim — closeness to G-d.

kivrei tzaddikim — the graves of righteous individuals.

Klal Yisrael — Jewish people in general; the Jewish nation.

ko'ach — strength; ability; energy.

kol hakavod — lit., *all the honor*; roughly, "good for you."

Kol Yachol — the Omnipotent (G-d).

kollel — academy of higher Jewish study, usually for married men.

Kosel — the Western Wall.

kovei'a ittim (laTorah) — establishes set times (to learn Torah).

kriah — 1. reading 2. tearing one's clothing on hearing of the death of a close relative or at the funeral of a close relative.

Krias HaTorah — the reading of the Torah in the synagogue.

krias Shema — 1. the three paragraphs of the Torah recited twice daily, beginning with the words *"Shema Yisrael,* Hear, O Israel." 2. the recitation of this liturgy.

kvittel — a written petition for help or spiritual guidance.

l'chaim — lit., *to life.* 1. party celebrating an engagement 2. toast over a drink of wine or whiskey.

l'havdil bein chaim l'chaim — lit., *to differentiate between life and life*; expression used to make a separation between mentioning a person who has passed away and one who is still living.

L'sheim mitzvas succah — for the sake of performing the *mitzvah* of dwelling in the *succah*.

Lag BaOmer — 18 Iyar, the 33rd day of the *Omer* (the period between Passover and Shavuot; the anniversary of the death of Rabbi Shimon bar Yochai, a day that is often marked by bonfires in Israel and, in Hassidic circles, by the first haircut of 3-year-old boys.

lashon hara — lit., *evil speech*; derogatory speech; slander; gossip; harmful speech.

Lechah Dodi — part of the traditional prayer recited at the beginning of the Sabbath service on Friday evening.

leining — (Yiddish) the reading of the Torah portion.

leiv tov — a good heart.

levayah — a funeral.

licht bentching — (Yiddish) candle-lighting.

limudei kodesh — study of Torah subjects (as opposed to secular studies).

litvishe — following the litvish tradition; the traditions of the Lithuanian yeshivos of pre-war Europe.

lo aleinu — lit., *not on us*; Heaven protect us.

lo baShamayim hi — lit., *it is not in the Heavens*; referring to the Torah, which is on Earth for the edification of mankind.

Lo sa'amod al dam rei'echa — "You shall not stand aside while your fellow's blood is shed" (*Vayikra* 19:16).

luchos — tablets inscribed with the Ten Commandments.

Ma'ariv — the evening prayer service.

machalah — illness; euphemism for cancer.

machlokes — an argument; a dispute.

maggid shiur — a lecturer.

Mah Tovu — prayer recited upon entering the synagogue.

Mah tovu ohalecha Yaakov — "How goodly are your tents, O Jacob" (*Bamidbar* 24:5).

malach (pl. *malachim*) — angel; heavenly angel.

mashgiach — 1. (cap.) dean of students in a yeshivah who oversees students' spiritual and ethical development. 2. *kashrut* supervisor.

Mashiach – Messiah, the awaited redeemer of Israel, who will usher in an era of universal recognition of the Kingship of Hashem.

masmid — exceptionally diligent student.

mattan b'seiser — to give charity anonymously.

mazel — good fortune.

mazel tov — congratulations.

mechanech (m.) (pl. *mechanchim*) (f. *mechaneches*) — an educator.

mechazeik — to strengthen, often spiritually.

mechilah — forgiveness.

mechutan (pl. *mechutanim*) — parent of one's in-law children; one's relative through marriage.

mechuteiniste — one's child's mother-in-law; a relative through marriage.

medakdeik — to be stringent (usually in reference to the performance of *mitzvos*).

mefarshim — commentaries on the Torah.

megillah — literally, scroll; also refers to the Scroll of *Esther* read on Purim.

mekarev — to bring closer to religious observance.

mekubal (pl. *mekubalim*) — a Kabbalist.

melachah (pl. *melachos*) — labor; any of the 39 labors forbidden to be performed on the Sabbath.

melaveh malkah — meal eaten on Saturday night in honor of the departure of the Sabbath Queen.

menachem avel — to comfort a mourner; to pay a condolence call.

menahel (m.) (f. *menaheles*) — a school principal.

mentch — (Yiddish) all-around good person.

Mesilas Yesharim — *The Way of the Upright,* a classic work of Jewish thought and ethics, authored by Rabbi Moshe Chaim Luzzatto in the 18th century.

mesorah — Jewish heritage; the received tradition; tradition.

mevater— to nullify.

mezuzah (pl. *mezuzos*) – small parchment scroll in a casing, affixed to a doorpost and containing the first two paragraphs of the *Shema* prayer.

Mi k'amcha Yisrael — Who is like Your nation Israel?

middah (pl. *middos*) — character trait; attribute.

min haShamayim — *(decreed) from Heaven.*

Minchah — the afternoon prayer service.

minyan (pl. *minyanim*) — quorum of 10 men necessary for conducting a prayer service; the group for communal prayer service.

mishlo'ach manos — gifts of food sent to friends on Purim.

mishnah (pl. *mishnayos*) — (cap.) the six sections of the Oral Law compiled by Rabbi Yehudah HaNasi (the Prince). (l.c.) a passage from the Mishnah.

mispallel (pl. *mispallelim*) — 1. to pray. 2. one who prays.

mitzvah (pl. *mitzvos*) — commandment; merit; good deed; a religious obligation; a Biblical or Rabbinic commandment.

mochel — to forgive.

Modeh Ani — "I admit in front of You"; prayer upon awakening in the morning, expressing gratitude for life.

morah — a woman teacher.

moser nefesh — self-sacrificing.

Moshe Rabbeinu — Moses, Our Teacher.

mossad — Jewish institution, esp. educational institution.

motza'ei Shabbos — Saturday night; the time of the departure of the Sabbath.

Mussaf — additional prayer service recited after Shacharis on Shabbos, Rosh Chodesh, and Festivals.

mussar — ethical teachings geared toward self-refinement; reproof; reprimand.

nachas — pleasure, usually from one's children; spiritual or emotional pleasure.

narishkeit — (Yiddish) foolishness.

navi — a prophet. (cap.) one of the Books of the Prophets.

nebbach — (Yiddish) (n.) pitiful, ineffectual, and timid person. (adj.) poor; unfortunate. (interjection) how unfortunate!

neitz — sunrise, the most preferable time to recite *Shemoneh Esrei* during the morning prayer service.

nekudah (pl. *nekudos*) — 1. a Hebrew vowel. 2. a point.

neshamah (pl. neshamos) — the soul.

niftar — (n.) a person who has died. (v.) died.

nisayon (pl. nisyonos) — a test, esp. a spiritual test.

Nishmas — prayer recited during the Sabbath and holiday morning service.

nisht Shabbos geredt — lit., *not to be spoken of on Shabbos*; expression used when one is about to speak of secular matters on Shabbos.

Nshei — lit., *women of*; women's organization.

Olam Haba — the World to Come

oleh (pl. *olim*) — 1. one who immigrates to Israel. 2. one called to the Torah during prayer services.

Oma — (German) Grandmother.

Opa — (German) Grandfather.

parashah — the weekly Torah portion.

Parashas — the Torah portion of....

parnassah — livelihood.

parve — food which is neither meat nor dairy.

pasach — a Hebrew vowel.

pasuk (pl. *pesukim*) — verse in the *Tanach* or liturgy.

pasul — invalid; inadequate.

penimiyus — inward; internal.

perek — a chapter.

Pesukei D'Zimrah – Verses of Praise; a section of the morning prayer service.

petirah — lit., *departure*; death; the moment of death.

peyos — sideburns or side curls, worn by Orthodox Jewish males.

pidyon — redemption.

pidyon haben — redemption of the (firstborn) son: the ceremony of the redemption of the firstborn son.

poritz — landowner; nobleman.

posek — halachic authority.

protektzia — lit., *protection*; influence.

psak — a halachic ruling.

pulka — a thigh.

pushka — (Yiddish) a charity collection box.

Rabbosai — lit., *gentlemen*, a polite term of address.

rav (pl. *rabbanim*) — a rabbi; a spiritual leader.

rebbe (pl. *rebbeim*) — a *rav*; a rabbi; (cap.) Hassidic Grand Rabbi.

rebbi — teacher.

rebbetzin — (Yiddish) rabbi's wife; also used to refer to a respected Jewish woman.

rechilus — tale-bearing.

redt — to suggest a possible shidduch.

refuah sheleimah — lit., *a full/complete recovery*; a blessing for a complete/speedy recovery extended to an ailing person.

reish — a letter in the Hebrew alphabet.

reshus hayachid — an individual's domain.

revi'is — halachically significant amount of liquid.

Ribbono shel Olam — lit., *Master of the World*; i.e., Hashem.

rosh yeshivah — the dean of a yeshivah; senior lecturer in a yeshivah.

ruach — spirit; enthusiasm.

ruach hakodesh — Divine inspiration.

ruchniyus — spirituality; spiritual growth.

Saba — Grandfather.

sabra — a native-born Israeli; a cactus fruit.

savlanus/savlanut — patience.

Savta — Grandmother.

schach — the roof of a *succah*, generally made from leaves, branches, or bamboo.

seder (pl. *sedarim*) — 1. study period. 2. set time, usually for learning. 3. (u.c.) Pesach-night ritual during which the Haggadah is recited.

sefer (pl. *sefarim*) — a book, specifically a book on holy subjects; a book, esp. on a learned topic.

segulah (pl. *segulos*) — a spiritual remedy; a valuable tool.

seichel — insight; intelligence; common sense; rationality; one's rational side.

Sephard — style of prayer service used by Jews of Eastern European descent, particularly Chassidic communities.

seudah — a festive meal, esp. one served on the Sabbath or a holiday

Sha'ar HaBitachon — section in *Chovos HaLevavos* (*Duties of the Heart*), on the subject of trust in G-d.

Shabbat Shalom — greeting, "have a peaceful Shabbos."

Shabbaton — inspirational weekend.

Shabbos, Shabbat (pl. *Shabbosim, Shabbosos*) — Saturday or the Sabbath; the Jewish day of rest; the Sabbath, which is a day of total rest from all forms of work.

Shabbos Mevarchim — the Shabbos on which a blessing for the upcoming month is recited.

Shacharis — the morning prayer service.

shadchan (pl. *shadchanim*) (f. *shadchante*) — a matchmaker.

shalom — peace; often said on meeting or leave-taking.

shalom aleichem — lit., *peace be on you*; traditional greeting; (cap.) Friday-evening song of welcome to the ministering angels.

shalom bayis — peace and harmony in the home; marital harmony.

shalom zocher — celebration of the birth of a boy, held on Friday night.

shalosh seudos — the third Shabbos meal, eaten on Shabbos afternoon.

Shamayim — Heaven.

shanah rishonah — the first year of marriage.

Shas — the Talmud.

Shavuos — festival commemorating the giving of the Torah on Mount Sinai.

Shechinah — Divine Presence; the spirit of the Omnipresent manifested on earth.

shechitah — ritual slaughter; the ritual manner in which an animal is slaughtered.

she'eilah (pl. she'eilos) — question, esp. a question asked of a rabbinical authority regarding a halachic issue.

shefa — abundant blessing.

shehecheyanu — blessing recited on certain occasions, expressing gratitude to G-d.

sheitel — (Yiddish) wig.

sheitel macher — (Yiddish) wigmaker.

Shema Yisrael —"Hear O Israel"; this prayer, recited twice daily, expresses the essence of Jewish faith.

shemirah — protection.

shemiras halashon — guarding against improper speech, , such as gossip, slander, and other forms of forbidden speech.

Shemoneh Esrei — lit., eighteen; the prayer, originally eighteen blessings but now nineteen, that forms the central core of each weekday prayer service.

sheva berachos — 1. the seven blessings recited at a wedding. 2. the festive meals, celebrated during the week after a wedding, at which the seven blessings are recited. 3. the seven blessings recited under the chuppah.

Shevat — a month in the Jewish calendar.

shidduch (pl. shidduchim) — 1. match, esp. a marriage match. 2. proposed marriage match. 3. one's betrothed.

shir — a song.

Shir shel Yom — lit., the daily song; the specific psalm said at the conclusion of the morning prayer service.

shiur (pl. shiurim) — (a) a Torah lecture. (b) the required amount (e.g., of eating forbidden food to be considered a punishable act). (c) halachic amount. (d) lecture on Torah subject.

shivah — lit., seven; the seven-day mourning period immediately following the death of a close relative.

shkoyach (yasher koach)—(informal) "thanks a lot."

shlita — acronym for (Hebrew) "May he live a long and good life."

shlep — (Yiddish) to drag.

shmatte— (Yiddish) a rag.

shomer Shabbos — one who observes the laws of Shabbos.

shtar mechilah — document in which one declares that he grants forgiveness.

shtark — (Yiddish) strong.

shteiging — (Yiddish) advancing in learning.

shtick – (Yiddish) 1. mischievous actions or behavior, often done in the spirit of the holiday. 2. foolishness.

shtiebel — (Yiddish) lit., room; a small synagogue, often situated in a house; small synagogue, used mainly by chassidim.

shul — (Yiddish) synagogue; house of prayer.

Shulchan Aruch — Code of Jewish Law.

shver — a father-in-law.

shvigger— a mother-in-law.

siddur — a prayer book.

simchah (pl. simchahs) — 1. happiness, joy; a joyous occasion. 2. a happy occasion; a celebration, esp. a celebration of a family milestone such as a wedding, bar mitzvah, or a birth.

simchas hachaim — joie de vivre; a positive attitude toward life; happiness in life.

Simchas Torah — the festival honoring the cycle of the Torah reading. 2. the festival immediately following Succos, honoring the cycle of the Torah.

simchas yom tov — joy of celebrating a Yom Tov.

sinas chinam — unwarranted hatred of one Yid for another; unwarranted hatred.

siyatta d'Shmaya — Heavenly assistance; Divine Providence; help from Hashem.

siyum — celebration marking the completion of a course of Torah or Talmud study.

succah — booth in which Jews are commanded to dwell during Succos.

Succos — the festival during which one dwells in a succah.

sugya — (Aramaic) a topic; conceptual unit in Talmud study; topic in Talmud.

tafkid — purpose; job; calling.

tallis/tallit — four-cornered prayer shawls with fringes at each corner, worn by (married) men during morning prayers.

talmid chacham (pl. talmidei chachamim) — lit., the student of a wise person; a person learned in Torah and Talmud; a Torah scholar.

Tamim tihyeh im Hashem Elokecha — "You shall be wholehearted with Hashem, your G-d" (Devarim 19:13).

tatty — (Yiddish) father.

tefillah (pl. tefillos) — Jewish prayer.

tefillin — phylacteries.

Tehillim — 1. the Book of Psalms. 2. (l.c.) psalms.

Three Weeks—the semimourning period between the fast of the 17th of Tammuz and Tishah B'Av.

tietch — (Yiddish) (v.) to translate. (n.) translation.

tikkun — rectification.

tikkun olam — perfecting the world.

Tishah B'Av — [the fast of] the Ninth of Av; day of mourning for the destruction of the Holy Temples.

tofei'ach al menas l'hatfiach — something saturated to the point that it can saturate something else.

toivel – to ritually purify via immersion in a mikveh.

Torahdik — (Yiddish) lit., Torah-like; in the Torah spirit.

Tosafos — 1. critical and explanatory notes on the Talmud by French and German scholars of the 12th–14th centuries. 2. The authors of those notes, collectively.

treif — colloquial term for nonkosher.

tza'ar — pain; suffering.

tzaddik (pl. tzaddikim) — righteous man; righteous person.

tzarah (pl. tzaros) — difficult, painful situation.

tzedakah — charity.

tzibbur — congregation; the community as a whole.

tzidkus — righteousness.

tzitzis — fringed garment worn by Jewish men and boys; fringes at the corners of a tallis.

tznius — modesty standard in speech, behavior, and dress.

tzugepast — (Yiddish) suitable; appropriate.

upsheren — (Yiddish) lit., shearing; the first haircut given to a boy at the age of 3.

va'ad – group symposium on a Torah or mussar topic.

vachnacht — (Yiddish) lit., night of watching; the night before an infant's circumcision, when children recite the Shema in front of the cradle.

vatranus — the act of giving in.

vort — 1. a Torah thought. 2. an engagement celebration.

yahrtzeit — (Yiddish) the anniversary of a death.

yarei Shamayim (pl. *yirei Shamayim*) — one who fears (is in awe of) G-d; connotes reverence for G-d, an all-pervasive attitude of piety.

yarmulke — (Yiddish) a skullcap.

yasher ko'ach — idiom expressing gratitude.

yehupitz — jocular term indicating a far-off location.

Yerushalayim — Jerusalem.

yeshivah (pl. yeshivos) — a school of Jewish studies; a Torah academy.

yeshivish — of or pertaining to a yeshivah; typical of a yeshivah student.

yeshuah (pl. *yeshuos*) — salvation; rescue; remedy.

yetzer hara — evil inclination; the negative impulse to behave contrary to the Torah's commandments

yichus — lineage.

Yid (pl. Yidden) — a Jew.

Yiddishkeit — (Yiddish) Judaism; the Jewish way of life.

yiras Shamayim — lit., *fear of Heaven*; connotes reverence for G-d, an all-pervasive attitude of piety.

yishuv — a settlement.

Yom HaAtzma'ut — Israeli Independence Day.

yom hadin — the day of judgment; Yom Kippur.

Yom Tov (pl. *Yamim Tovim*) — a Jewish holiday; a Festival.

yungerman — (Yiddish) young married man, usually referring to one studying in a yeshivah or *kollel*.

z''l – acronym for "*zichrono livrachah*," lit., *may the righteous person be remembered as a blessing*, appended to the name of a deceased righteous person.

Zachreinu l'chaim — remember us for life.

zechus (pl. *zechusim, zechuyos*) — merit; privilege.

zeidy — (pl. *zeidies*) (Yiddish) grandfather; Grandpa; Grandfather.

zeman (pl. *zemanim*) — lit., *time*; 1. the time the Sabbath or a holiday begins. 2. a school semester.

zeman krias Shema — the time when it is permitted to recite the *Shema*.

zemiros — songs sung at Shabbos and festive meals.

zichron — remembrance.

zivug — one's destined marriage partner.

zivug hagun — proper marriage partner.

zocheh — to merit.

Zohar — fundamental work of mystical Jewish thought.

zt''l — acronym for *zecher tzaddik livrachah*, may the righteous person be remembered as a blessing.